THE WORLD BANK GROUP

A TO Z

THE WORLD BANK GROUP

A TO Z

2015

ISBN (paper): 978-1-4648-0382-6
ISBN (e-book): 978-1-4648- 0383-3
ISBN (fixed-format e-book): 978-1-4648-0416-8
DOI: 10.1596/978-1-4648-0382-6

Cover and interior design: Debra Naylor, Naylor Design Inc.

Library of Congress Cataloging-in-Publication Data has been requested.

CONTENTS

CONTENTS FROM A TO Z

CONTENTS BY TOPIC

FOREWORD

Over the last year, the World Bank Group has made progress toward achieving our twin goals of eliminating extreme poverty by 2030 and boosting shared prosperity for the poorest 40 percent in every developing country. From managing a portfolio of more than $9 billion for education, to nearly tripling funds for maternal and early childhood nutrition programs, to collaborating with more than 130 countries on climate change, we have had a very strong year.

Increased collaboration among all four institutions of the World Bank Group made these advancements possible. For the first time in our history, we have devised a plan to make the Bank's different bodies work in tandem. Comprising the International Bank for Reconstruction and Development, International Finance Corporation, Multilateral Investment Guarantee Agency, and International Centre for Settlement of Investment Disputes, this network will now operate under a single, unifying corporate strategy.

The strategy lays out a blueprint for how we will deliver global knowledge to help countries and businesses solve local challenges. Our approach stems from decades of hands-on experience and proven results in promoting economic development. Our strategy also spells out a plan for strengthening ties with key partners, including civil society and the private sector. Tackling the world's toughest development challenges requires collaboration not only across our own institution, but also with stakeholders across the development landscape.

Another key feature of our new strategy is the creation of global practices that will spread knowledge across sectors, regions, and the entire institution. In the past, operational silos too often prevented our staff from sharing vital knowledge and technical skills. By breaking down these silos, our global practices will allow Bank Group experts from diverse areas of expertise and geographical locations to work together more seamlessly.

These changes mark a shift from an institution focused on completing projects to one that values delivering solutions. We're becoming more nimble, evidence-based, and financially viable. Operating as one group, we will work with other development partners to bend the arc of history toward justice by ending extreme poverty and boosting shared prosperity across the world.

At this transformative time for our institution, I am pleased to present *The World Bank Group A to Z*. This publication provides need-to-know information about the World Bank Group, and does so in a concise, approachable manner. I'm convinced that this book will serve as a valuable resource for all those interested in development.

Jim Yong Kim
World Bank Group President

PREFACE

The *World Bank Group A to Z* provides the most concise and essential information about the mission, policies, procedures, products, and services of the new World Bank Group. With more than 280 entries arranged in encyclopedic A-to-Z format, readers can easily find up-to-date information about the five agencies of the World Bank Group and the wide range of areas in which we work: from agriculture, education, energy, health, social protection and labor to gender, jobs, conflict, private sector development, trade, water, and climate change. The World Bank Group's work in all of these areas now focuses on our twin goals: eliminating extreme poverty by 2030 and boosting shared prosperity of the bottom 40 percent of each developing country's population.

Building on previous editions of *A Guide to the World Bank*, this new volume has been completely revised and updated to include features not found in its predecessors, including examples and photos of Bank Group projects and programs, and introductory content that highlights the new World Bank Group's goals, financials, regions, and results. The book also reflects the wide ranging reforms within the World Bank Group in recent years, including the launch of the new World Bank Group Strategy; new approaches to development; the establishment of new Global Practice Groups and Cross-Cutting Solution Areas; and the goal of becoming a "Solutions Bank," one that will marshal the vast reserves of evidence and experiential knowledge across the five World Bank Group agencies and apply them to local problems.

If you are interested in understanding what the World Bank Group does and how it does it, this book will serve as an indispensable guide. Join us in our ambitious mission to end extreme poverty in a single generation: connect with us on

Facebook, Twitter, and LinkedIn, and join the conversation at World Bank Live, an online space to discuss and debate key development topics in real time.

Facebook: facebook.com/worldbank
Twitter: twitter.com/worldbank
LinkedIn: www.linkedin.com/company/the-world-bank
LiveChat: live.worldbank.org

Cyril Muller
Vice President
External and Corporate Relations
World Bank Group

ABOUT THIS BOOK

The *World Bank Group A to Z* has been designed with a number of features to guide you to the information you are looking for, even if you don't know exactly what that is:

Tables of contents: Two tables of contents open the volume. The first provides a high-level look at how the book is structured, and the second presents all of the main entries listed in alphabetical order with their corresponding page numbers.

Contents by topic: These pages bring together entries into 15 major topic areas to guide you to key information including the new structure of the World Bank Group (Cross-Cutting Solution Areas, Global Practices, and Institutions of the World Bank Group); policies, procedures, financial services, and knowledge products (Accountability Mechanisms, Products and Services, Safeguards, and Transparency and Openness); and how the Bank Group classifies and organizes countries and regions for operational and analytical purposes (Regions of the World Bank Group and Terms for Countries or Areas).

Introduction to the World Bank Group: A 12-page graphical presentation will orient you to the Bank Group and its work. It includes:

- The five World Bank Group agencies and their financials
- The Bank Group's new twin goals
- Bank Group financial commitments broken down by region
- Maps of Bank regions and of global poverty
- Highlights of key development results of the World Bank Group in different topical areas from across the globe

Alphabetical arrangement of entries: As the book title suggests, the entries in this volume are arranged alphabetically, which makes it easy to find information on a specific topic. The core of the volume is formed by more than 280 main text entries, which cover every area of the Bank Group's work as well as details about the institution's new structure following the 2014 reorganization.

Cross-referencing: Entries in the main body of the volume are extensively cross-referenced, providing a further aid to locating related articles and entries on a particular subject. Two types of cross-references are provided to help the reader locate a given entry under its proper title: *See* directs you to the active entry; *See also* points you to other related entries in the volume.

Web links to additional information: There are hundreds of links that accompany the entries throughout the volume, leading you to more detailed and updated information online.

Appendixes: At the end of the volume, you will find information about how to contact the World Bank Group and a timeline of key Bank Group events since the institution was created in 1944.

Index: In addition to the features described above, a detailed index following the appendix of the book provides quick access to hundreds of entries and sub-entries.

To learn more about this book and the World Bank Group, download the free augmented reality app Blippar, then point your device at the book's front cover.

The *World Bank Group A to Z* will be updated every six months—in October and April of each year—and is available in print and electronic versions. Readers who purchase an e-book will receive a notification for a free e-book update six months after the original e-book purchase.

Connect with us on Facebook, Twitter, Instagram, and LinkedIn and let us know what you think of *The World Bank Group A to Z.*

Facebook: facebook.com/worldbankpublications
Twitter: twitter.com/WBPubs
LinkedIn: www.linkedin.com/company/the-world-bank

ACKNOWLEDGMENTS

The *World Bank Group A to Z* was produced by a team led by Stephen McGroarty, together with Jewel McFadden, in the Bank Group's Publishing and Knowledge Division. Dana Lane was indispensable in researching, writing, editing, and fact checking. Many people in the World Bank Group's Publishing and Knowledge Division contributed to or provided assistance with this project. Cindy Fisher and Rumit Pancholi expertly managed the design and editorial production of the book. Thanks also go to Shana Wagger, who helped with the conceptualization and development of the volume, and Randi Park, who managed the e-book design and production. Denise Bergeron adeptly coordinated the printing process and dissemination. We would also like to thank Jose de Buerba and Yulia Ivanova for the book's promotion and marketing. A special thanks to Carlos Rossel, Publisher, and Nancy Lammers, head of Editorial, Design, and Production for their continuous support and guidance, as well as to Cyril Muller, Vice President, External and Corporate Relations.

Many individuals across the World Bank Group provided advice, content, and feedback on the draft manuscript. We are extremely grateful to Ghislaine Baghdadi, Dominique Bichara, Lucie Blyth, Sebastien Boitreaud, Susan C. Botha, Yanina Budkin, Diana Ya-Wai Chung, Mason Denton, John Donnelly, Connie Eysenck, Alexander Anthony Ferguson, Melissa Fossberg, Nicole Frost, Chisako Fukuda, Clare Lloyd Gardoll, John W. Garrison, Hannah George, Elena Gex, Sarah Jackson-Han, Sonu Jain, Sarwat Hussain, Nicholas K. W. Jones, Agron Kelmendi, Yoko Kobayashi Chandra Kumar, Dale Lautenbach, Maura K. Leary, Jeffrey N. Lecksell, Maureen Shields Lorenzetti, Ana Elisa Luna Barros, Heba Mahmoud, Flore Martinant, Tomoko Matsukawa, Devika Seecharran McWalters, Brenda Mejia, April Miller, Thoko Moko, Xenia Zia Morales, Chris Neal, Daniel Nikolits, Michael J. O'Connell, Sona V. Panajyan, Emmanuel E. Quintos, Sumithra Rajendra, Jamile A. Ramadan, Joseph Rebello, Carolyn Reynolds, Mauricio Rios, Lara Saade, Mallory Lee Saleson, Kristyn Schrader, Mokhtar Shamseldin, Angelica Silvero, Paschal Ssemaganda, Noel Sta. Ines, Arathi Sundaravadanan, Ekaterina Svirina, Anissa Amador Tria, Yasusuke Tsukagoshi, Mario Trubiano, Stuart Tucker, Christopher Walsh, and Fernanda Zavaleta.

WORLD BANK GROUP TWIN GOALS

END EXTREME POVERTY

Goal: Decrease the percentage of people living on less than $1.25 a day to no more than 3 percent by 2030.

36%
1990

28%
2000

18%
2010

+ ENVIRONMENTAL, SOCIAL, AND ECONOM

PROMOTE SHARED PROSPERITY

Goal: Foster the welfare and income growth of the bottom 40 percent of the population in every developing country.

Opportunity   Inclusion   Sustainability

WHERE DO THE EXTREME POOR LIVE?

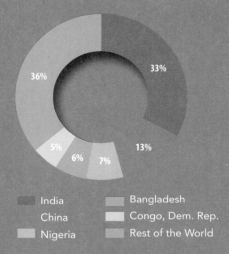

- India — 33%
- China
- Nigeria
- Bangladesh
- Congo, Dem. Rep.
- Rest of the World — 36%

13%

5% 6% 7%

9%
2020

3%
2030

SUSTAINABILITY

2030

The twin goals will be pursued in an
environmentally, socially, and economically
sustainable manner to ensure that development
gains do not harm the welfare of current
and future generations.

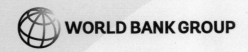**WORLD BANK GROUP**

FIVE INSTITUTIONS, ONE GROUP

THE INTERNATIONAL BANK FOR RECONSTRUCTION AND DEVELOPMENT
The International Bank for Reconstruction and Development (IBRD) lends to governments of middle-income and creditworthy low-income countries.
⮕ www.worldbank.org

THE INTERNATIONAL DEVELOPMENT ASSOCIATION
The International Development Association (IDA) provides interest-free loans—called credits—and grants to governments of the poorest countries.
⮕ www.worldbank.org

Together, IBRD and IDA make up the World Bank.

THE INTERNATIONAL FINANCE CORPORATION
The International Finance Corporation (IFC) is the largest global development institution focused exclusively on the private sector.
⮕ www.ifc.org

THE MULTILATERAL INVESTMENT GUARANTEE AGENCY
The Multilateral Investment Guarantee Agency (MIGA) was created in 1988 to promote foreign direct investment into developing countries to support economic growth, reduce poverty, and improve people's lives.
⮕ www.miga.org

THE INTERNATIONAL CENTRE FOR SETTLEMENT OF INVESTMENT DISPUTES
The International Centre for Settlement of Investment Disputes (ICSID) provides international facilities for conciliation and arbitration of investment disputes.
⮕ www.icsid.org

FINANCING FOR PARTNER COUNTRIES

FISCAL 2010–14
MILLIONS OF DOLLARS

	2010	2011	2012	2013	2014
WORLD BANK GROUP					
Commitments[a]	76,482	61,120	57,450	57,587	65,579
Disbursements[b]	50,234	42,028	42,390	40,570	44,399
IBRD					
Commitments	44,197	26,737	20,582	15,249	18,604
Disbursements	28,855	21,879	19,777	16,030	18,761
IDA					
Commitments	14,550	16,269	14,753	16,298	22,239
Disbursements	11,460	10,282	11,061	11,228	13,432
IFC					
Commitments[c]	12,664	12,186	15,462	18,349	17,261
Disbursements	6,793	6,715	7,891	9,971	8,904
MIGA					
Gross issuance	1,464	2,099	2,657	2,781	3,155
RECIPIENT EXECUTED TRUST FUNDS					
Commitments	3,607	3,829	3,996	4,910	4,319
Disbursements	3,126	3,152	3,571	3,341	3,302

a. Includes IBRD, IDA, IFC, Recipient Executed Trust Funds (RETF) commitments, and MIGA gross issuance. RETF commitments include all recipient executed grants, and therefore total WBG commitments differ from the amount reported in the WBG Corporate Scorecard, which includes only a subset of trust funded activities.

b. Includes IBRD, IDA, IFC, and RETF disbursements.

c. IFC's own account, not including funds mobilized from third parties.

GLOBAL COMMITMENTS

The World Bank Group's support for developing countries grew sharply over the past year as the organization focused on delivering results more quickly, increasing its relevance for its clients and partners, and bringing global solutions to local challenges.

LATIN AMERICA AND THE CARIBBEAN

$9.8 billion

EUROPE AND CENTRAL ASIA
$10.0 billion

EAST ASIA AND PACIFIC
$10.0 billion

MIDDLE EAST AND NORTH AFRICA
$4.8 billion

SOUTH ASIA
$13.6 billion

SUB-SAHARAN AFRICA
$16.1 billion

$**65.6** billion

in loans, grants, equity investments, and guarantees to partner countries and private businesses. (This number includes multiregional and global projects.)

Note: Regional breakdowns reflect World Bank country classifications.

WORLD BANK REGIONS

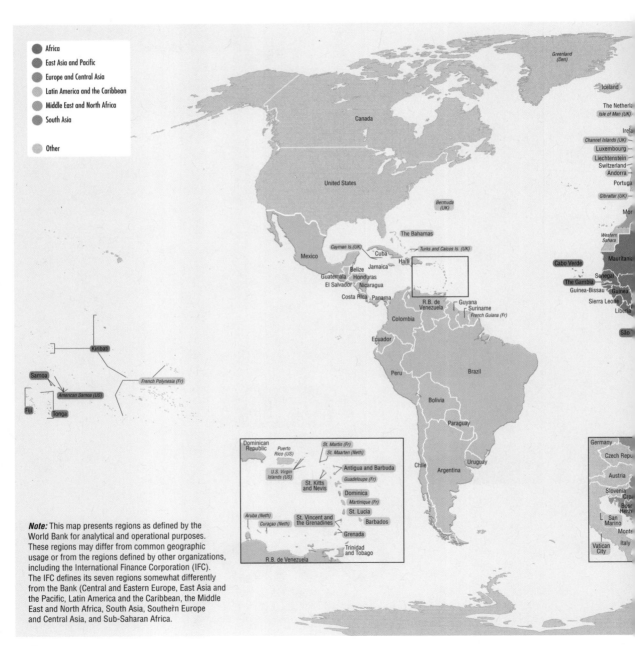

Africa
East Asia and Pacific
Europe and Central Asia
Latin America and the Caribbean
Middle East and North Africa
South Asia

Other

Note: This map presents regions as defined by the World Bank for analytical and operational purposes. These regions may differ from common geographic usage or from the regions defined by other organizations, including the International Finance Corporation (IFC). The IFC defines its seven regions somewhat differently from the Bank (Central and Eastern Europe, East Asia and the Pacific, Latin America and the Caribbean, the Middle East and North Africa, South Asia, Southern Europe and Central Asia, and Sub-Saharan Africa.

IBRD 41130 SEPTEMBER 2014

WORLD BANK GROUP POVERTY MAP

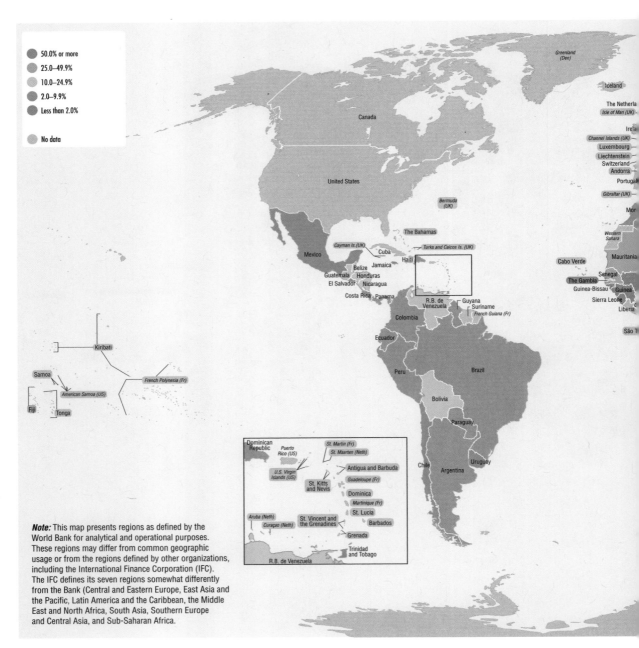

Note: This map presents regions as defined by the World Bank for analytical and operational purposes. These regions may differ from common geographic usage or from the regions defined by other organizations, including the International Finance Corporation (IFC). The IFC defines its seven regions somewhat differently from the Bank (Central and Eastern Europe, East Asia and the Pacific, Latin America and the Caribbean, the Middle East and North Africa, South Asia, Southern Europe and Central Asia, and Sub-Saharan Africa).

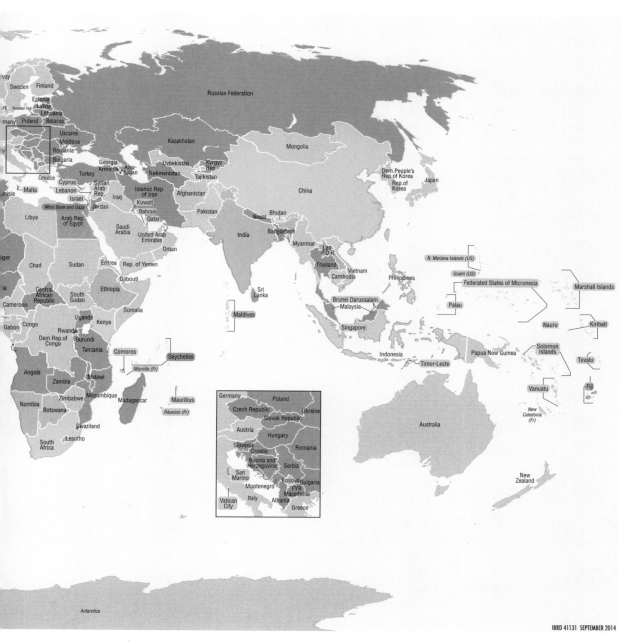

WORLD BANK GROUP RESULTS

The World Bank Group leverages its strengths, expertise, and resources to help countries and other partners make a real impact on development—by driving economic growth, promoting inclusiveness, and ensuring sustainability.

DRIVING ECONOMIC GROWTH	PROMOTING INCLUSIVENESS	ENSURING SUSTAINABILITY
IBRD/IDA		
95,000 kilometers of roads constructed and rehabilitated	**250.9** million people received health, nutrition, and population services	**903** million tons of CO$_2$ equivalent emissions expected to be reduced annually
15.3 million people and micro, small, and medium enterprises reached with financial services	**37.4** million beneficiaries covered by social safety net programs	**57** countries with strengthened public financial management systems
IFC		
2.6 million jobs provided	**2.9** million farmers assisted	**5.5** million metric tons of greenhouse emissions expected to be reduced
170 million customers supplied with power, water, and gas	**2.5** million students received educational benefits	**$18.7** billion in government revenues generated by IFC clients
MIGA		
52,000 jobs provided	**47** million people provided access to power	**3.3** million people provided access to clean water
$170 million in new loans provided by MIGA clients	**15** million people provided access to transport	**$1.6** billion in government revenues generated by MIGA client

WORLD BANK

 Nearly tripled financing for maternal and early childhood nutrition programs to $600 million

 Provided $35.3 million people with access to an improved water source

 Helped $6.9 million people gain direct access to electricity

 Recruited or trained $1 million teachers worldwide between 2011 and 2013

 Supported $1.8 million farmers in adopting improved agricultural technology

 Constructed or rehabilitated 95,000 kilometers of roads

IFC

 Supported $2.6 million jobs

 Provided $181 million phone connections

 Educated $2.5 million students

 Cared for $27 million patients

 Made 300 billion in loans to micro, small, and medium enterprises

 Supplied $30.3 million customers with water

MIGA

 Supported shipment of 5.6 million metric tons of freight and cargo

 New or rehabilitated roads used by 87,000 vehicles per day

 Purchased $2 billion in goods and services from domestic suppliers

 Connected 65.4 million subscribers to mobile networks

A

Access to Information Policies
World Bank

The World Bank Policy on Access to Information (AI) became effective on July 1, 2010. In 2013, the AI Policy was modified to include changes to align with the World Bank Group's commitment to greater transparency, accountability, and access to information.

The AI Policy is based on the following five principles:

- Maximizing access to information
- Setting out a clear list of exceptions
- Safeguarding the deliberative process
- Providing clear procedures for making information available
- Recognizing requesters' right to an appeals process

The AI Policy allows public access to any information in the World Bank's possession that is not on its list of 10 exceptions, enabling the Bank to proactively release a wealth of information to the public. The AI Policy has provided the policy framework and the enabling environment necessary for the World Bank to emerge as a convener, leader, and partner in global transparency and openness.

IFC

IFC's Access to Information Policy (AIP) went into effect on January 1, 2012, and superseded the IFC Disclosure of Information Policy (April 2006). Through the AIP, IFC seeks to provide accurate and timely information on its investment and advisory services activities to its clients, partners, and stakeholders.

For each proposed investment, IFC discloses relevant information pertaining to project, environmental, and social implications and expected development impact before consideration by IFC's Board of Directors. For investment projects, IFC discloses a summary of investment information and, if relevant, an environmental and social review summary, depending on the risk category assigned:

- For all Category A investments (that is, those projects expected to have significant adverse social or environmental impacts), disclosure occurs 60 days before Board discussion.

- For all other investments, disclosure occurs 30 days before Board discussion.

In addition, IFC has special disclosure requirements for investments made through financial intermediaries. For advisory services projects, IFC discloses a summary of Advisory Services Project Information within 60 days of approval of the project. IFC's Access to Information Policy allows users to search IFC projects, submit inquiries, subscribe to disclosure documents, and link to related sites.

MIGA

MIGA's Access to Information Policy, updated in December 2013, aims to enhance transparency and promote good governance with a view toward increasing the Agency's development effectiveness and strengthening public trust. The policy defines MIGA's obligations to disclose information about itself and its activities. In accordance with the policy, MIGA discloses summaries of proposed guarantees through its website before consideration by its Board of Directors (or other relevant internal authority). The lead time for this disclosure is as follows:

- Category A projects (that is, those projects expected to have significant adverse social or environmental impacts) are disclosed not less than 60 days before Board consideration.

- All other projects are disclosed not less than 30 days before Board consideration.

The summary of proposed guarantees includes a brief description of the prospective project; its location, purpose, and anticipated development impact; as well as information about the investors and lenders seeking guarantee coverage and about the project enterprise. These summaries are disclosed up until the time of contract signing, at which point a project brief is disclosed. MIGA will cease disclosure of information on a prospective project if it is determined before issuing a guarantee that the Agency will not be involved.

MIGA's Access to Information website provides links to project information, MIGA's

Performance Standards, and the Compliance Advisor Ombudsman.

Evolution of World Bank's Disclosure Policies
http://tinyurl.com/WBG002

IFC's Access to Information Policy
http://tinyurl.com/WBG0044

MIGA's Access to Information Policy
http://tinyurl.com/WBG079

World Bank Policy on Access to Information
http://www.worldbank.org/wbaccess

Accra Agenda for Action The Accra Agenda for Action is designed to strengthen and deepen implementation of the Paris Declaration on Aid Effectiveness. It proposes the following main areas for improvement:

- *Ownership.* Countries have more say over their development processes through wider participation in development policy formulation, stronger leadership on aid coordination, and more use of country systems for aid delivery.

- *Inclusive partnerships.* All partners—including donor agencies and civil society organizations—participate fully.

- *Delivering results.* Aid is focused on real and measurable impact on development.

- *Capacity development.* The ability of countries to manage their own future should be supported.

http://tinyurl.com/WBG0047

ADePT ADePT is a software program that automates and standardizes the production of analytical reports using microlevel data from various types of surveys, such as household budget surveys, demographic and health surveys, and labor force surveys. The results are used to produce rich sets of tables and graphs for a particular area of economic research.

ADePT dramatically reduces the time required for the production of analytical reports, minimizes human errors, allows easy introduction of new techniques to a wide audience of policy practitioners, and allows users to free up resources for other activities such as drawing policy implications from the empirical evidence.

⊃ http://www.worldbank.org/adept

AFR (*See* Africa, Sub-Saharan.)

Africa, Sub-Saharan
World Bank Group in Africa
Sub-Saharan Africa features significant diversity among its 48 countries: the region includes 17 fragile and conflict-affected states, 26 low-income countries, 14 lower-middle-income countries, 7 upper-middle-income countries, and 1 high-income country. Development challenges in these countries vary greatly. The World Bank Group (WBG) continues to engage with all countries across this range to support the broad-based eradication of extreme poverty and to help generate shared prosperity across the region.

With a strong emphasis on increasing regional and national competitiveness and on creating more jobs and opportunities for families—at the same time reducing vulnerability and improving resilience—the WBG works to deepen the impact of its development mission and complement the efforts of other key partners, including African governments, the private sector, civil society, academia, donor agencies, and others.

World Bank in Africa
The World Bank Africa Regional Vice Presidency works selectively and focuses on results, flexibility, efficient delivery, and innovation while increasing the use of programmatic approaches and maximizing the performance of its portfolio. The Bank's assistance to Africa reached a record high in fiscal 2014 with the approval of $10.6 billion for 160 projects. Among the regional priorities are the following:

- *Energy.* Increasing access to affordable, reliable, and sustainable energy is a primary objective of the Bank's work in Africa's energy sector. Sub-Saharan Africa is blessed with large hydropower resources that can create electricity; yet only 10 percent of its potential has been mobilized. Hydropower projects—such as Rusumo Falls in Burundi, Rwanda, and Tanzania and the Jiji-Mulembwe in Burundi—will increase generation capacity, benefiting millions of Africans. The Banda gas-to-power project will produce and convert natural gas from offshore gas fields in Mauritania into 300 megawatts of new electricity. This first-of-its-kind combination of guarantees also mobilizes private investment in gas extraction and energy generation by facilitating power trade among Mali, Mauritania, and Senegal.

- *Agriculture.* The World Bank works to strengthen the resilience of agricultural production systems through landscape approaches, including irrigation, to improve the quality of agricultural policies and public spending and to facilitate inclusive private sector investments in agriculture that focus on land administration programs. Pastoralism and agribusiness are other important areas. In fiscal 2014, the Bank provided more than $1.4 billion in agricultural assistance to Sub-Saharan Africa, a 35 percent increase over the prior two years. Priority projects included support in Ethiopia for improving pastoralism through community development and livelihoods and subregional support for boosting agribusiness in Senegal

AFRICA REGION SNAPSHOT

911.5 million	Total population
2.7 percent	Population growth
$1,345	Gross national income per capita
48.5 percent	Population living below $1.25 per day
56 years	Life expectancy at birth
59.3 percent	Adult (15+) literacy rate

This region includes the following countries:*

Angola
Benin
Botswana
Burkina Faso
Burundi
Cabo Verde
Cameroon
Central African Republic
Chad
Comoros
Democratic Republic of Congo
Republic of Congo
Côte d'Ivoire
Equatorial Guinea
Eritrea
Ethiopia
Gabon
The Gambia
Ghana
Guinea
Guinea-Bissau
Kenya
Lesotho
Liberia
Madagascar
Malawi
Mali
Mauritania
Mauritius
Mozambique
Namibia
Niger
Nigeria
Rwanda
São Tomé and Príncipe
Senegal
Seychelles
Sierra Leone
Somalia
South Africa
South Sudan
Sudan
Swaziland
Tanzania
Togo
Uganda
Zambia
Zimbabwe

*Regions are defined for analytical and operational purposes and may differ from common geographic usage. Variances also exist across the five World Bank Group institutions.

Member Countries by WBG Institution
⟳ www.worldbank.org/en/about/leadership/members#1

and meeting food security and emergency needs in the Central African Republic and Madagascar.

- *Social protection.* Extending coverage of social protection systems to help households mitigate shocks and build human capital is critical, as reflected in the Bank's quickly expanding social protection portfolio, including investments in fragile and conflict-affected situations.

- *Higher education, science, and technology.* Investing in skills and education is crucial to the region. It is particularly important to improve the quality of education and of science and technology training, to spend funds wisely, and to explore appropriate private sector links. The World Bank's new Africa Higher-Education Centers of Excellence Project is funding 19 university-based centers for advanced education in West and Central Africa. It will support regional specialization among participating universities in mathematics, science, engineering, and information and communication technology to address regional challenges. The Bank has long supported Africa's new partners— Brazil, China, the Republic of Korea, and India—in their development. In July 2013, it proposed that these same countries and Japan create a Partnership for Skills in Applied Sciences, Engineering, and Technology to work toward closing skills gaps in Africa's workforce.

IFC in Africa

IFC supports private sector development in Sub-Saharan Africa through innovative investments and advisory services. To help strengthen the private sector role in Africa's development, IFC draws on all its core functions: investing, advising, mobilizing capital, and managing assets. Its work helps simplify business procedures, attract investment, create jobs, and stimulate growth.

IFC supports health, education, agriculture, and infrastructure projects and helps economies recover from conflict. Its strategy is built on three pillars:

- Improving the investment climate by working at both the national and the regional level to remove the barriers to greater private investment. This effort forms the basis for the increased job creation and earning power that lead to poverty reduction.

- Encouraging entrepreneurship by expanding the access of micro, small, and medium enterprise owners to finance, markets, and management skills. IFC places a special emphasis on women entrepreneurs and inclusive business for those who need the most help.

- Transforming key markets and industries through strategic initiatives in priority areas where private sector participation is currently low, beginning with a major focus on infrastructure, food, and agribusiness.

IFC works to increase incomes across Africa through sustainable, inclusive growth, building on the momentum in more successful countries. In others, IFC helps put some of the essential building blocks of private sector development in place: basic infrastructure (especially power and transport) to support agribusiness and manufacturing competitiveness, the improved investment climates and access to finance needed to scale up business growth, and expanded private participation in health and education to serve a growing African population.

MIGA in Africa

Sub-Saharan Africa is a priority area for MIGA, which works to attract new private sector investment in the region by providing political risk insurance (guarantees) and credit enhancement for projects with high development impact in a broad range of sectors. MIGA's support for projects on the continent underscores its commitment to the poorest countries, its capacity to assist fragile situations and countries emerging from conflict, and its ability to work with middle-income countries, including support to local investors planning cross-border investments. Projects it supports create jobs and promote growth and development. Recent guarantees issued by MIGA support investments in infrastructure (in particular power and transport), agribusiness, oil and gas, telecommunications, and services.

Data Resources on Africa
➲ http://data.worldbank.org/region/SSA

Research on Africa
➲ http://www.worldbank.org/en/region/afr/research

Agriculture (*See also* Global Practices.) One of 14 new World Bank Group Global Practices, Agriculture is the most powerful tool available for ending global poverty and boosting shared prosperity.

World Bank Group and Agriculture
Seventy-five percent of the world's poor people live in rural areas; most are involved in farming; and agriculture remains fundamental in the 21st century to eliminating poverty, increasing economic growth, boosting shared prosperity, and promoting environmental sustainability, especially in the context of climate change.

Agriculture accounts for one-third of gross domestic product and three-quarters of employment in Sub-Saharan Africa. Agricultural development is an especially pro-poor source of economic growth—about two to four times more effective in raising incomes among very poor people than growth in other sectors.

Agriculture is more vulnerable to climate change than any other sector, and it is the only sector that can take carbon out of the atmosphere. Worldwide, almost 70 percent of freshwater is used for agriculture. Agriculture and changes in land use are responsible for between 19 and 29 percent of global greenhouse gas emissions. Global food prices remain near historic peaks, and food price volatility needs to be seen as the "new normal." A food system that shifts from being a major contributor to climate change to being part of the solution is needed.

The Bank Group's updated Agriculture Action Plan 2013–15 emphasizes five key areas for action: raising agricultural productivity; linking farmers to markets; reducing risk, vulnerability, and gender inequality; improving nonfarm rural employment; and making agriculture more environmentally sustainable, as well as a source of positive environmental services.

To help countries meet food and nutrition needs and to raise the incomes of smallholder farmers, the World Bank Group is expanding its support to agriculture and related sectors, reaching $8–10 billion per year during 2013–15, up from an average of $7 billion per year during 2010–12. World Bank and IDA agricultural assistance to Sub-Saharan Africa was particularly strong, reaching $1.4 billion, a 35 percent increase over average assistance during fiscal 2010–13. All of IFC's agricultural lending, $3.8 billion in fiscal 2014, goes to agribusiness value chains.

World Bank and Agriculture
In response to the 2008 food crisis, the World Bank launched the Global Food Crisis Response Program (GFRP) to provide immediate relief to countries hard hit by high food prices. The GFRP has reached nearly 70 million people in 49 countries—through $1.6 billion in emergency support—directly for farming, for example, for seeds and fertilizer, and for social safety nets such as emergency school feeding programs. From July 2012 onward, the Bank's emergency response has been channeled through the International Development Association's Crisis Response Window and the recently approved Immediate

The West Africa Agricultural Productivity Program (WAAPP) works with governments and researchers to boost research, farmer education, and advisory services around agricultural innovations. To date, 37 new technologies have improved yields by at least 15 percent on 166,938 hectares of land in Ghana, Mali, Senegal, Sierra Leone, and other West African countries. © World Bank / Arne Hoel (photographer). Permission required for reuse.

Response Mechanism that will provide the basis for emergency assistance in the future.

The Bank administers the Global Agriculture and Food Security Program (GAFSP), which supports country-led agriculture and food security plans and helps promote investments, especially for small-holder farmers. So far, nine countries and the Gates Foundation have pledged about $1.4 billion over three years, with $1.2 billion received.

The World Bank is increasingly employing land-scape approaches to agriculture by taking both a geographical and socioeconomic approach to managing the land, water, and forest resources that form the foundation—the natural capital—for meeting goals of food security and inclusive green growth. The Bank helps promote these integrated approaches, for example, through advocating for climate-smart agriculture, which seeks to increase productivity, enhance resilience, and lower agriculture's footprint—a triple win—by working across landscapes such as crops, livestock, forests, and fisheries. The goal is for farms to thrive without negatively affecting forests, streams, and biodiversity. In addition, the Bank is a strong supporter of the global public goods agenda, such as agricultural research through the Consultative Group on International Agricultural Research (CGIAR), zoonotic diseases, food safety, and community-driven development, among other initiatives.

IFC and Agriculture

IFC has made agribusiness a priority because of its potential for broad development impact and especially strong role in poverty reduction. It combines investments and advisory services to help the sector address higher demand and escalating food prices in an environmentally sustainable and socially inclusive way. IFC also supports global initiatives for sustainable production of agricultural commodities.

IFC provides support for the private sector to address rising demand in an environmentally sustainable and socially inclusive way. To help clients finance inventories, seeds, fertilizers, chemicals, and fuel for farmers, IFC offers working-capital facilities. To facilitate trade and lower costs, IFC pursues investments in infrastructure such as warehouses and cold-storage facilities, and to bring land into sustainable production, IFC works to improve productivity by transferring technologies and making the best use of resources.

MIGA and Agriculture

MIGA guarantees mitigate the noncommercial risks of agribusiness investments, thereby lowering the cost of capital and helping to secure financing. Its insurance reassures lenders that their investments are protected and helps equity owners overcome hesitations that may loom large prior to deal signing, particularly for costly investments in high-risk countries.

Once a deal is in place, MIGA guarantees, backed by the World Bank Group, provide an added measure of security that can stabilize a project's risk profile and reinforce positive relations with host governments. MIGA can also help guide agribusiness

companies as they face challenges related to the environmental and social aspects of their investments. MIGA also advises its agribusiness clients on implementing social and environmental best practices in their operations.

Consultative Group on International Agricultural Research
⮩ http://www.cgiar.org

Data on Agriculture
⮩ http://tinyurl.com/WBG080

Global Agriculture and Food Safety Program
⮩ http://www.gafspfund.org

IFC and Agriculture
⮩ http://tinyurl.com/WBG0046

Research on Agriculture
⮩ http://www.worldbank.org/en/topic/agriculture/research

World Bank Work in Agriculture
⮩ http://worldbank.org/agriculture

World Bank Work in Food Security
⮩ http://www.worldbank.org/foodsecurity

Aid Effectiveness Aid effectiveness is the impact that aid has in reducing poverty and inequality, increasing growth, building capacity, and accelerating achievement of the Millennium Development Goals set by the international community. Aid effectiveness is about improving the delivery and management of aid so that partner countries can more easily achieve their development objectives.

Since the formal inception of the global aid effectiveness agenda through the 2005 Paris Declaration, the World Bank has embraced and championed it, continuously improving its own processes to implement aid effectiveness principles at the country and institutional levels and shaping the global agenda to focus attention on selected key substantive issues:

- A shift from a discussion about traditional donor harmonization and alignment to one of supporting country-led management with a focus on results

- The expanding role of new development partners, such as middle-income countries and the private sector

- The growing importance of aid as a resource for catalytic change and institutional development

- The emergence of new technologies to increase transparency and accountability

The World Bank Group has focused on promoting the leadership and ownership of its partner countries, improved aid management and more effective institutions, development partnerships beyond aid, transparency, and results.

Recognizing that progress on aid effectiveness at the global, institutional, and country levels is linked, the Bank Group continues its engagement and leadership by participating in international initiatives, partnerships, and platforms; leads and innovates through institutional reforms, policies, and practices; and promotes support for country-led and -owned development efforts.

⮑ http://data.worldbank.org/topic/aid-effectiveness

Analytic and Advisory Activities (*See also* Products and Services.)

World Bank Advisory Services

The vast research, analytical, and technical capabilities of the World Bank are a vital part of its contribution to development. Use of these services can help member governments adopt better policies, programs, and reforms that lead to greater economic growth and poverty reduction. Products range from reports on key economic and social issues, to

policy notes, to knowledge-sharing workshops and conferences.

Most of the Bank's analytic and advisory services—that is, its nonlending activities—consist of economic and sector work and technical assistance. Economic and sector analysis examines a country's economic prospects—including, for example, its banking or financial sectors—and its trade, poverty, and social safety net issues. The results often form the basis for assistance strategies, government investment programs, and projects supported by IBRD and IDA lending and guarantees. Much of this economic research output is available through the World Bank's research website.

The Bank's advisory services provide information on such topics as environmentally and socially sustainable development; the financial sector; health, nutrition, and population; and law and justice. Advisory services serve the Bank's clients and staff members, other development organizations, and the general public.

⮑ http://econ.worldbank.org

IFC Advisory Services

IFC's work includes advising national and local governments on how to improve their investment climate and strengthen basic infrastructure. The Corporation helps companies improve corporate governance, strengthen risk management, and become more sustainable—financially, environmentally, and socially.

At the end of fiscal 2014, IFC had an active portfolio of more than 700 advisory services projects in more than 100 countries. Almost two-thirds of the fiscal 2014 program was in IDA countries, and 20 percent was in fragile and conflict-affected areas. During fiscal 2014, IFC provided advice in four broad areas:

- Helping increase the availability and affordability of financial services for individuals and for micro, small, and medium enterprises. IFC helps its financial clients provide broad-based financial services and build the financial infrastructure necessary for sustainable growth and employment.

- Helping governments implement reforms that improve the business environment and encourage and retain investment, thereby fostering competitive markets, growth, and job creation. IFC also helps resolve legal and policy weaknesses that inhibit investment.

- Helping clients promote sound environmental, social, governance, and industry standards; catalyze investment in clean energy and resource efficiency; and support sustainable supply chains and community investment.

- Helping governments design and implement public-private partnerships in infrastructure and other basic public services. IFC's advice helps maximize the potential of the private sector to increase access to public services such as electricity, water, health, and education while enhancing their quality and efficiency.

Annual Bank Conference on Development Economics The Annual Bank Conference on Development Economics (ABCDE) is organized by the World Bank Development Economics Vice Presidency and is one of the world's best-known series of conferences for the presentation and discussion of new knowledge on development. First held in Washington, D.C., in 1988, the series has become broader in scope and aims to promote the exchange of cutting-edge research among researchers, policy makers, and development practitioners.

⮕ http://go.worldbank.org/ICHUVIP8C0

Annual Meetings The Boards of Governors of the World Bank Group and International Monetary Fund hold Annual Meetings each autumn to discuss a range of issues related to poverty reduction,

international economic development, and finance. The Annual Meetings provide a forum for international cooperation and enable the Bank Group and IMF to better serve their member countries.

The Bank Group and the IMF organize a number of opportunities to facilitate the interaction of governments and World Bank–IMF staff with representatives of civil society organizations, journalists, private sector executives, academics, and representatives of other international organizations. Every effort is made to ensure that the Annual Meetings provide an effective forum for explaining to the public the activities, challenges, and achievements of both institutions. The meetings also aim to open up the meetings to the public through live-streamed events and online conversations on World Bank Live, Twitter, and other platforms.

⮕ http://worldbank.org/annualmeetings

Annual Reports Annual reports of World Bank Group organizations and programs are available online. The World Bank, IFC, MIGA, and ICSID each publish an annual report. The reports are available in multiple languages, and the websites include past editions.

ICSID Annual Report
⮕ http://tinyurl.com/WBG0045

IFC Annual Report
⮕ http://www.ifc.org/annualreport

MIGA Annual Report
⮕ http://www.miga.org/resources/index.cfm?stid=1854

World Bank Annual Report
⮕ http://www.worldbank.org/annualreport

Apps World Bank Group apps make it easier to find and use information about the Bank Group and its work, including World Bank documents, reports, policy recommendations, and more. Apps such as World Development Report 2014, Doing Business at a Glance 2014, World Bank DataFinder, World Bank Integrity, Health Stats DataFinder, and World Bank Finances provide resourceful up-to-date information that is accessible with iPhone, iPad, Android, and the mobile Web.

⟳ http://apps.worldbank.org

Archives World Bank Group archives contain records, oral history interviews, policy files, films, videos, photographs, lending project files, video case studies, and learning tools, as well as exhibits from collections and the archives of partner institutions. The expanding collection contains 193,000 linear feet of development information related to World Bank Group member countries dating from 1946 to the present.

⟳ http://worldbank.org/archives

Asset Management (*See also* Products and Services.) IFC's Asset Management Company (AMC) manages funds on behalf of a wide variety of institutional investors, including sovereign funds, pension funds, and development finance institutions. Formed in 2009, the AMC manages third-party capital across six funds that invest in IFC transactions in developing countries. The company uses a strong governance structure and an innovative business model to marry commercial capital with development finance.

⟳ http://www.ifcamc.org

Avian Influenza (*See* Pandemics.)

B

Biodiversity The world's biodiversity is in trouble, with wildlife crime, the spread of invasive species, and loss of habitat reducing the number of species. The loss has economywide consequences, but biodiversity is especially important for the 870 million rural poor whose livelihoods and safety nets are inextricably linked to natural and seminatural ecosystems.

The loss of biodiversity has negative effects on livelihoods, clean water supply, food security, and resilience to environmental disasters. It has consequences for 75 percent of the world's poor—some 870 million people—who live in rural areas and rely on ecosystems and the goods they produce to make a living.

The World Bank is one of the largest international financiers of biodiversity conservation, with a portfolio of 245 projects worth $1.058 billion in the 10 years from fiscal 2004 to 2013. These projects have been undertaken in 74 countries, with the majority in Africa and Latin America and the Caribbean.

The World Bank works with countries to put policies in place so that biodiversity is valued as a key driver of sustainable development. It helps countries improve their administration to better conserve and sustainably use their biodiversity. The Bank invests in those aspects of biodiversity and ecosystem services—such as watershed management and protected areas—that help countries achieve their development goals. The Bank also helps countries find ways to generate revenues from biodiversity—including through tourism payments for environmental services—that will cover the cost of managing their biodiversity and improve economies.

World Bank biodiversity projects include providing support for protected areas, institution building, integrating biodiversity conservation into production landscapes, designing sustainable financing schemes for conservation, promoting nature tourism, and fighting wildlife crime and the spread of invasive species.

⮕ http://www.worldbank.org/en/topic/biodiversity

Black, Eugene (*See* Presidents of the World Bank Group).

Boards of Directors (*See also* Organizational Structure.) General operations of IBRD are delegated to 25 resident Executive Directors, representing the World Bank's 188 member countries. Executive Directors fulfill an important role in deciding on the policies that guide the general operations of the World Bank and its strategic direction, representing the member countries'

RELATIONSHIP OF MEMBER COUNTRIES AND THE WORLD BANK GROUP

Member countries

Boards of Governors

Boards of Executive Directors

President

Bank Group management and staff

viewpoints on the Bank's role. They consider and decide on proposals made by the President for IBRD and IDA loans, credits, and guarantees; new policies; the administrative budget, and financial matters. They also discuss country assistance strategies and are responsible for presenting to the Board of Governors an audit of accounts, an administrative budget, and the *World Bank Annual Report* on fiscal year results.

Boards of Governors (*See also* Organizational Structure.) The World Bank Group operates under the authority of its Boards of Governors. Each member of the Bank appoints a Governor and an Alternate. If the member of the Bank is also a member of IFC and/or IDA, the appointed Governor of the Bank and his or her alternate serve ex officio as Governor and Alternate on the IFC and/or IDA Boards of Governors. MIGA Governors and Alternates are appointed separately. For ICSID, the Bank Governor and Alternate also serve as a member and alternate on the

Administrative Council of ICSID, in the absence of a contrary designation.

Under the Articles of Agreement, all the powers of the Bank shall be vested in the Board of Governors. By a provision in the Bank's bylaws, the Board of Governors has delegated to the Executive Directors all its powers, except those reserved to it under the Articles, or specifically mentioned in the Articles as pertaining to the Board of Governors.

Powers specifically reserved by the Articles for the Governors are those to admit and suspend members, to increase or decrease the authorized capital stock, to determine the distribution of the net income of the Bank, to decide appeals from interpretations of the Articles by the Executive Directors, to make formal comprehensive arrangements to cooperate with other international organizations, and to suspend permanently the operations of the Bank. Other matters specifically mentioned in the Articles as requiring decision by the Board of Governors include increasing the number of elected Executive Directors.

The Board of Governors is also assigned responsibility for approving amendments to the Articles of Agreement of the Bank.

Bretton Woods Institutions (1944) The World Bank and the IMF were both created in 1944 at a conference of world leaders in Bretton Woods, New Hampshire, in the United States. Originally called the United Nations Monetary and Financial Conference, the Bretton Woods Conference—which took place July 1–22, 1944—drafted the Articles of Agreement for IBRD and the IMF with the aim of placing the international economy on a sound footing after World War II.

As a result of their shared origin, the two entities— the IMF and the expanded World Bank Group—are sometimes referred to collectively as the Bretton Woods institutions. The Bank Group and the IMF work closely together, have similar governance structures, have a similar relationship with the United Nations, and have headquarters in close proximity in

The Bretton Woods Conference took place at Mount Washington Hotel, situated in Bretton Woods, New Hampshire. © World Bank. Permission required for reuse.

Washington, D.C. Although membership in the Bank Group's institutions is open only to countries that are already members of the IMF, the Bank Group and the IMF remain separate institutions. Their work is complementary, but their individual roles are quite different.

The Bank Group lends only to developing or transition economies, whereas all member countries, rich or poor, can draw on the IMF's services and resources. The IMF's loans address short-term economic problems: they provide general support for a country's balance of payments and international reserves while the country takes policy action to address its difficulties. The Bank Group is concerned mainly with longer-term issues: it seeks to integrate countries into the wider world economy and to promote economic growth that reduces poverty.

The IMF focuses on the macroeconomic performance of economies, as well as on macroeconomic and financial sector policy. The Bank Group's focus extends further into the particular sectors of a country's economy, and its work includes specific development projects as well as broader policy issues.

Busan Partnership for Effective Development Cooperation In 2011, the Global Partnership for Effective Development Cooperation built on a range of international efforts, including those begun in the Monterrey Consensus of 2002, the Rome Declaration on Harmonisation (2003), the Paris Declaration on Aid Effectiveness (2005), and the Accra Agenda for Action in 2008. The Busan Partnership agreement sets out principles, commitments, and actions that offer a foundation for effective cooperation in support of international development.

The Busan Partnership for Effective Development Cooperation for the first time established an agreed framework for development cooperation that embraces traditional donors, South-South cooperators, the BRICS (that is, Brazil, the Russian Federation, India, and China), civil society organizations, and private funders.

⟳ http://effectivecooperation.org

C

Cai, Jin-Yong Jin-Yong Cai is the Executive Vice President and CEO of IFC, the largest global development institution focused on private sector development and the fight against poverty. Cai, a Chinese national, joined IFC on October 1, 2012. He has extensive experience in private sector development in emerging markets across the globe and a record of success in managing highly complex business transactions with clients in developed and developing markets alike. Throughout his career, he has been recognized for his role in major transactions in financing, restructuring, and mergers and acquisitions.

Before joining IFC, Cai worked in the financial services industry for 20 years. Cai, who began his professional career in the World Bank Group in 1990, has a PhD in economics from Boston University and a BS from Peking University.

Chief Economist (*See also* Regional Chief Economists.) The World Bank's Chief Economist and Senior Vice President heads the main research and knowledge-generation Vice Presidency. Development Economics (known as DEC) provides data, analyses of macroeconomic and development prospects, research findings, analytical tools, and policy advice in support of Bank operations, as well as advice to clients. DEC produces the annual *World Development Report*, prepared each year by a team comprising Bank staff members and experts from outside the Bank Group. Kaushik Basu is the current Chief Economist of the World Bank.

Citizens Engagement The World Bank Group has established an Advisory Council to guide the development and implementation of a Strategic Framework for Mainstreaming Citizen Engagement in World Bank Group Operations. The framework is a follow-up to the Bank's strategy commitment to increase engagement with citizens for improved results and achieve 100 percent beneficiary feedback in projects with clearly identifiable beneficiaries.

The Advisory Council's remit is to provide its guidance and expertise on how citizen engagement, including beneficiary feedback, can improve the results of World Bank Group–financed development interventions. Members are expected to meet every six months to discuss the implementation of the strategic framework, provide recommendations, and assist in evaluating lessons learned.

The Participation and Civic Engagement Group
The Participation and Civic Engagement Group works to enhance capacity for participatory

processes and social accountability and develops analytical instruments to assess constraints to the effectiveness of civil society. The group focuses on the following themes:

- Social accountability promotes the participation of citizens and communities in exacting accountability.

- An enabling environment for civic engagement promotes conditions that facilitate the effective engagement of civil society in development policies and projects.

- Participatory monitoring and evaluation promote the participation of local beneficiaries in the monitoring and evaluation of projects and programs.

- Participation at the project, program, and policy levels promotes participatory processes and stakeholder engagement in projects, programs, and policies.

Civil Society Organizations (*See also* Nongovernmental Organizations.) The World Bank Group interacts with thousands of country, regional, and global civil society organizations (CSOs) throughout the world. These CSOs include nongovernmental organizations, trade unions, faith-based organizations, indigenous peoples' organizations, foundations, and many others. These interactions range from CSOs that critically monitor the Bank's work and engage the Bank Group in policy discussions to those that actively collaborate with the Bank in operational activities. There are many examples of active partnerships in the areas of forest conservation, AIDS vaccines, rural poverty, microcredit, and Internet development.

Classification of Countries Several designations for member countries commonly used by the World Bank Group reflect important distinctions among them. Although the meanings of the terms overlap—and they are all based on wealth—they are not interchangeable.

Low-Income, Middle-Income, and High-Income Economies
In its analytical and operational work, the Bank Group characterizes country economies as low income, middle income (subdivided into lower-middle income and upper-middle income), and high income. It makes these classifications for most nonsovereign territories as well as for independent countries. Low-income and middle-income economies are sometimes referred to as developing economies.

In fiscal 2015, low-income economies are defined as those with a gross national income (GNI) per capita, calculated using the World Bank Atlas method, of $1,045 or less in 2013; middle-income economies are those with a GNI per capita of more than $1,045 but less than $12,746; high-income economies are those with a GNI per capita of $12,746 or more. Lower-middle-income and upper-middle-income economies are separated at a GNI per capita of $4,125. Classification by income does not necessarily reflect development status.

Developing and Industrial Countries
In general, the term *developing* refers to countries whose economies are classified as low income or middle income. The terms *industrial* or *developed* refer to countries whose economies are high income. The use of these terms is not intended to imply that all economies in the group are experiencing similar development or that other economies have reached a preferred or final stage of development.

Part I and Part II Countries
In IDA, countries choose whether they are Part I or Part II primarily on the basis of their economic standing. Part I countries are almost all industrial countries and donors to IDA, and they pay their contributions in freely convertible currency. Part II countries are

almost all developing countries, some of which are donors to IDA. Part II countries are entitled to pay most of their contributions to IDA in local currency.

MIGA makes a similar distinction between Category I and Category II member countries. The breakdown of countries into these categories differs slightly from the breakdown within IDA.

Donors and Borrowers

In general, the term *donor* refers to a country that makes contributions specifically to IDA. In contrast, the term *borrower* refers to a country that borrows from IDA or IBRD or both. However, all member countries pay capital subscriptions, and this payment is distinct from a given country's lending and borrowing.

IBRD, IDA, and Blend Countries and Graduates

The distinctions between IBRD and IDA borrowers—and the circumstances in which a country may be eligible to receive a blend of IBRD loans and IDA credits and grants—are based on per capita income and the country's creditworthiness. Note that as a country's per capita income increases, it can graduate out of eligibility for IDA credits and grants and, in turn, become eligible for IBRD loans. Wealthier countries remain members of Bank Group organizations, however, even if they or the enterprises operating within their borders do not draw on Bank Group services.

⮕ http://data.worldbank.org/news/new-country-classifications

Clausen, Alden W. (*See* Presidents of the World Bank Group).

Climate Change (*See also* Cross-Cutting Solution Areas.)

World Bank Group and Climate Change

Climate Change—one of five new Cross-Cutting Solution Areas—is a fundamental threat to development and the fight against poverty. The World Bank Group is concerned that without bold action now, the warming planet could put prosperity out of the reach of millions and roll back decades of development.

The science is unequivocal that humans are the cause of global warming, and that major changes are already being observed. The intensity of extreme weather-related events has also increased. Recent experience is a stark reminder that no country—rich or poor—is immune to the impacts of climate-related disasters today. The Bank Group is therefore stepping up its mitigation, adaptation, and disaster risk management work and will increasingly look at all its business through a climate lens.

The Bank is trustee of 15 carbon finance initiatives that have supported more than 145 active projects in 70 client countries. Since 2000, these initiatives have reduced the equivalent of 187 million tons of carbon dioxide emissions through the projects they support. The Bank is also supporting work on ending fossil fuel subsidies.

The World Bank Treasury and IFC are also the world's largest issuers of green bonds, which support climate-related projects such as increasing energy efficiency and the development of renewable energy—with more than $6.3 billion with green bonds raised by the World Bank Treasury. IBRD has issued 66 World Bank Green Bonds in 17 currencies, supporting 50 projects in 17 member countries.

The World Bank Group has successfully mobilized additional resources to finance climate action by working with partners. These resources include the $8 billion Climate Investment Funds, which are designed to provide scaled-up financing through the multilateral development banks to initiate transformational change toward climate-resilient, low-carbon development.

The World Bank Climate Vice Presidency, established in January 2014, is working to leverage both public and private sources of climate finance to support climate-smart policy and investments and help countries and businesses adapt to a changing climate.

The Third Climate Change Development Policy Operation Program supports the government of Vietnam in its efforts to address climate change by strengthening institutional capacity to promote climate resilience and lower carbon intensity development. The project contributes to Vietnam's efforts to move toward more environmentally sustainable growth as outlined in the Socio-Economic Development Plan for 2011–2015. © World Bank / Tran Thi Hoa (photographer). Permission required for reuse.

World Bank and Climate Change

To help get prices right, get finance flowing, and make progress where it matters most, the Bank focuses on five key areas:

- Building low-carbon, climate-resilient cities—particularly through assistance with low-carbon planning, energy-efficiency assessments, and finance—targets the fast-growing metropolitan areas, which are connected to 70 percent of global emissions

- Moving forward on climate-smart agriculture improves yields to feed a growing global population, reduces emissions, and adds carbon storage

- Accelerating energy efficiency and investment in renewable energy helps shifts the world away from high-carbon fossil fuels

- Developing carbon pricing helps set the right prices on emissions

Another important move that can make a difference quickly is reducing short-lived climate pollutants (SLCP)—such as soot from fires and diesel vehicles and methane from landfills and extractive industries. Countries can reap the added reward of reducing the impact on snow and glaciers and of lowering the costs to human health and crops.

Through the Global Facility for Disaster Reduction and Recovery, the Bank is helping developing countries reduce their vulnerability to natural hazards and adapt to climate change by mainstreaming disaster risk reduction and climate change adaptation in country development strategies.

Knowledge portals—including the Climate Change Knowledge Portal, the Climate Finance Options Platform, and the Platform for Climate Smart Planning—provide countries with cutting-edge information, analysis, and tools on climate change.

To tackle short-lived climate pollutants, the Bank launched a review of its own portfolio to identify ways to do more through its projects to reduce the emission of these pollutants and found that 7.7 percent of World Bank commitments, or approximately $18 billion, went into "SLCP-relevant" activities between 2007 and 2012.

Following the Bank's own Strategic Framework for Development and Climate Change in 2008 and the *World Development Report* on climate change in 2010, the Bank is developing a new Climate Action Plan that will enhance the resilience of countries, support inclusive green growth, and integrate climate risk assessments in investment decisions across the Bank Group's portfolio.

IFC and Climate Change

IFC works to support renewable power, energy efficiency, and other climate-smart solutions for developing countries. IFC has invested more than $13 billion in climate-related projects since 2005, including about $2.5 billion in fiscal 2014. Specific initiatives illustrate the ways in which IFC is responding to the need to address climate change through private sector approaches:

- *Leveraging climate financing.* IFC is helping commercial banks in Armenia, China, Lebanon, and elsewhere increase their lending for clean and efficient energy and is working to support trade finance for climate-related goods and services.

- *Green bonds.* IFC's Treasury has issued more than $3 billion in green bonds, including two $1 billion issuances in 2013, and is working with investment banks and other issuers to grow the market for this new asset class.

- *Catalyst Fund.* IFC's Asset Management Company has raised some $400 million from six investors, including sovereign wealth and pension funds, for this private equity fund of funds supporting renewable energy and energy efficiency.

- *Blended finance.* In rare circumstances, IFC uses funds from donor governments to invest in high-impact climate projects on concessional terms to help overcome market barriers or perceived risk that would otherwise make projects impossible.

MIGA and Climate Change

MIGA's work to reduce the impact of climate change focuses on moving developing countries onto a lower carbon path by exploiting renewable energy resources, supporting energy conservation, and increasing efficiency. MIGA's added value is especially evident in green infrastructure development. MIGA is supporting energy transformation by insuring sustainable power investments in all regions of the world. Geothermal energy in Kenya, wind energy in Nicaragua, waste-to-energy in China, hydropower in Angola and Pakistan, and public transport in Panama and Turkey—these are all examples of MIGA-insured projects that demonstrate the Agency's commitment to this critical sector.

Community-Driven Development Community-driven development (CDD) is an approach that gives control over planning decisions and investment resources for local development projects to community groups.

CDD programs operate on the principles of local empowerment, participatory governance, demand-responsiveness, administrative autonomy, greater downward accountability, and enhanced local capacity.

Experience has shown that when given clear explanations of the process, access to information, and appropriate capacity and financial support, poor men and women can effectively organize to identify community priorities and address local problems by working in partnership with local governments and other supportive institutions.

The World Bank recognizes that CDD approaches and actions are important elements of an effective poverty reduction and sustainable development strategy. Over the past decade, the Bank has increasingly focused on lending to CDD programs in order to reach local communities directly. The Bank has used the CDD approach across a range of countries to support a variety of urgent needs, including water supply and sewer rehabilitation, school and health post construction, nutrition programs for mothers and infants, building of rural access roads, and support for microenterprise.

⮕ http://tinyurl.com/WBG0043

Compliance Advisor Ombudsman The Compliance Advisor Ombudsman (CAO) is the independent recourse mechanism for IFC and MIGA. The CAO responds to complaints from project-affected communities with the goal of enhancing social and environmental outcomes on the ground.

The CAO works to:

- Address the concerns of individuals or communities affected by IFC and MIGA projects

- Enhance the social and environmental outcomes of IFC and MIGA projects

- Foster greater public accountability of IFC and MIGA

⟳ http://www.cao-ombudsman.org

Compliance Mechanisms and Monitoring In 2010, the World Bank Integrity Vice Presidency appointed an Integrity Compliance Officer to monitor integrity compliance by sanctioned companies (or codes of conduct for individuals). The officer also decides whether the compliance condition—and/or others established by the Sanctions Board or a World Bank Group (WBG) evaluation and suspension officer as part of a debarment—has been satisfied.

The WBG Integrity Compliance Guidelines incorporate standards, principles, and components commonly recognized by many institutions and entities as good governance and antifraud and anticorruption practices. They are not intended to be all-inclusive, exclusive, or prescriptive; rather, a party's adoption of these guidelines, or variants thereof, should be determined based on that party's own circumstances.

As part of the WBG's continuing effort to improve its sanctions regime, the existing sanction of debarment with conditional release has become the default or baseline WBG sanction for cases initiated under the Bank Group's revised Sanctions Procedures effective September 2010. The establishment (or improvement) and implementation of an integrity compliance program satisfactory to the WBG is a principal condition to ending a debarment (or conditional nondebarment) or, in the case of some existing debarments, early termination of the debarment.

Conable, Barber B. (*See* Presidents of the World Bank Group.)

Concessional Finance and Global Partnerships (*See* Development Finance.)

Concessional Lending (*See also* Products and Services.) IDA lends money on concessional terms. This means that IDA charges little or no interest and repayments are stretched over 25–40 years, including a 5- to 10-year grace period. IDA has become the leading source of concessional lending to 82 of the world's poorest countries, with 40 countries in Africa.

Conciliation and Arbitration ICSID provides facilities for and coordination of the conciliation and arbitration of investment disputes between contracting states and nationals of other contracting states. ICSID's objective in making such facilities available is to promote an atmosphere of mutual confidence between states and foreign investors—an atmosphere that is conducive to increasing the flow of private international investment.

Conferences (*See* Events.)

Conflict Countries (*See* Fragile and Conflict-Affected Countries and Situations.)

Conflict Resolution System (*See also* Enabling Services.) Because of immunities, the World Bank cannot be sued in national courts by staff members with employment claims. Therefore, the Bank Group established the Conflict Resolution System (CRS) to handle such concerns. The CRS is a group of independent offices that addresses workplace problems such as disputes regarding staff rules, pay, career advancement, performance evaluation, and benefits.

The CRS includes the Respectful Workplace Advisors Program, the Ombuds Services Office, the Office of Mediation Services, and Peer Review Services. Another component of the CRS is the Administrative Tribunal, which handles formal claims and is an independent judicial forum of last resort staffed by seven external judges. The Office of Ethics and Business Conduct and the World

Bank Integrity Vice Presidency also form part of the CRS.

Connect4Climate Connect4Climate (C4C) is a campaign, a coalition, and a community that cares about climate change. The goal of Connect4Climate is to create a participatory, open knowledge platform that engages the global community in climate change conversation to drive local action through advocacy, operational support, research, and capacity building.

⟳ http://www.connect4climate.org

Consultations The World Bank Group Consultation Hub provides a one-stop shop for those interested in consultations hosted by the World Bank Group. On the hub are listed all ongoing and planned consultations as well as those that were closed within the past year. Information on the subject of consultation, on the scope and process of consultation, and on how to contribute to the World Bank Group's decision-making process is available. Feedback submitted by World Bank Group stakeholders can be viewed on a range of topics.

⟳ http://consultations.worldbank.org

Consultative Group to Assist the Poorest Consultative Group to Assist the Poorest (CGAP) is a global partnership of 34 leading organizations that seek to advance financial inclusion. CGAP develops innovative solutions through practical research and active engagement with financial service providers, policy makers, and funders to enable approaches at scale. CGAP combines a pragmatic approach to responsible market development with an evidence-based advocacy platform to increase access to the financial services the poor need to improve their lives.

⟳ http://www.cgap.org

Corporate Governance Improving corporate governance is a priority for IFC. Good corporate governance contributes to sustainable economic development by enhancing the performance of companies and increasing their access to outside capital. Increased access to capital encourages new investments, boosts economic growth, and provides employment opportunities. Good corporate governance also helps companies operate more efficiently, mitigates risk, and safeguards against mismanagement. Well-governed companies are therefore more accountable and transparent to investors and have the tools to respond to stakeholder concerns.

IFC was the first development finance institution to require corporate governance analysis of every investment transaction as part of its due diligence process. IFC provides investment support and advice on good practices for improving board effectiveness, strengthening shareholder rights, and enhancing the governance of risk management, internal controls, and corporate disclosure.

IFC works in close collaboration with the World Bank to ensure that regulation in emerging markets is developed using IFC's frontline experience as an investor. As such, IFC also advises regulators, stock market administrators, and others with an interest in improving corporate governance.

The IFC Corporate Governance Methodology is a system for evaluating corporate governance risks and opportunities that is recognized as the most advanced of its kind among development finance institutions. This methodology is the basis for a coordinated approach to corporate governance now implemented by more than 30 development finance institutions. IFC also helps strengthen local partners who will continue to provide corporate governance services over the long term. This includes training materials and institution-building tools in the areas of corporate governance associations, codes and scorecards, board leadership training, dispute resolution, the training of business reporters, and implementation of good governance practices in firms.

Strong corporate governance depends on diversity in board leadership. IFC strives to increase the number of women who serve as nominee directors on the boards of its clients. Nearly 24 percent of IFC nominee directors are women, and IFC is committed to increasing that share to 30 percent by 2015.

Corporate Scorecard (*See also* Results Measurement.) The World Bank Group (WBG) Corporate Scorecard provides a high-level and strategic overview of the Bank Group's progress toward achieving two strategic goals: ending extreme poverty by reducing the percentage of people living on less than $1.25 a day to 3 percent by 2030, and boosting shared prosperity by fostering income growth for the bottom 40 percent of the population in every country.

The scorecard is structured in three tiers:

* The goals and development context tier provides an overview of progress on key development challenges faced by WBG client countries.

* The results tier reports on the key sectoral and multisectoral results achieved by WBG clients with support of Bank Group operations in pursuit of the goals.

* The performance tier captures WBG performance in implementation of Bank Group strategy and includes measures of both operational and organizational effectiveness.

These three tiers are the components of a unified results and performance monitoring framework with indicators grouped along the results chain as follows: the scorecard monitors in aggregate how the Bank Group implements its strategy and improves its performance (Tier III) to support clients in achieving results (Tier II) in the context of global development progress (Tier I).

The indicators in the first two tiers are grouped into three categories encompassing growth, inclusiveness, and sustainability/resilience. The Bank Group strategy recognizes the importance of each of these three areas for the achievement of the two goals. The economic growth that creates good jobs requires action to strengthen both the private and the public sectors. Inclusion entails empowering all citizens to participate in, and benefit from, the development process and removing barriers against those who are often excluded. Sustainability ensures that today's development progress is not reversed tomorrow; it implies securing the long-term future of the planet and its resources, ensuring social inclusion, and limiting the economic burdens on future generations. In recognition of the importance that the strategy places on fragility and gender, scorecard indicators are disaggregated by gender and by fragile and conflict-affected situations, when feasible.

⤵ http://corporatescorecard.worldbank.org

Corporate Secretariat (*See also* Enabling Services.) The Corporate Secretariat (SEC) Vice Presidency of the World Bank Group supports the Board of Governors and the Executive Directors of IBRD/IDA, IFC, and MIGA in executing their fiduciary and governance responsibilities. SEC therefore maintains relations across all the World Bank Group institutions and serves as the key interlocutor between the Board of Governors, the Executive Directors, the President and Senior Management, Operational Management, and staff. SEC's primary purpose is to facilitate effective, efficient, and strategically focused interactions between the Board and management to achieve the goals of the World Bank Group.

Corruption (*See also* Integrity Vice Presidency.) The World Bank Group views good governance and anticorruption as critical to its mission of ending extreme poverty and boosting shared prosperity. Many governance and anticorruption initiatives are taking place throughout the Bank Group. These initiatives focus on ensuring internal organizational integrity, minimizing corruption on World Bank–funded projects, and assisting countries in promoting openness and enhancing efficiency.

The Bank Group does this by providing policy and institutional advice and support to countries in their formulation of action programs and by building the capacity of a wide range of stakeholders to advance openness and accountability. Using a strategic and multidisciplinary approach, the Bank applies action-learning methods to link empirical diagnostic surveys, their practical application, collective action, and prevention. Concrete results are emphasized in its learning programs and clinics as well as through the periodic release of the Worldwide Governance Indicators and country diagnostics. This integrated approach is supported by operational research and a comprehensive governance databank.

Fighting corruption by promoting good governance has become a policy priority for the development community over the past two decades, and extensive reform efforts have been launched. These reforms build on the idea that corruption is a dysfunction of public administration, which in turn can be curbed by promoting accountability and transparency.

The World Bank Group is committed to improving governance and fighting corruption in its member countries through the Governance Anticorruption Framework, which has three main pillars:

- Helping countries build capable, transparent, open, and accountable institutions

- Expanding partnerships with multilateral and bilateral development institutions, civil society, the private sector, and other actors in joint initiatives to address corruption

- Minimizing corruption in World Bank–funded projects by assessing corruption risk in projects upstream, actively investigating allegations of fraud and corruption, and strengthening project oversight and supervision

Any person can report allegations of fraud and corruption involving World Bank Group–financed operations, supported activities, or staff by contacting 1 (800) 831-0463.

Country Assistance Strategy (*See also* Country Partnership Framework.) The Country Assistance Strategy was discontinued in 2014.

Country Economic Memorandum The Country Economic Memorandum (CEM) provides a comprehensive analysis of a country's economic developments, prospects, and policy agenda, and it identifies policy reforms for key economic sectors. The CEM also serves as a basis for dialogue with government on critical policy issues and provides background information and analysis to members of aid groups and other donors.

Country Engagement Model (*See also* Comprehensive Development Framework; Country Partnership Strategy.)

Systematic Country Diagnostic

The Systematic Country Diagnostic (SCD) is intended to become a reference point for client consultations on priorities for WBG country engagement. It is intended to help the country, the WBG, and other development partners establish a dialogue to focus their efforts around goals and activities that have high impact and are aligned with the global goals of ending absolute poverty and boosting shared prosperity in a sustainable manner.

Country Partnership Framework

In 2014, the Country Partnership Framework (CPF) replaced the Country Assistance/Partnership Strategy (CAS/CPS). The CPF is a four- to six-year strategy that the World Bank Group develops for a country to guide its operational activities. The CPF focuses on the Bank Group's added value in that country and is produced in close coordination with the Bank's counterpart in government (usually the Ministry of Planning/International Cooperation or Ministry of Finance). All projects and programs that the Bank finances within the time frame of this strategy must be aligned with it.

The CPF is built around a results framework that identifies the objectives that the WBG activities are expected to help the country achieve, the results chain that links the objectives to the country's development goals, and indicators of progress. It also lays out how the objectives will contribute to the Bank Group's twin goals of reducing absolute poverty and boosting shared prosperity in a sustainable manner.

Country Management Units Each of the six Regional Vice Presidencies within the World Bank—Africa, East Asia and Pacific, Europe and Central Asia, Latin America and the Caribbean, Middle East and North Africa, and South Asia—has several Country Management Units (CMUs). Each CMU is responsible for Bank dialogue with the country government and the preparation of the country assistance strategy, which is the basis for the Bank's financial support to the country.

Country Offices The Bank has established country offices in most of the borrowing countries. Over 50 Country Management Units (CMUs) and their respective Country Directors are located at the country level. These CMUs provide information on Bank activities and business opportunities in the respective countries and improve the Bank's institutional footprint in those countries.

⮕ http://go.worldbank.org/Q0CG1KOW90

Country Partnership Strategy (*See also* Comprehensive Development Framework) The Country Partnership Strategy was discontinued in 2014.

Country Policy and Institutional Assessment The Country Policy and Institutional Assessment (CPIA) is a diagnostic tool intended to capture the quality of a country's policies and institutional arrangements—that is, its focus is on the key elements that are within the country's control rather than on outcomes (such as growth rates) that are influenced by elements outside the country's control. More specifically, the CPIA measures the extent to which a country's policy and institutional framework support sustainable growth and poverty reduction and consequently the effective use of development assistance.

Credit Enhancement (*See also* Guarantees; Products and Services.) A World Bank guarantee is seen by investors as a stabilizing factor in transactions with sovereign governments. By covering a government or government entity's failure to meet specific contractual obligations to a project, World Bank guarantees help attract private sector investment in oil, gas, and mining; power; telecommunications; transport; and water projects; and they enhance private sector participation in privatizations and public-private partnerships. Guarantees also help governments and projects access international capital markets or local financing on more favorable terms. In addition to the leverage effect, guarantees have also played a valuable role in easing the entry of emerging economies into international capital markets by helping them acquire a track record of credible policy performance.

MIGA also supplies credit enhancement through its nonhonoring of financial obligations coverage to encourage and support cross-border investment in its developing member countries.

MIGA Credit Enhancement
⮕ http://www.miga.org/documents/NHFObrief.pdf

World Bank Credit Enhancement
⮕ http://tinyurl.com/WBG0042

Cross-Cutting Solution Areas (*See also* Global Practices.) In 2014, the World Bank Group (WBG) adopted a new strategy for achieving two ambitious goals: eradicating extreme poverty by reducing the number of people living on less than $1.25 a day to

3 percent by 2030, and promoting shared prosperity by fostering the income growth of the bottom 40 percent in every country. That strategy leverages the strengths of Bank Group institutions and their unique ability to partner with the public and private sectors to deliver customized development solutions backed by finance, world-class knowledge, and convening services.

Underpinning the strategy are 14 Global Practices and 5 Cross-Cutting Solution Areas (CCSAs), all newly created. The Global Practices and CCSAs, in concert with the WBG regions, will pool their expertise to address clients' most pressing developmental challenges and ultimately enable the WBG to meet its goals. The five CCSAs are Climate Change; Fragility, Conflict, and Violence; Gender; Jobs; and Public-Private Partnerships:

Climate Change

The first priority of this area is to ensure that solutions are fit-for-purpose and that the CCSA is able to deliver the best evidence of the impact of climate on the poorest, the most valuable tools for all those working on climate action, and the best assessment of climate risk and opportunity for clients. The key question will be how the Climate Change CSSA can make the Global Practices, the regions, and the external clients successful in what they do. Recognizing that climate finance must come from both the public and the private sectors, the Climate Change CCSA is committed to making sure every action is vital to helping the World Bank Group achieve its key goals. Alliances will be a critical part of success, since the goals cannot be achieved by working alone.

Fragility, Conflict, and Violence (*See also* Conflict Countries.)

To achieve the full potential of Bank-wide engagement on issues of fragility, conflict, and violence, the WBG will focus on the following areas: maximizing the role of the private sector for inclusive growth and job creation; integrating considerations of fragile and conflict-affected situations into country partnership frameworks and projects; building a knowledge base on development interventions that support the clients' transition out of fragility, conflict, and violence; building appropriate frontline staffing and skills and a security and support infrastructure and exploiting flexibility in the robust policy framework; working with countries and partners on analysis and support for adequate public financial management and macro and fiscal frameworks; and enhancing existing and forging new and closer partnerships with a wide range of external actors who have both the mandate and the comparative advantage to engage on all sides of the complex political, social, and security questions.

Gender

The WBG seeks stronger, better-resourced, and more evidence-based efforts to address gender inequalities in human development and access to services and sustainable development, especially for the poorest. The Gender CCSA also seeks to focus on areas that could have transformational impacts in areas such as gender-based violence; inequality at work; entrepreneurship; leadership; access to financing and financial services; and discrimination under the law that prevents women from signing a contract, taking out a loan, or inheriting property, for example.

Jobs

The WBG regards the issue of sustainable jobs as critical to its mission. Ending poverty and boosting shared prosperity require that people—particularly vulnerable groups such as women and youth—have access to jobs. The challenge is to create enough jobs to have a transformational effect on living standards, productivity, and social cohesion. The WBG can help governments develop integrated and tailored jobs strategies by interpreting development challenges through a jobs lens and fully engaging the private sector in finding solutions to the jobs challenge, as well as by proposing holistic and multisectoral approaches. The WBG can also work directly with private sector companies by helping strengthen domestic value chains, by reducing critical constraints such as infrastructure or finance, or by designing training programs.

Public-Private Partnerships

Public-private partnerships (PPPs) are one of the WBG's core cross-cutting tools for addressing pressing development challenges. The PPP CCSA will support the delivery of advice and technical assistance to governments on the design of PPPs that are consistent with emerging lessons of global experience. A focus on improved outcomes (including mobilization of private sector investment), rather than on individual enabling steps, is expected to improve the extent and quality of the WBG's services to clients. Expected results of the PPP CCSA are greater internal coordination and greater client satisfaction with Bank Group advice on service provision and financing modalities as well as greater financial leverage and expansion of access to basic services.

D

Development Committee The Development Committee is a ministerial forum of the World Bank Group and the International Monetary Fund for intergovernmental consensus building on development issues. Known formally as the Joint Ministerial Committee of the Boards of Governors of the Bank and the Fund on the Transfer of Real Resources to Developing Countries, the committee was established in 1974.

The committee's mandate is to advise the Boards of Governors of the Bank and the Fund on critical development issues and on the financial resources required to promote economic development in developing countries. Over the years, the committee has interpreted this mandate to include trade and global environmental issues in addition to traditional development matters.

➲ http://tinyurl.com/WBG075

Development Economics (*See also* Enabling Services.) The World Bank's Chief Economist and Senior Vice President heads this main research and knowledge-generation Vice Presidential Unit. The Development Economics (DEC) Vice Presidency provides data, analyses of macroeconomic and development prospects, research findings, analytical tools, and policy advice in support of Bank operations, as well as advice to clients. DEC produces the annual *World Development Report*, prepared each year by a team comprising Bank staff members and experts from outside the Bank Group.

Development Finance The Development Finance (DFi) Vice Presidency is responsible for managing and monitoring policies and procedures for World Bank development financing vehicles. DFi engages in strategic resource mobilization, playing an intermediation role to help align the needs of recipients, World Bank Group institutional priorities, and priorities of funding partners through a variety of funding instruments. These include IDA and trust funds, including financing intermediary funds.

Previously known as Concessional Finance and Global Partnerships (CFP), DFi has moved from an exclusive focus on concessional finance to a broader focus on development finance. The new approach is geared toward leveraging the financial resources and instruments of the entire World Bank Group to increase the pool and types of funding available to clients, particularly for transformative projects.

➲ http://tinyurl.com/WBG009

Development Marketplace For more than 15 years, the World Bank Group's Development Marketplace (DM) has identified innovative social entrepreneurs who tackle service delivery bottlenecks that disproportionately affect the world's poorest populations. Originally a competitive grants program, the DM has evolved into a multifaceted, consultative program that identifies these entrepreneurs and analyzes their specific needs to provide capacity development and technical assistance. The DM aims to map these innovative solutions to identify quickly and efficiently service delivery problems that exist around the world and to provide the most effective solution possible. Since its inception in 1998, the DM has awarded more than $65 million in grants to more than 1,200 innovative projects.

⟳ http://wbi.worldbank.org/developmentmarketplace

Development Policy Operations Development Policy Operations provide direct budget support to governments for policy and institutional reforms aimed at achieving a set of specific development results. These operations provide rapid financial assistance to allow countries to deal with actual or anticipated development financing requirements. The operations are supportive of, and consistent with, the country's economic and sectoral policies and institutions aimed at accelerated sustainable growth and efficient resource allocation. They typically support a program of policy and institutional actions, for example, to improve the investment climate, diversify the economy, create employment, and meet applicable international commitments. Any investment financing subcomponent included in a development policy operation is subject to the relevant operational policies for investment financing.

Development policy operations are delivered as a series of annual loans, credits, or guarantees to support a government's medium-term program of policy reforms. Lending funds from each operation are disbursed against (or raised after, in the case of guarantee operations) the achievement of a mutually agreed set of policy and institutional actions. In low-income countries where a national poverty reduction strategy has been adopted by the government and where a development policy series supports implementation of that strategy, development policy operations may also be called poverty reduction support credits.

The World Bank's policy for Development Policy Lending (DPL) was updated in February 2012 to provide a unified framework for all development policy operations. It is a single lending instrument, leaving room for customizing content and design to country circumstances.

DPL aims to help a borrower achieve sustainable reductions in poverty through a program of policy and institutional actions that promote growth and enhance the well-being and increase the incomes of poor people. Every three years, the World Bank reviews its use of Development Policy Lending. The "2012 Development Policy Lending Retrospective" was the third such retrospective since Development Policy Operations was introduced in 2004. It covers 221 development policy operations approved by the Board between 2009 and 2012.

Disability One billion people, or 15 percent of the world's population, experience some form of disability. Persons with disabilities, on average, are more likely to experience adverse socioeconomic outcomes than persons without disabilities, such as lower rates of education, worse health outcomes, less employment, and higher poverty levels.

Disability and poverty are complex, dynamic, and intricately linked phenomena. Therefore, integrating disability into existing World Bank work is key to addressing disability issues. World Bank development initiatives—including in education, employment, safety nets, transport, infrastructure, health, water and sanitation, post-conflict, and natural disasters—contribute to removing barriers that limit the functioning and participation of persons with disabilities.

Inadequate or lack of physical access to the workplace, schools, clinics, transportation, and buildings poses barriers for people with disabilities. Significant improvements in accessibility can be achieved if civil works—both new construction and refurbishment of existing infrastructure—consider persons with disabilities as beneficiaries and stakeholders. The World Bank supports this use of "universal design" in its projects to improve accessibility for people with disabilities.

Disability and development is one of seven emerging topics that are being addressed by the World Bank review of safeguard policies and procedures. In addition to soliciting comments from an expert group of practitioners and civil society representatives, the World Bank is encouraging input from individuals and organizations.

In addition to World Bank project financing, World Bank trust funds contribute to disability and development. The Japanese Policy and Human Resources Development Fund (PHRD) has financed the mainstreaming of disability in World Bank projects, and the Multi Donor Trust Fund on Global Partnership for Disability and Development (GPDD) and the World Bank have coordinated the Disability and Development Donor Forum, which includes all major bilateral and multilateral development agencies with the objective of fostering international cooperation for the implementation of the United Nations' Convention on the Rights of Persons with Disabilities. The World Bank also continues to work with partners on key global events such as the United Nations High-Level Meeting on Disability and Development (September 2013). The World Bank integrates disability into development through its analytical work, data, and good-practice policies. In collaboration with the World Health Organization, the World Bank published the *World Report on Disability*. These organizations are also developing the Model Disability Survey (MDS). The MDS will address the lack of accurate and comparable data on disability both at national and international levels, identified by the *World Report on Disability* as one of the major impediments to a better understanding of disability and to the development and implementation of disability inclusion policies.

The World Bank also produces independent empirical studies on poverty and disability in developing countries, disability and education, and disability and labor markets (e.g., "Disability and Poverty in Developing Countries: A Snapshot from the World Health Survey"). In progress is review and research on the basics of disability assessment and certification, which will address the knowledge gap, develop knowledge tools, and build the capacity of the World Bank and counterpart governments for improving these systems.

⊃ http://www.worldbank.org/en/topic/disability

Disaster Risk Management (*See also* Products and Services.) Disasters hurt the poor and vulnerable the most. Low-income countries account for more than 70 percent of the world's disaster "hotspots." The economic impact can be devastating for developing countries. Analysis carried out for *Natural Hazards, UnNatural Disasters*, a report funded by the World Bank and Global Facility for Disaster Reduction and Recovery (GFDRR), shows that disasters' impact on gross domestic product (GDP) is 20 times higher in developing countries than in industrialized nations.

The Bank has emerged as the global leader in disaster risk management (DRM), supporting client countries in assessing exposure to hazards and addressing disaster risks. It provides technical and financial support for risk assessments, risk reduction, preparedness, financial protection, and resilient recovery and reconstruction. The Bank's DRM portfolio has grown about 20 percent annually for the past four years to nearly $4 billion in fiscal 2013. In providing support for DRM, the World

Bank promotes a comprehensive, multidimensional approach to managing disaster risk.

The GFDRR, a growing partnership of 41 countries and 8 international organizations, is the World Bank's institutional mechanism for DRM. A World Bank–GFDRR DRM Hub in Tokyo was established in February 2014 under a new $100 million DRM program supported by Japan. The Hub will help to match relevant expertise with World Bank DRM operations and clients.

Disclosure Policies (*See* Access to Information Policies.)

Dispute Resolution and Prevention (*See also* Products and Services.) The Dispute Resolution and Prevention (DRP) team at the World Bank assists task teams in predicting, preventing, and resolving potential disputes on Bank-supported projects. The office offers staff advice, training, research, tools, and access to regional dispute resolution professionals. By connecting task teams to the resources and expertise they need, DRP helps manage risk, strengthen relationships, and deliver results.

From the smallest informal complaint to outright conflict, the DRP team helps World Bank staff members manage disputes on their projects. While formal mechanisms such as the World Bank's Inspection Panel and local or national courts are always ready to deal with conflict, faster and more cost-effective dispute resolution can often be achieved through feedback, dialogue, facilitation, and mediation.

Further resources—such as publications, frequently asked questions, and a report on mechanisms for redressing grievances in World Bank projects—are available on the Dispute Resolution and Prevention website.

⟳ http://go.worldbank.org/GN2MUUF750

Documents and Reports Previously known as World Development Sources (WDS), Documents

and Reports contains more than 145,000 publicly available World Bank documents that enable the sharing of the institution's extensive knowledge base. Documents in both text and downloadable pdf format can be accessed by browsing or searching. Most documents are also available in depository libraries around the world.

The types of information included in Documents and Reports include the following:

- *Board documents.* These are items related to meetings of the Bank's Board of Directors.

- *Country focus.* These documents concern strategic priorities and directions for lending activities.

- *Economic and sector work.* These reports provide in-depth background, strategic priorities, and direction for lending activities.

- *Project documents.* These documents are released to the public in the course of a project, according to the stage in the project cycle.

- *Publications and research.* These include formal publications, working papers, and informal series from departments around the Bank Group.

⟳ http://documents.worldbank.org/curated/en/about

Doing Business The Doing Business Project provides objective measures of business regulations and their enforcement across 189 economies and selected cities at the subnational and regional level. The Doing Business Project, launched in 2002, looks at small and medium domestic companies and measures the regulations that apply to them throughout their life cycle.

By gathering and analyzing comprehensive quantitative data to compare business regulation environments across economies and over time, Doing Business encourages countries to compete toward more efficient regulation, offers measurable benchmarks for reform, and serves as a resource for academics, journalists, private sector researchers, and others interested in the business climate of each country.

In addition, Doing Business offers detailed subnational reports, which exhaustively cover business regulation and reform in different cities and regions within a nation. These reports provide data on the ease of doing business, rank each location, and recommend reforms to improve performance in each of the indicator areas. Selected cities can compare their business regulations with other cities in the country or region and with the 189 economies that Doing Business has ranked.

The first Doing Business report, published in 2003, covered 5 indicator sets and 133 economies. The 2014 report covers 11 indicator sets and 189 economies. The project has benefited from feedback from governments, academics, practitioners, and reviewers. The initial goal remains: to provide an objective basis for understanding and improving the regulatory environment for business around the world.

⮌ **www.doingbusiness.org**

E

EAP (*See* East Asia and Pacific.)

Early Childhood Development The potential benefits from supporting early childhood development range from improved growth and development to better schooling outcomes to increased productivity in life. The World Bank supports early childhood development (ECD) through financing, policy advice, technical support, and partnership activities at the country, regional, and global levels.

In response to convincing evidence on the benefits of investing in young children, as well as demand from client countries, the World Bank is increasingly supporting ECD around the world. It does so through financing, policy advice, technical support, and partnership activities at the country, regional, and global levels.

ECD features prominently within the Bank's Education Strategy 2020, which sets the goal of Learning for All through three pillars: Invest Early, Invest Smartly, Invest for All. ECD is also a strong component of the Bank's health and nutrition and social protection strategies.

Between 2001 and 2013, the World Bank invested more than $3.3 billion ($1.9 billion supporting the poorest countries through IDA) in 273 ECD activities, including education, health, and social protection activities, which targeted pregnant women, young children, and their families.

The Bank uses a range of entry points to influence young children's development. They include investments in health care, hygiene, nutrition, and parental training to promote a child's physical, cognitive, linguistic, and socio-emotional development. Programs can target the pregnant woman, the child, the caregiver, or the family as a whole and can take place in many environments, including at home, at a preschool or child care center, at a health facility, or at a community center.

⮑ http://tinyurl.com/WBG010

East Asia and Pacific
World Bank Group in East Asia and Pacific

The East Asia and Pacific region remains the world's growth engine despite a challenging external environment, with developing economies growing at a healthy pace. The proportion of people living in poverty in the region has steadily declined—less than 10 percent of the population now lives on $1.25 a day—but much more needs to be done as there are still close to half a billion people living on $2 a day.

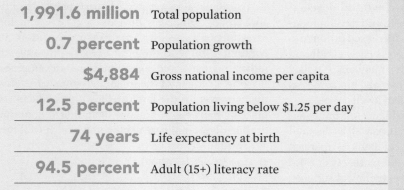

EAST ASIA AND PACIFIC REGION SNAPSHOT

1,991.6 million	Total population
0.7 percent	Population growth
$4,884	Gross national income per capita
12.5 percent	Population living below $1.25 per day
74 years	Life expectancy at birth
94.5 percent	Adult (15+) literacy rate

This region includes the following countries:*

American Samoa
Cambodia
China
Fiji
Indonesia
Kiribati
Democratic People's Republic of Korea
Republic of Korea
Lao People's Democratic Republic
Malaysia
Marshall Islands
Federated States of Micronesia
Mongolia
Myanmar
Palau
Papua New Guinea
Philippines
Samoa
Solomon Islands
Thailand
Timor-Leste
Tonga
Tuvalu
Vanuatu
Vietnam

*Regions are defined for analytical and operational purposes and may differ from common geographic usage. Variances also exist across the five World Bank Group institutions.

Member Countries by WBG Institution
⟳ www.worldbank.org/en/about/leadership/members#1

The World Bank Group's strategic priorities for development in the East Asia and Pacific region include the following:

- Poverty reduction and shared prosperity
- Disaster risk mitigation and climate change
- Infrastructure and urbanization
- Job creation and private sector–led growth
- Governance and institutions

The region's diversity requires delivering a customized combination of solutions to meet each country's unique challenges and build on opportunities. The region is increasing collaboration among the Bank, IFC, and MIGA by pursuing joint WBG business strategies in six countries—in Indonesia, to build the financial sector; in Mongolia, to improve livelihoods through agriculture; in the Pacific, to increase women's empowerment; in the Philippines, to improve agribusiness in Bangsamoro, a postconflict zone; in Vietnam, to promote efficiency and value addition in agriculture; and in Myanmar, to expand access to electricity and health care.

A priority for the region has been reengagement with Myanmar. After a nearly 25-year absence, the groundwork for reengagement in the country was laid when the Bank's Board of Executive Directors endorsed an interim strategy in 2012, reaffirming support for government reforms aimed at improving the lives of the people of Myanmar. This strategy focuses on helping reform institutions so that they can deliver better services during the country's critical transition period.

The region's strategy also focuses on fragile and conflict-affected areas and on disaster risk management. To address fragility in the Pacific Islands, the Bank Group is promoting good economic management; global and regional integration by supporting airports, telecommunications, and fisheries; resilience to natural disasters and economic shocks; and women's economic empowerment. To help the Philippines' reconstruction efforts after Typhoon Haiyan, the World Bank Group is providing almost $1 billion.

In January 2014, the World Bank Group announced plans for a $2 billion multiyear development program to support the government's plan to deliver universal health care to its citizens and to help everyone in the country gain access to electricity by 2030.

World Bank in East Asia and Pacific
In line with the WBG strategy, the Bank is supporting the $80 million National Community Driven Development Project to help realize the government's goal of "people-centered" development and the $140 million Myanmar Electric Power Project to help address the country's urgent energy needs. The Bank is also helping the government improve economic governance and create conditions for growth and jobs by providing policy advice and technical assistance.

Recent World Bank projects in East Asia and Pacific include those in the health care, power, and education sectors:

- *The China Tuberculosis Control Project* was the largest tuberculosis control project funded by the World Bank in the world, covering 668 million people in 16 provinces. It registered and treated close to 1.6 million new patients. More than 1.5 million of these patients completed treatment (94.2 percent), and nearly 1.5 million patients were cured (93.8 percent).

- *The Renewable Energy and Rural Electricity Access Project (REAP)* helped the government of Mongolia complete its National 100,000 Solar Ger Electrification Program, which provided over half a million nomadic herders with access to electricity through portable solar home systems.

- *The Rural Education and Development (READ) Project* has helped set up classroom libraries in all 383 primary schools in rural Mongolia, which until 2006 had almost no books. The project also helped put 200 new titles of children's books on the local market, delivered more than 676,000 books to classrooms, and essentially turned students in grades 1–5 into regular readers and book authors.

IFC in East Asia and Pacific

In East Asia and Pacific, IFC focuses on supporting sustainable, private sector–led development to ensure that the region's economic growth reaches all segments of society.

Economic growth in the East Asia and Pacific region has lifted millions out of poverty over the past decades. Yet, high income inequality remains a challenge. Supporting inclusive growth is one of IFC's priorities in the region—where its commitments reached a record $4.2 billion in fiscal 2014, including $1.4 billion mobilized from other investors.

IFC's clients provided employment for over 550,000 people, helped educate more than 3,000 students, and supplied power to over 33 million people in the region. In the financial sector, they provided nearly 6.5 million loans, totaling more than $100 billion, to micro, small, and medium enterprises.

MIGA in East Asia and Pacific

Recent guarantees issued by MIGA for investments in East Asia and Pacific supported a range of sectors, including water and wastewater in China, mining in Indonesia, banking in Thailand, and transportation, chemicals, and manufacturing in Vietnam. The Agency has a business hub in Singapore and representatives in other Asian capitals to provide support for inbound and outward investments.

Data Resources on East Asia and Pacific

⟳ http://data.worldbank.org/region/EAP

Research on East Asia and Pacific

⟳ http://www.worldbank.org/en/region/eap/research

Ebola Virus (*See* Pandemics.)

ECA (*See* Europe and Central Asia.)

Economic and Sector Work (*See also* Finance and Markets.) The World Bank has committed itself to becoming a "global knowledge bank," using knowledge to improve the development effectiveness of its work. Two of the analytical and advisory ways the Bank provides knowledge to its client countries are economic and sector work (ESW) and nonlending technical assistance (TA). ESW and TA are an essential part of the Bank's engagement with its clients.

The Bank produces a range of ESW products. These include the core diagnostic reports such as country economic memorandums, poverty assessments, and public expenditure reviews; other diagnostic reports such as sector reviews and investment climate assessments; advisory reports; and policy notes.

The data provide a starting point for policy and strategic discussions with borrowers and help enhance a country's capacity and knowledge. Studies and analytical reports help the Bank support clients to plan and implement effective development programs and projects. ESW underpins the Bank's policy dialogue with clients, its development of country strategies, and its formulation and implementation of lending programs and operations. ESW is also used as an instrument for building institutional capacity, especially when it is undertaken in partnership with local institutions.

Education (*See also* Global Practices.) One of 14 new World Bank Group Global Practices, Education is a powerful driver of development and one of the strongest instruments for reducing poverty and improving health, gender equality, peace, and stability.

World Bank Group and Education

There has been great progress in the past decade—many more children attend schools and girls' education has markedly improved—however, 57.8 million children are still out of school. Even when children complete school, they often do so without acquiring the basic skills necessary for work and life. This is particularly detrimental when unemployment is high and labor markets are demanding more skilled and agile workforces than ever before.

Today, amid a growing urgency prompted by widespread joblessness on the one hand and serious skills shortages on the other, the World Bank Group is more committed than ever to expanding opportunities for children and youth and nations alike through education.

World Bank and Education

The World Bank is one of the largest external education financiers for developing countries, managing a portfolio of $11.1 billion, with operations in 71 countries as of June 2014. The World Bank supports education through an average of $2.8 billion a year in new financing for the poorest countries as well as for middle-income countries. The World Bank helps countries achieve their education goals through finance and knowledge services in the form of analytic work, policy advice, and technical assistance. This support includes working with countries to help identify the role and contribution of education to their overall development and poverty reduction strategies. This means understanding countries' individual priorities and constraints and collaborating with governments, donor agencies, and development partners to design programs tailored to countries' particular needs.

In 2011, the World Bank launched its Education Sector Strategy 2020, "Learning for All." The strategy

The Rural Education and Development (READ) Project helped set up classroom libraries in all 383 primary schools in rural Mongolia, which until 2006 had almost no books. The project also helped put 200 new titles of children's books on the local market and delivered more than 676,000 books to classrooms. © World Bank / Khasar Sandag (photographer). Permission required for reuse.

recognizes that the knowledge and skills that children and youth gain through learning help lift them out of poverty and drive development. The strategy encourages countries to "invest early" because foundational skills acquired in childhood help lifelong learning, to "invest smartly" in efforts shown to improve learning, and to "invest for all" children and youth, not just the most privileged or gifted.

To achieve learning for all, the World Bank is promoting reforms of education systems and helping build a robust evidence base to guide those reforms. In over 100 countries, the World Bank is using a systems approach to achieving better educational results, with support from analytical tools developed under the Systems Approach for Better Education Results (SABER) initiative.

The World Bank supports a number of other important initiatives and programs, including, among others:

- The Millennium Development Goals
- The Global Education First Initiative
- The Global Partnership for Education
- Education for Global Development (blog)

IFC and Education

IFC is the world's largest multilateral investor in private education services. Its goal is to improve standards of quality and efficiency and create jobs for skilled professionals, thereby encouraging them to practice in their countries. To ease the burden on public educational systems, IFC works closely with the World Bank and developing country governments to design and tailor strategies that fit the needs of countries that do not have the resources to provide high-quality education services for all their people. IFC has also published several reports related to schools and education.

IFC's investment holdings cover all its regions and support K–12, tertiary, and technical education providers: for example, K–12 education in Kenya and Tanzania and tertiary education in Ghana; technical education in the Russian Federation and Turkey; technical education in the Philippines and K–12 education in Indonesia; tertiary education in Antigua and Barbuda, technical education in Brazil, and K–12 in Mexico; K–12 education in Egypt and Jordon and tertiary education in Morocco, Pakistan, and Saudi Arabia; and K–12 education in India.

Employment Opportunities at the World Bank Group

The World Bank Group employs experienced professionals with a demonstrated record of professional and academic achievement. A broad understanding of development issues and international work experience, preferably at the policy level, are desirable. In addition to proficiency in English, language skills are needed in Arabic, Chinese, French, Portuguese, Russian, or Spanish.

The Bank Group provides information on its job openings, employment opportunities for professionals, consultancies, internships, and secondments through a careers website maintained by Human Resources.

Learning Programs

- *Internships.* Providing graduate students with practical experience in global development.

- *Junior Professional Associates.* A unique opportunity to gain entry-level professional experience, with firsthand exposure to the challenges—and rewards—of international development and poverty reduction.

Development and Capacity Building Programs

- *Young Professional Program.* An opportunity for young people who have a passion for international development and who possess the potential for future global leadership.

- *Junior Professional Programs for Afro-Descendants.* Provides young and motivated individuals of Afro-descent, for example, blacks of Sub-Saharan African nationality or race or U.S. citizens from minority groups, who possess outstanding potential with a unique career opportunity to gain experience in a global development environment.

- *MIGA Professional Programs.* Opportunities for new professionals with diverse talent to work in the Multilateral Investment Guarantee Agency at entry-level professional positions for two years.

- *Legal Associates.* Opportunities for talented young legal professionals to gain exposure to the various areas of the World Bank's legal practice and to develop country expertise and skills.

- *Resource Management Fast Track Development Program.* Opportunities for professionals competent in finance and accounting.

Partnership Programs
- *Donor-Funded Staffing Program.* A donor-funded program enabling junior and mid-career professionals, of different nationalities, to gain valuable insights, exposure, and experience from the Bank's internal perspective.

- *Global Secondment Program.* Provides opportunities for partner organizations and the World Bank to stimulate knowledge sharing, strategic alliances, and capacity building.

- *Saudi Recruitment Program.* Targets Saudi nationals and allows participants to gain valuable insights, exposure, and experience from the Bank's internal perspective.

- *Voice Secondment Program.* Program for government officials to take part in a unique capacity -building and knowledge-sharing exchange between the Bank and its 180+ member countries.

IFC Career Opportunities
http://www.ifc.org/careers

MIGA Career Opportunities
http://www.miga.org/whoweare/index.cfm?stid=1791

World Bank Career Opportunities
http://www.worldbank.org/careers

Enabling Services In 2014, the World Bank Group adopted a new strategy for achieving two ambitious goals: eradicating extreme poverty by reducing the number of people living on less than $1.25 a day to 3 percent by 2030 and promoting shared prosperity by fostering the income growth of the bottom 40 percent in every country. That strategy leverages the strengths of Bank Group institutions and their unique ability to partner with the public and private sectors to deliver customized development solutions backed by finance, world-class knowledge, and convening services.

To support the new operating model, 13 different but essential groups from across the Bank Group were brought together to provide critical mission support functions. For more information, please see the individual entries for each of the following Enabling Services:

- Conflict Resolution System
- Corporate Secretariat
- Development Economics
- Ethics and Business Conduct
- External and Corporate Relations
- Financial Management
- General Services Department
- Human Resources
- Information and Technology Solutions
- Integrity Vice Presidency
- Internal Justice System
- Legal
- Operations Policy and Country Services

Energy and Extractives (*See also* Global Practices.) One of 14 new World Bank Group Global Practices, Energy and Extractives focuses on sustainable energy infrastructure, renewable energy generation, off-grid energy access, energy efficiency, and upstream oil and gas.

World Bank Group and Energy and Extractives
Providing reliable electricity to the unserved and inadequately served people of the world is central to the Bank Group's effort to eradicate extreme poverty and boost shared prosperity.

- *Poverty Reduction.* Energy is a key input to economic growth needed to end extreme poverty, while extractives generate substantial revenues for poverty reduction and socioeconomic development.

- **Shared Prosperity.** Universal access to affordable, reliable, and sustainable energy is key for ensuring economic opportunity and prosperity. The extractives sector, if managed well, can boost shared prosperity through co-development of infrastructure, local economic development, skills, and jobs.

- **Sustainability and Climate Change.** An environmentally and socially responsible approach to energy and extractives is critical to attaining sustainability objectives. The energy sector contributes about 40 percent of global carbon dioxide emissions, making the transition to a more sustainable energy mix critical for climate change mitigation. World Bank Group energy teams play a critical role in this process.

- **Sustainable Energy for All.** The WBG's co-leadership (with the UN) of the Sustainable

The $382 million District Heating Energy Efficiency Project focuses on rehabilitating boiler houses, replacing network pipes, and installing individual heat substations and building-level heat meters, with the overall aim of increasing the efficiency of district heating companies. The project will help to reduce costs, enhance reliability of service, and improve the overall quality of the heat supplied to more than 3 million Ukrainians. © World Bank / Yadviga Semikolenova (photographer). Permission required for reuse.

Energy for All Initiative leverages support for clients to achieve their 2030 goals:

- Universal access to modern energy services
- Double the rate of improvement in energy efficiency
- Double the share of renewable energy in the global mix

The Energy and Extractives Global Practice delivers comprehensive energy and extractive industry solutions.

Energy. Financing program of approximately $7 billion per year, complemented by Climate Investment Fund operations, a sizable Technical Assistance program, and a strong track record of One WBG engagements with MIGA and IFC to scale up and leverage greater resources. Energy priorities are:

- **Achieving universal access to reliable modern energy:** generation, transmission, electrification, and clean cooking solutions

- **Shifting energy systems to a more sustainable path:** renewable energy, natural gas, and energy efficiency

- **Improving the investment climate for energy:** sector reform and governance, strengthening utilities, enhancing investment framework and encouraging private sector participation, and rationalizing subsidies.

Extractives. Technical Assistance lending, advisory services, IFC investments, and partnership programs pave the way for transparent, responsible, and productive development of extractives industries. Extractives priorities are:

- Enhancing sustainability, transparency in revenue management, inclusive job creation and growth opportunities, and addressing conflicts related to resources

- Supporting the extractive industry through investments/interventions by IFC and MIGA, such as early equity in mining and oil and gas companies in fragile states; promoting domestic companies; and developing transformational projects

- Knowledge sharing and exercising a convening role with a view to promoting a best practice approach to sustainability

World Bank and Energy and Extractives

Some recent examples of IDA- and IBRD-financed projects are a power project in India, a renewable energy project in Turkey, and an energy-efficiency project in Mexico. Extending power to India's nearly 400 million people currently without electricity requires a massive expansion of transmission capacity. World Bank financing has helped India expand transmission across the country's regions by 52 billion kilowatt-hours. It has also supported a five-year program, led by India's Power Grid Corporation, to increase its circuit by 40,000 kilometers to reach 100,000 kilometers, raising interregional electric power transfer capacity from 21 to 37 gigawatts.

A $1 billion IBRD-financed project has supported expansion of five regional transmission systems to enable transfer of power from energy-surplus regions to towns and villages in underserved regions. This expansion has helped integrate the national grid, resulting in a more reliable system and reduced transmission losses.

With rising energy demand, reliance on imported fuel exposed Turkey to vulnerabilities by increasing the current account deficit as well as environmental consequences. As a result, the government developed a policy framework for attracting investments in the energy sector. As of August 2012, the Private Sector Renewable Energy and Energy Efficiency Project had supported construction of 969 megawatts of renewable energy and financed 20 energy-efficiency projects, resulting in energy savings of 1,840 tera calories or about 1 percent of electricity consumption in Turkey in 2009. Within this portfolio, the

Clean Technology Fund financing had supported development of nine small hydroelectric power plants, as well as six wind, one geothermal, and 20 energy-efficiency projects. The investments supported under the project are expected to contribute to reductions in greenhouse gas emissions of 3.3 million tons per year over the life of the project.

Mexico has achieved an energy-efficiency milestone by distributing almost 23 million free energy-saving light bulbs. The national program, partially financed by $185 million from the Global Environment Fund, established over 1,100 exchange points at which customers replaced their incandescent bulbs with compact fluorescent lamps. In total, more than 5.5 million Mexican families now use energy-saving lamps that consume only 20 percent of the energy and last 10 times longer than a traditional lightbulb. The first stage of the program, partially financed by the World Bank, resulted in savings of 1,400 gigawatt-hours (GWh). The program also enables families to save up to 18 percent on their electric bill. When the second stage ends, it is estimated that the saving will be of 2,800 GWh per year, preventing about 1.4 million tons of CO_2 emissions.

IFC and Oil, Gas, and Mining

IFC finances projects in the oil, gas, and mining sectors and also adds value to clients through advice on sustainability issues. Its mission is to help developing countries realize long-term economic benefits from natural resources. These sectors are important for many of the world's poorest countries as they can provide jobs, economic opportunities, infrastructure, revenues to government, energy, and other benefits for local communities. IFC coordinates closely with the World Bank's policy team that works with governments on oil, gas, and mining regulations and revenue use.

Industries that can harness natural resources are vital for many of the world's poorest countries. They are a key source of jobs, energy, government revenues, and a wide array of other benefits for local economies. In Africa, in particular, large-scale sustainable investments in these industries can create equally large-scale gains in economic development.

IFC's mission in the oil, gas, and mining sector is to help developing countries realize these benefits. IFC provides financing and advice for private sector clients, and also helps governments adopt effective regulations and strengthen their capacity to manage these industries across the value chain. IFC supports private investment in these industries and works to ensure that local communities enjoy concrete benefits. In fiscal 2014, IFC's new commitments in the oil, gas, and mining sector totaled $441 million.

MIGA and Oil, Gas, and Mining
MIGA's work in the oil, gas, and mining sectors has led to the development of guarantees that specifically target mining and oil- and gas-related concerns. These include those that protect against the revocation of leases or concessions; tariff, regulatory, and credit risks arising from a government's breach or repudiation of a contract; and disputes related to take-off agreements, production sharing, exploitation, and drilling rights.

Sound environmental performance, sustainability with respect to natural resource management, and social responsibility are critical to the success of these investments. Well-designed environmental and social programs can help manage reputational risks for project sponsors, reduce social conflicts within communities, protect the environment, and reduce political risks. MIGA helps clients take a responsible approach to their projects' environmental and social aspects.

MIGA has oil, gas, and mining projects in Côte d'Ivoire, Egypt, Indonesia, Mozambique, and the Russian Federation.

Environmental and Social Sustainability
IFC and Environmental and Social Sustainability
Growing public awareness of environmental, social, and corporate governance issues is driving changes in the products consumers buy, how companies do business, and how investment decisions are made. IFC's environmental, social, and corporate governance expertise helps private sector clients succeed in this changing global environment by realizing their financial potential while maintaining a strong focus on environmental, social, and governance issues such as climate change, access to water, disclosure and transparency, and the impact business operations may have on local communities.

IFC's expertise includes:

- *Risk management.* IFC helps companies identify, reduce, and manage the environmental, social, and corporate governance risks associated with their services, products, and business operations.

- *Advisory services in sustainable business.* IFC works with companies to adopt the environmental, social, and governance practices and technologies that create a competitive edge and promote the broad adoption of these practices to transform markets and improve people's lives.

- *Global environmental and social standard setting.* IFC's Policy and Performance Standards on Social and Environmental Sustainability set high standards for achieving sustainable development.

- *Global standard setting on corporate governance.* IFC's Corporate Governance Methodology has been widely adopted by other development finance institutions (DFIs). The DFI Working Group on Corporate Governance launched the DFI Toolkit on Corporate Governance, which is based on IFC's methodology.

MIGA and Environmental and Social Sustainability
MIGA strives for positive development outcomes in the investment projects it insures. An important component of such outcomes is the environmental and

social sustainability of projects, which the Agency expects to achieve by applying a comprehensive set of environmental and social performance standards.

MIGA's environmental and social sustainability policies are derived from its extensive experience insuring investments around the world. The policies are a powerful tool for identifying risks, reducing development costs, and improving project sustainability—benefiting affected communities and preserving the environment. During the underwriting process, MIGA identifies the policies and guidelines applicable to a project. Projects are expected to comply with those policies and guidelines, as well as applicable local, national, and international laws.

⤴ http://tinyurl.com/WBG0041

Environment and Natural Resources (*See also* Global Practices; Environmental and Social Sustainability.) One of 14 new World Bank Group Global Practices, Environment and Natural Resources ensures that the conservation and sustainable use of

The Integrated Coastal Zone Management Project balances development with the protection of vulnerable ecosystems in India. By June 2013, more than 9,000 hectares of mangroves had been planted, aerial photography of 78,000 square kilometers completed, and more than 100,000 sea turtles protected. © World Bank / Ray Witlin (photographer). Permission required for reuse.

the environment leads to sustainable growth, helping to lift people permanently out of poverty.

World Bank Group and Environment and Natural Resources

The World Bank Group's Environment Strategy for fiscal 2012–22 articulates a vision for a "Green, Clean, and Resilient World for All" and prioritizes scaled-up action in a number of key areas.

The green agenda focuses on supporting healthy, productive landscapes that nurture long-term growth, improve livelihoods, and sustain life:

- Enhancing countries' decision making through the Wealth Accounting and Valuation of Ecosystem Services global partnership, which supports valuing countries' natural capital assets and incorporating them into their systems of national accounts

- Finding ways to restore the world's oceans to health and economic productivity through working with a broad coalition of governments, international agencies, nongovernmental organizations, and private companies through the Global Partnership for Oceans

- Testing the market's willingness to encourage integrated landscapes and protect critical habitats while also providing carbon storage benefits through continuing innovative work on forests and land use linked to the Reducing Emissions from Deforestation and Forest Degradation program

Under the clean agenda, the focus is on providing continued support to countries to find low-pollution and low-emission development paths through:

- Supporting countries on river cleanup and legacy pollution issues

- Improving energy efficiency, encouraging a shift to renewable energies, finding climate-smart agricultural solutions, and building cleaner, lower-carbon cities

- Scaling up use of cleaner stoves to help reduce indoor air pollution

- Supporting South-South exchange on best practice for managing pollution

The resilience agenda aims to reduce vulnerability to climate risks through helping countries find climate change adaptation solutions, such as better coastal zone management; minimizing loss of life and structural damage from natural disasters; and improving the resilience of small island and developing states.

World Bank and Environment and Natural Resources

Between fiscal 2012 and 2014, the World Bank committed loans for $11.7 billion, from which IDA's contribution was $5.4 billion, to support investment in environment and natural resource management, including taking action on climate change and strengthening governance, policies, and institutions.

A large share of the World Bank's environment and natural resource management loans were directed to water resources management (38 percent) and to pollution management and environmental health (9 percent).

Continued investment in nature is critical to ending extreme poverty and accelerating inclusive growth for shared prosperity. Over the past 10 years, the Bank has funded almost 300 forest-related projects in 75 countries, a quarter of which have supported the establishment or expansion of forest protected areas. For example, in Brazil the Bank worked with its partners to support the creation of 18 million hectares of new protected areas in the Amazon, while working with the communities living in them to use their natural capital sustainably to boost their own growth and prosperity.

The World Bank and Bank-managed trust funds are increasingly supporting initiatives to rebuild the ocean's natural capital, which is fundamental to delivering essential goods and services that underpin millions of livelihoods, social equity, and food security. Many of the Bank's investments in the oceans over the past five years promote the sustainable governance of marine fisheries, the establishment of coastal and marine protected areas, and integrated coastal resource management.

World Bank pollution management priorities focus on air pollution, river basin cleanup, and legacy pollution. Such projects have included managing hospital waste in Vietnam; managing coastal zones and river basins in India, Pakistan, and Vietnam; reducing indoor air pollution in Bangladesh, Madagascar, and Uganda; lowering industrial pollution in India; and reducing particulate matter concentrations in Ulaanbaatar, Mongolia—a city with one of the highest concentrations of particulate matter in the world.

IFC and Environment and Natural Resources

A strong commitment to protecting the environment underlies all of IFC's private sector investments and shapes the way it does business.

Sustainability Framework. The IFC Sustainability Framework articulates the Corporation's strategic commitment to sustainable development and is an integral part of its approach to risk management. The Framework helps IFC clients do business in a sustainable way, promotes sound environmental and social practices, encourages transparency and accountability, and contributes to positive development impacts. IFC's Performance Standards, which are part of the Sustainability Framework, have become globally recognized as a benchmark for environmental and social risk management in the private sector.

Following are a few of the ways IFC maintains best environmental practices in all its investments and advisory services.

Climate Change. IFC is stepping up its investments in climate change mitigation and adaptation and helping clients understand and manage the risks and opportunities climate change presents.

Since 2005, IFC has invested more than $13 billion in climate-related projects, including nearly $2.5 billion in fiscal 2014. IFC made its first investment in renewable energy in 1989 and is now one of the world's largest financiers of wind and solar power for emerging markets.

Sustainable Forestry. IFC defines sustainable forestry practices as balancing the current and future economic value of forests with enduring commitments to social responsibility and environmental stewardship, including conservation, biodiversity, and protection of ecosystems. IFC's results in sustainable forestry include:

- Plantations sequestering several million tons of carbon dioxide per year

- Projects involving collection and re-use of waste paper reducing annual methane emissions equivalent to 1 million tons of CO_2 emissions

- Combined heat and power projects using carbon-neutral waste wood to replace fossil fuel

Renewable Energy Finance. IFC, a leader in emerging market renewable energy finance, is uniquely positioned to help countries transition to a low-carbon future. As part of a wider program to help mitigate climate change, IFC is investing in and providing advisory services to private enterprises in the renewable energy sector throughout emerging markets and across all parts of the supply chain.

MIGA and Environment and Natural Resources

MIGA strives for positive development outcomes in the investment projects it insures. An important component of positive development outcomes is the environmental and social sustainability of projects, which MIGA expects to achieve by applying a comprehensive set of environmental and social performance standards.

MIGA's environmental and social sustainability policies are derived from its extensive experience insuring investments around the world. They are a powerful tool for identifying risks, reducing development costs, and improving project sustainability—benefiting affected communities and preserving the environment. During the underwriting process, MIGA identifies the policies and guidelines that are applicable to a project. Projects are expected to comply with those policies and guidelines, as well as applicable local, national, and international laws.

Through its Policy on Environmental and Social Sustainability, MIGA puts into practice its commitment to these issues. This policy applies to all investment guarantees initiated after October 2013. The 2007 editions of the Policy on Social and Environmental Sustainability and Performance Standards apply to investment guarantees for which definitive applications were received after October 2007 and prior to October 2013.

MIGA also adheres to the World Bank Group's Environmental, Health, and Safety Guidelines, which are available on IFC's website.

Equity IFC takes equity stakes in private sector companies and other entities such as financial institutions and portfolio and investment funds in developing countries. It risks its own capital and does not accept government guarantees. IFC is a long-term investor and usually maintains equity investments for a period of 8–15 years. When the time comes to sell, IFC prefers to exit by selling its shares through the domestic stock market in such a way that will benefit the enterprise, often in a public offering.

To ensure the participation of other private investors, the Corporation generally subscribes between 5 percent and 20 percent of a project's equity. The Corporation encourages the companies in which it invests to broaden share ownership through public listing, thereby deepening local capital markets. IFC's equity investments are based on project needs and anticipated returns. IFC does not take an active role in company management.

IFC also backs private equity funds in emerging markets because funds, with their unique provision of both equity capital and expertise, have a significant impact on company growth and job creation. The majority of private equity in emerging markets is growth equity, using little leverage and depending on sustained growth of companies to generate returns. The private equity fund helps companies improve focus and negotiate the transformations and risks of rapid growth.

MIGA also supports private equity funds seeking to attract capital for investments in emerging and frontier markets.

Ethics and Business Conduct (*See also* Enabling Services.) The Office of Ethics and Business Conduct (EBC) ensures that staff members understand their ethical obligations to the World Bank Group as embodied in its core values and the various rules, policies, and guidelines under which they operate.

EBC helps ensure that WBG staff members are aware of their ethics and business conduct obligations to the Bank Group in four key ways:

- Providing training, outreach, and communication on business conduct

- Managing programs to promote transparency and trust, including conflicts of interest and financial disclosure

- Responding to and investigates certain allegations of staff misconduct

- Tracking trends and provides insights to senior management

Europe and Central Asia
World Bank Group in Europe and Central Asia
To reach the World Bank Group's goals of ending extreme poverty within a generation and boosting shared prosperity, the strategy of the Europe and Central Asia (ECA) Regional Vice Presidency focuses on two main areas: competitiveness and shared prosperity through jobs; and environmental, social, and fiscal sustainability. The World Bank Group provided $11.9 billion to ECA during fiscal 2014.

Competitiveness and Shared Prosperity through Jobs. In the past decade, most ECA countries have done well, and the incomes of the lower-earning 40 percent of the population have grown. Jobs and access to quality public services are essential to ensuring that economic growth benefits the less well-off. Creating good-quality jobs is a challenge in many ECA economies, especially in Central and Southeastern Europe, where unemployment has remained stubbornly high since the economic crisis. Creating new, quality jobs will require structural reforms to strengthen the competitiveness of ECA's economies. Such reforms include improving governance and the investment climate, ensuring the stability of the financial sector, upgrading the skills of the labor force, building and maintaining energy and transport infrastructure, and maintaining a sound macroeconomic framework.

To achieve these ends, the World Bank Group has helped improve workers' skills and create new job opportunities, modernize tax administrations, improve roads, strengthen the business environment and policies conducive to innovation, increase access to finance for small and medium enterprises, stabilize public finances, and strengthen financial sector regulations in the region.

Environmental, Social, and Fiscal Sustainability. To be sustainable in the longer term, economic growth and shared prosperity need to be fiscally affordable, environmentally responsible, and conducive to social inclusion. The Bank Group supports ECA countries in designing and implementing reforms to improve the efficiency and fiscal sustainability of their pension, social protection, and health care systems, so that these systems can adapt

EUROPE AND CENTRAL ASIA REGION SNAPSHOT

270.8 million	Total population
0.7 percent	Population growth
$6,664	Gross national income per capita
0.7 percent	Population living below $1.25 per day
72 years	Life expectancy at birth
98.1 percent	Adult (15+) literacy rate

This region includes the
following countries:*

Albania
Armenia
Azerbaijan
Belarus
Bosnia and Herzegovina
Bulgaria
Croatia
Georgia
Hungary
Kazakhstan
Kosovo
Kyrgyz Republic
Former Yugoslav Republic of
Macedonia
Moldova
Montenegro
Poland
Romania
Russian Federation
Serbia
Tajikistan
Turkey
Turkmenistan
Ukraine
Uzbekistan

*Regions are defined for analytical and
operational purposes and may differ
from common geographic usage.
Variances also exist across the five
World Bank Group institutions.

Member Countries by WBG Institution
www.worldbank.org/en/about/leadership/members#1

successfully and continue to benefit the people of these countries for generations to come.

World Bank in Europe and Central Asia

The Bank is working with ECA clients to strengthen social cohesion through supporting community-driven development and social accountability, which will allow citizens' voices to be heard in the design of social policies and the improvement of public services. Increasing economic opportunities and public services for disadvantaged communities is also an important element of the Bank's social sustainability work; for example, the Bank supports Roma inclusion in countries of Central and Southeastern Europe through advocacy and evidence-based analysis as well as through lending and technical assistance from the Bank's budget.

Climate adaptation and energy efficiency remain strategic priorities for the region. Despite significant progress in the past decade, ECA remains the most energy-intensive region in the world. Better energy efficiency will bring both environmental and economic gains. The Bank is working with ECA clients to achieve these gains through policy reforms (for example, energy pricing) and investments in both public infrastructure and private industry. Adaptation efforts focus on improved water resource management (flood protection, water loss reduction, irrigation efficiency), disaster risk mitigation, climate-smart agriculture (a shift to more resilient crops, for instance), and increasing institutional capacity for improving weather forecasting and climate change monitoring.

Examples of recent World Bank projects in ECA include work in Greece, the former Yugoslav Republic of Macedonia, and Poland:

- In Greece, technical support from the WBG has helped the country climb 28 ranks in the past two Doing Business rankings through the reimbursable advisory services work on improving the business environment.

- In FYR Macedonia, the conditional cash transfer program (CCT) has increased secondary education enrollment by 10 percentage points. Approximately 7,500 children from poor families, who would not otherwise attend school, regularly attended secondary school in the school year 2013–14, thanks to the CCT benefit. The coverage of the CCT secondary education program increased from about 67 percent of eligible children in the first year of implementation to about 86 percent in 2012–13.

- In Poland, following 200 years of flooding of the Odra River Basin, thousands of homes—and millions of residents—are now protected, and 60,000 ancient artifacts were found and conserved during archaeological excavations as part of the flood protection project work along Poland's Odra River.

IFC in Europe and Central Asia

In Europe and Central Asia, IFC supports economic development by expanding access to finance, improving infrastructure, and tackling climate change through a combination of investments and advisory services. With continued volatility in the Euro Area, IFC promotes diversification and works to ensure access to basic goods and services for people in the region. IFC invested $4.2 billion in Europe and Central Asia in fiscal 2014, including nearly $1 billion mobilized from other investors. IFC supported the region's sustainable growth by helping the private sector improve competitiveness and create more and better jobs and also helped expand access to finance, services, and infrastructure—and contributed to increasing the region's resilience to climate change.

IFC's clients supported more than 430,000 jobs and provided assistance to nearly 230,000 farmers. In the financial sector, they provided more than 4 million loans valued at about $70 billion to micro, small, and medium enterprises in the region.

MIGA in Europe and Central Asia

Recent political risk guarantees issued by MIGA for companies investing in Europe and Central Asia have supported a range of sectors, including capital markets in Hungary, leasing in Ukraine, financial services in the Russian Federation, banking in Serbia, transportation in Turkey, and services in Croatia.

Data resources on Europe and Central Asia

⤵ http://data.worldbank.org/region/ECA

Research on Europe and Central Asia

⤵ http://www.worldbank.org/en/region/eca/research

Events: Conferences, Forums, and Summits

The Bank sponsors, hosts, and participates in numerous conferences, forums, and summits both on its own and in conjunction with other notable organizations.

⤵ http://www.worldbank.org/en/events

Executive Directors The Board of Executive Directors resides in Washington, D.C. Executive Directors have a dual responsibility, as individual representatives of the Bank's member country or countries that appointed or elected them and as Bank officials who represent the interests and concerns of those countries.

The 25 resident Executive Directors, representing the 188 World Bank member countries, are responsible for the conduct of the World Bank's general operations under delegated powers from the Board of Governors. The Executive Directors select a President, who serves as Chairman of the Board.

Executive Directors fulfill an important role in deciding on the policies that guide the general operations of the World Bank Group (WBG) and its strategic direction, and they represent member countries' viewpoints on the WBG. They consider and decide on proposals made by the President for loans, credits, and guarantees; new policies; and the administrative budget. They also discuss Country Strategies—the central tool with which management and the Board review and guide the WBG's support for a country's development programs. They are responsible for presenting to the Board of Governors an audit of accounts, an administrative budget, and the annual report on fiscal year results.

Executive Directors serve on one or more standing committees. The committees help the Board discharge its oversight responsibilities through in-depth examinations of policies and practices. The Executive Directors' Steering Committee plays an important role in preparing the Board's work program. The Board, through its committees, attends to the effectiveness of the WBG's activities by regularly engaging with the independent Inspection Panel and the Independent Evaluation Group—which report directly to the Board—as well as with the Internal Audit Department and the external auditor.

External and Corporate Relations (*See also* Enabling Services.) The mandate of the External and Corporate Relations (ECR) Vice Presidency is to strengthen the World Bank Group's development impact by increasing public support for, and awareness of, the mission and work of the Bank Group. ECR manages corporate communications and relationships with key stakeholders, including the media, civil society, the private sector, donor countries, and international organizations, as well as staff communication within the Bank Group.

ECR publishes the Bank Group's research and knowledge products and manages its corporate identity and branding. ECR is also responsible for the Bank Group's corporate online and social media presence and produces content for a wide variety of platforms, including print, broadcast, and Web.

Extractive Industries Transparency Initiative
The Extractive Industries Transparency Initiative (EITI), established in 2003, promotes and supports improved governance in resource-rich countries through the full publication and verification of company payments and government revenues from oil, gas, and mining.

The EITI is both part of the World Bank's response to its own Extractive Industries Review and one of the many tools identified in the Bank's recent Governance and Anticorruption Strategy. In this context, the Bank also works with governments on EITI issues as part of broader Bank-supported programs on extractive industries reform, natural resource management, and good governance and anticorruption. In addition to supporting the governments involved in the EITI, the Bank has also provided financial support from its own funds to a number of civil society groups concerned with EITI implementation.

⟳ http://eiti.org

F

Fiduciary Policies The fiduciary policies of the World Bank Group, set forth in the Operational Manual, govern the use and flow of Bank funds, including financial management, procurement, and disbursement. The Operations Policy and Country Services Vice Presidency provides guidelines for the procurement of goods and services in Bank projects. The guidelines help ensure that funds are used for the intended purposes and with economy, efficiency, and transparency. They also ensure competitive bidding and help protect Bank-funded projects from fraud and corruption.

Finance and Markets (*See also* Global Practices; Products and Services.) One of the 14 new World Bank Group Global Practices, Finance and Markets helps to create opportunity for jobs, growth, and reducing poverty.

World Bank Group and Finance and Markets

Stable, efficient, and inclusive financial markets are essential to promoting economic growth and reducing poverty and increasing shared prosperity.

As an integrated World Bank Group practice, the value of Finance and Markets comes from delivering public and private sector tailored solutions to

The Deep Dive approach helps countries mobilize funds from diversified sources by building local-currency and private bond markets that can help finance long-term development needs. Colombia was selected for the Deep Dive Initiative because it has substantial financing needs for infrastructure and housing. © World Bank / Charlotte Kesl (photographer). Permission required for reuse.

development challenges by leveraging the whole range of the Bank Group's financial, knowledge, advisory, and convening services for clients. The practice implements comprehensive solutions that integrate World Bank services (loans, credits, guarantees, and risk management products) and IFC services (advisory services and investments in private sector firms). The Finance and Markets Global Practice is also an enabler of all the other Global Practices and Cross-Cutting Solution Areas, given the essential role that finance plays in delivering solutions and partnering with the broader World Bank Group finance team.

World Bank and Finance and Markets

Government policies have a decisive impact on shaping the business environment for the private sector. The international development community can best support government policies for the business environment in five key areas:

- Developing a regulatory environment that fosters opportunities for entrepreneurship and job creation

- Facilitating access to a broad range of financial services—for firms and for households

- Mobilizing the private sector to offer better services, such as housing finance and insurance, to the poor as consumers

- Supporting developing countries in building robust financial systems that are resilient to shocks

- Measuring the development results of the World Bank Group's private sector activities and helping to advance results measurement in the development community

Financing Instruments. Financing instruments include the following:

- Investment project financing provides IBRD loan, IDA credit/grant, and guarantee financing to countries for activities that create the physical and social infrastructure necessary to reducing poverty and creating sustainable development.

- Development policy financing provides IBRD loan, IDA credit/grant, and guarantee budget support to governments (or a political subdivision) for a program of policy and institutional actions that help achieve sustainable shared growth and poverty reduction.

- Program-for-Results links disbursement of funds directly to the delivery of defined results, helping countries improve the design and implementation of their own development programs and achieve lasting results by strengthening institutions and building capacity.

- Trust funds and grants allow scaling up of activities, notably in fragile and crisis-affected situations; enable the Bank Group to provide support when its ability to lend is limited; provide immediate assistance in response to natural disasters and other emergencies; and pilot innovations that are later mainstreamed into Bank Group operations.

- Private sector options for financing, direct investment, and guarantees are provided by IBRD, IDA, IFC, and MIGA.

- Customized options and risk management.

- Investment project financing is used in all sectors, with a concentration in the infrastructure, human development, agriculture, and public administration sectors. It is focused on the long term (5- to 10-year horizon) and supports a wide range of activities, including capital-intensive investments, agricultural development, service delivery, credit and grant delivery (including microcredit), community-based development, and institution building.

The Bank's investment project financing not only supplies developing countries with needed financing but also serves as a vehicle for sustained global knowledge transfer and technical assistance. This assistance includes support to analytical and design work in the conceptual stages of project preparation, technical support and expertise (including project management and fiduciary and safeguards activities) during implementation, and institution building throughout the project.

Technical Assistance. The World Bank Group's professional technical advice supports legal, policy, management, governance, and other reforms needed for a country's development goals. The Bank Group's wide-ranging knowledge and skills help countries build accountable, efficient public sector institutions to sustain development in ways that benefit their citizens over the long term. Bank staff members offer advice and support governments in the preparation of documents, such as draft legislation, institutional development plans, country-level strategies, and implementation action plans. The Bank Group can also assist governments in shaping or putting new policies and programs in place.

Reimbursable Advisory Services. By client request, the World Bank can provide reimbursable advisory services, which can be used when the Bank cannot fully fund an activity within the existing budget. This service can include traditional knowledge and advisory work as well as convening services. Subject to appropriate safeguards and risk management, the Bank may provide technical assistance for project-related preparation and implementation support services—except for advice directly related to engineering or final design.

Economic and Sector Work. In collaboration with country clients and development partners, Bank country staff members gather and evaluate information (data, policies, and statistics) about the existing economy, government institutions, or social services systems. These data provide a starting point for policy and strategic discussions with borrowers and help enhance a country's capacity and knowledge. Studies and analytical reports support clients in planning and implementing effective development programs and projects.

Donor Aid Coordination. The World Bank Group acts on occasion as a coordinator of organized regular interaction among donors (governments, aid agencies, humanitarian groups, foundations, development banks). Activities range from simple information sharing and brainstorming, to cofinancing a particular project, to joint strategic programming in a country or region. It also includes the preparation of donor coordination events such as consultative group meetings (joint meetings of partners) focused on a particular issue or country.

IFC and Finance and Markets

IFC blends investment with advice to help the private sector find solutions to today's greatest development challenges. IFC's three business services—investment, advisory, and asset management—are mutually reinforcing, delivering global expertise to clients in more than 100 developing countries.

Sound, inclusive, and sustainable financial markets are vital to development because they ensure efficient resource allocation. IFC's work with financial intermediaries has helped strengthen financial institutions and overall financial systems. It has also allowed IFC to support far more micro, small, and medium enterprises than it would be able to on its own.

Working through financial intermediaries enables IFC to encourage them to become more involved in sectors that are strategic priorities—such as women-owned businesses and climate change—and in underserved regions such as fragile and conflict-affected states as well as in housing, infrastructure, and social services.

In fiscal 2014, IFC commitments in financial markets totaled more than $3.4 billion, about 20 percent of commitments for IFC's own account.

Financial Management (*See also* Enabling Services.) The Financial Management (FM) Sector at the World Bank focuses on two strategic objectives: providing assurance that borrowers are using the Bank-provided funds for intended purposes and assisting countries in building improved financial management capacity.

For countries, financial management refers to the budgeting, accounting, internal control, funds flow, financial reporting, and auditing arrangements by which they receive funds, allocate them, and record their use. Good financial management is important to a country's development because it gives assurance to citizens that their taxes are being used appropriately, to donors and lenders that the funds they provide are being used appropriately, and to the private sector that there is an appropriate environment for investment and growth.

To carry out this work, the Bank Group's FM sector works at many levels:

- At the global level, participating in organizations that set financial management standards and working with other donors and lenders to harmonize financial management requirements and build capacity of clients

- At the country level, helping countries improve financial management performance based on the country's development priorities and institutional environment

- In operations, ensuring that appropriate financial management arrangements are in place and that the borrower complies with financial management requirements in ways that maintain financial integrity and support the development of sustainable FM capacity in client countries

- On cross-cutting issues that are important for financial management work in all sectors

- Internally, sponsoring the World Bank policies and procedures that support this work and improving the ability of staff members to carry it out.

The Financial Management Sector Board (FMSB) has overall responsibility for financial management in World Bank operations, including the sector strategy and related World Bank Operational Policies and Procedures and guidance to staff members; the quality of operational work; human resources; learning, knowledge management, and outreach; and internal and external partnerships.

The FMSB is chaired by the Chief Financial Management Officer and comprises the seven regional financial managers and representatives from the Loan Department, Procurement Group, Public Sector Group, and Legal Operations Policy. The following committees support the sector's strategic priorities and key activities:

- Knowledge, Learning, and Outreach Committee
- Operational Practices Committee
- Financial Management Operations Review Committee
- Human Resources Committee
- Public Financial Management Capacity Committee
- Professional Accountancy Development Committee

⟳ http://go.worldbank.org/0HI4LODL60

Financial Products and Services (*See also* Products and Services; Finance and Markets.) The World Bank Group offers a number of innovative financing instruments and banking products for a wide variety of projects, sectors, and investors:

- ***Investment project financing*** provides IBRD loan, IDA credit/grant, and guarantee financing to countries for activities that create the physical and social infrastructure necessary to reducing poverty and creating sustainable development.

- *Development policy financing* provides IBRD loan, IDA credit/grant, and guarantee budget support to governments (or a political subdivision) for a program of policy and institutional actions that help achieve sustainable shared growth and poverty reduction.

- *Program-for-Results* links disbursement of funds directly to the delivery of defined results, helping countries improve the design and implementation of their own development programs and achieve lasting results by strengthening institutions and building capacity.

- *Trust funds and grants* allow scaling up of activities, notably in fragile and crisis-affected situations; enable the Bank Group to provide support when its ability to lend is limited; provide immediate assistance in response to natural disasters and other emergencies; and pilot innovations that are later mainstreamed into Bank Group operations.

- *Private sector options* for financing, direct investment, and guarantees are provided by IBRD, IDA, IFC, and MIGA.

- *Customized options and risk management.*

Financial Reporting (*See also* Annual Reports.) Each World Bank Group institution provides detailed financial statements in its annual report. The reports catalog financial performance and new activities. They also include comparative information on the regions and development sectors in which the institutions have provided assistance. The reports are available free to the public, both in print and on the Internet. The reports are published in multiple languages, and the websites include past editions.

Fiscal Year The fiscal year for the World Bank Group runs from July 1 of a given calendar year to June 30 of the following calendar year.

Food Security Investment in agriculture and rural development to boost food production and nutrition is a priority for the World Bank Group, which works through several partnerships to improve food security—from encouraging climate-smart farming techniques and restoring degraded farmland to breeding more resilient and nutritious crops to improving storage and supply chains for less food loss.

The World Bank has engaged in policy dialogue with more than 40 countries, at their request, to assist them in addressing the food crises of 2008 and 2010 and the "new normal" of high and volatile food prices. Instruments include rapid country diagnostics, high-level dialogue, public communications, and in-depth analytical work. In the Middle East and North Africa, the World Bank, in collaboration with the Food and Agriculture Organization and the International Fund for Agricultural Development, released a paper titled "Improving Food Security in Arab Countries." Further analytical work was undertaken in response to food price volatility and subsequently summarized in the Economic and Sector Work report "Responding to Higher and More Volatile World Food Prices."

The World Bank is also improving global collaboration in the generation and sharing of knowledge between agriculture, food security, and nutrition sectors through the SecureNutrition knowledge platform. As a part of the Scaling Up Nutrition movement, 100 partners—including the World Bank—have endorsed the Scaling Up Nutrition Framework for Action to address undernutrition.

Food Security
⟳ http://www.worldbank.org/en/topic/foodsecurity

SecureNutrition
⟳ https://www.securenutritionplatform.org

Forests If the world is to confront the challenges of mitigating and adapting to climate change while meeting the demands of a rapidly growing global population, it is vital that the balance between conserving and regenerating forest areas and supporting economic growth for poverty reduction be found. This is what the World Bank's work on forests aims to achieve.

Forests represent an important safety net for rural populations in times of economic or agricultural stress. About 350 million people who live within or close to dense forests depend on them for their subsistence and income. Of those, about 60 million people (especially indigenous communities) are wholly dependent on forests. They are key custodians of the world's remaining intact natural forests.

Forests are also an economic good, providing jobs for rural populations with few alternative off-farm employment options. Formal employment in the forest sector has been estimated at 14 million jobs worldwide, with 10 times that in the informal sector. Forest industries contribute about 1 percent to global gross domestic product, while in some regions and countries it is much higher (for example, in Sub-Saharan Africa it is up to 6 percent).

Forests are an important source of energy for many countries; 65 percent of the total primary energy supply in Africa comes from solid biomass such as firewood and charcoal. Wood-based fuel will continue to represent a principle source of energy in low-income countries and is increasingly viewed as a green alternative to fossil fuels in developed countries.

The World Bank's Forests Strategy pledges to support countries in their efforts to harness the potential of forests to reduce poverty, better integrate forests into their economies, and protect and strengthen the environmental role forests play—locally and globally. A new Forests Action Plan that lays out how the Bank's work on forests and trees will contribute to resilient and sustainable landscapes is under way, building on the current Forests Strategy and taking into account the evolving global context.

⊃ http://www.worldbank.org/en/topic/forests

Fragile and Conflict-Affected Countries and Situations

World Bank Group and Conflict Countries

Fragile and conflict-affected situations (FCS) are a key priority for the World Bank Group's poverty-fighting mission as they face severe development challenges and lag behind on many Millennium Development Goals (MDGs). One in four people in the world—more than 1.5 billion—live in fragile and conflict-affected situations; by 2015, an estimated 32 percent of the world's poor will live in such conditions. Only 20 percent of FCS countries are expected to achieve the goal of halving poverty and hunger.

Fragile and conflict-affected situations account for:

- A third of the deaths from HIV/AIDS in poor countries
- A third of the people who lack access to clean water
- A third of children who do not complete primary school
- Half of all child deaths

Despite overwhelming challenges, there has been important progress: 20 fragile and conflict-affected states have recently met one or more targets under the MDGs, and an additional 6 countries are on track to meet individual MDG targets ahead of the 2015 deadline.

World Bank and Conflict Countries

The Bank has embarked on a series of internal reforms to enhance its effectiveness in fragile and conflict-affected states, which include the following:

- Designing country strategies to better address the drivers of conflict and fragility and leveraging instruments across the Bank Group to support countries, especially in job creation and private sector development. For instance, joint business plans are being developed in Côte-d'Ivoire, Haiti, Myanmar, and Nepal.

- Adopting operational policies and practices specially designed for fragile and conflict-affected states to recognize the unique challenge of working in these volatile, high-risk, and low-capacity environments.

- Strengthening staffing policies to get the right people to the right places at the right time in a cost effective and sustainable manner.

- Supporting a global community of practice on fragility and conflict to generate knowledge. The Center on Conflict, Security, and Development (CCSD), with staff in Nairobi and Washington, is supporting frontline teams, encouraging the flow of knowledge, and improving how the Bank can learn from implementation, including promoting global communities of practice around jobs, security, justice, and natural resource revenue management.

- Putting in place an intensive monitoring system to track progress in fragile and conflict-affected states.

IFC and Conflict Countries

The private sector, which provides 90 percent of the jobs worldwide, also has a key role to play in addressing fragile and conflict-affected situations. Economic growth and increased employment are essential to reducing fragility. IFC and MIGA are both working to stimulate private investment and economic growth in fragile and conflict-affected situations (FCS), together with the World Bank, other development partners, and their clients. IFC's activities in FCS have grown significantly in recent years. IFC's annual investments in fragile and conflict-affected areas have climbed 20 percent over the past two years— to nearly $950 million, including funds IFC mobilized from other investors.

MIGA and Fragility and Conflict
➲ http://www.miga.org/documents/conflict.pdf

World Bank and Fragility and Conflict
➲ http://www.worldbank.org/fcs

Fragility, Conflict, and Violence (*See also* Cross-Cutting Solution Areas.)

World Bank Group and Fragility, Conflict, and Violence

One of five new Cross-Cutting Solution Areas, Fragility, Conflict, and Violence reaches those in fragile and conflict-affected situations and is a key priority for the institution's poverty-fighting mission.

The World Bank Group launched the Center on Conflict, Security, and Development (CCSD) in 2012 to strengthen the Bank's work on fragile and conflict-affected situations. Since the Bank's organizational change of July 2014, the CCSD team has become the Fragility, Conflict, and Violence (FCV) Group and—from its co-located offices in Nairobi and Washington, D.C.—serves as a global hub providing knowledge and resources to FCS clients and practitioners.

The FCV Group comprises a cadre of dedicated staff with deep experience working on conflict and fragility. The team's competencies span a wide range, including conflict and violence, governance, social protection, gender-based violence, private sector development, operations policy, financial management, procurement, safeguards, and monitoring and evaluation. From Nairobi and Washington, D.C., the FCV team is set up to facilitate just-in-time support to country teams around the world working in FCS.

FCV Group staff work to:

- Provide rapid analytical and operational support to country teams working in fragile situations

The Second Kosovo Youth Development Project promotes social cohesion through inter-ethnic collaboration among young people, and it improves economic opportunities and sustainable access to youth services. More than 800 young people in Kosovo received vocational and entrepreneurship training as part of this project and more than 300 youths received apprenticeships. © World Bank. Permission required for reuse.

- Design and advocate for more agile operational policies and practices to improve results in FCS

- Build a global community of practice to share knowledge and experience of delivering effectively in FCS

- Leverage existing funds and reduce the volatility of financing for FCS

- Coordinate and build effective partnerships to address the core issues of security, justice, and jobs in FCS

Strategy Support. The FCV Group enables quick deployment of seasoned staff to the frontline of development in FCS countries. Since 2012, its conflict experts have helped shape the Bank's engagement strategies in more than 20 FCS countries, conducted in-country clinics to integrate conflict and fragility analysis in regional programs, and helped engage FCS governments in policy dialogues to feed into development plans.

Operational Support. To complement the critical work done at the strategy level, the FCV Group created an FCS Operations Support Team to provide just-in-time support to Bank projects. The team serves as a "live help desk" for operations teams to assist the delivery of quicker and more effective development results for the poor and vulnerable. The team also mentors field-based staff and helps develop policies and practices to improve the Bank's impact in fragile states.

IFC and Fragility, Conflict, and Violence

In recognition of the importance of the private sector in addressing the needs of those living in fragile and conflict situations, IFC has made economic growth and increased employment in these areas a priority. Together with the World Bank, MIGA, other development partners, and its clients, the Corporation is working to stimulate private investment and growth and meet acute challenges to private sector development.

For example, 56 percent of firms in FCS report access to power as a major constraint to their business. Alleviating the barriers to business growth—specifically access to power, access to finance, access to markets, enabling environments for business, and transparency and rule of law—underpins IFC's approach in FCS. By providing financing and advisory services and by working with governments to improve business environments, IFC can help reduce those barriers.

IFC's activities in FCS have grown significantly in recent years. During 2013, IFC's activities in FCS included investments of $577 million and advisory services of more than $39 million. IFC has committed to increasing its own account investments by 50 percent over fiscal 2012 levels by the end of fiscal 2016 with investments of at least $806 million. Recent projects include a power project in Côte d'Ivoire, which will provide power to more than 2 million people in that country; a new microfinance institution in Myanmar, which will address the significant demand for financing by providing loans to more than 200,000 people, mostly micro

and small businesses run by women; and a telecommunications company in Afghanistan to expand Internet access.

Beyond investments, IFC has worked with the government to improve Afghanistan's investment climate, including support in launching its first electronic collateral registry, which helps make it possible for smaller businesses to get the loans they need to grow and create jobs. Its support has also extended to farmers—one IFC advisory services project helped 1,500 pomegranate growers improve their farming practices, resulting in a 60 percent increase in their incomes, links to exporters, and access to new markets.

MIGA and Fragility, Conflict, and Violence

Supporting investments into fragile and conflict-affected areas remains a strategic priority for MIGA. The Agency has supported investments into many countries that have experienced conflict, including Afghanistan, Bosnia and Herzegovina, Côte d'Ivoire, Iraq, Libya, Mozambique, Rwanda, and Sierra Leone.

Years of conflict can color investors' perceptions of risks, particularly those of a noncommercial nature. A survey of foreign corporate investors conducted by MIGA in 2010 for its World Investment and Political Risk report found that political risk was by far their principal concern when investing in fragile and conflict-affected economies. MIGA was created in 1988 to encourage foreign direct investment in its developing member countries by providing political risk insurance for developmentally sound projects, including those in the most challenging environments.

Over the years, MIGA has played an important role in conflict-affected and fragile economies, providing coverage where other insurers are often not willing or able to go. *The World Development Report 2011* finds that investment and private sector engagement are important for creating economic opportunities and reducing the risk of relapse into conflict. But, because of perceived risks, these essential projects are often hindered by the inability of investors to secure financing, including equity participation and long-term lending from commercial banks.

The presence of a MIGA guarantee can help make an investment more attractive to potential investors and lenders by lowering its overall risk profile. Equally important, the projects supported by MIGA create confidence among the international and domestic business communities, helping to attract even more investment and encouraging the return of flight capital.

MIGA insures foreign direct investments against losses related to currency inconvertibility and transfer restrictions; expropriation; war, civil disturbance, terrorism, and sabotage; breach of contract; and nonhonoring of financial obligations. MIGA also provides dispute resolution services for guaranteed investments to prevent disruptions to developmentally beneficial projects.

⊃ http://go.worldbank.org/ZEPJOFJEW0

G

Gender (*See also* Cross-Cutting Solution Areas.) One of the five new World Bank Group Cross-Cutting Solution Areas, Gender is at the forefront of World Bank Group efforts to address inequality as a whole.

World Bank Group and Gender

Progress toward gender equality is a prerequisite to achieving the World Bank Group's twin corporate goals of ending extreme poverty by 2030 and boosting shared prosperity. Although the World Bank Group has been promoting gender equality in development since 1977, in many parts of the world, women continue to lack voice and decision-making ability and their economic opportunities remain very constrained.

Although it is true that many more girls are going to school and living longer, healthier lives than 30 or even 10 years ago, this improvement has not translated into broader gains. Too many women still lack basic freedoms and face huge inequalities in the world of work. Girls and women have far fewer assets and opportunities. They typically farm smaller plots, work in less profitable sectors, and face discriminatory laws and norms that constrain their time and choices, as well as their ability to own or inherit property or open a bank account. Many lack any say in their own homes, in their communities, or in their countries, while hundreds of millions of girls and women have experienced gender-based violence.

Progress toward gender equality is a prerequisite to achieving the World Bank Group's twin corporate goals of ending extreme poverty by 2030 and boosting shared prosperity. Public and private policies and actions can promote equality, starting early and extending over a lifetime. Leadership, innovation, and scaled-up efforts are needed. This agenda is urgent, and failure to fully take up the challenge would represent a huge missed opportunity.

The World Bank Group's strong commitments on gender have highlighted a need for better data to measure equality for women and girls. The World Bank is committed to improving data collection in key areas such as women's earnings, property ownership, and political voice.

World Bank and Gender

All recent country assistance strategies have been gender informed—meaning that gender has been integrated into the analysis. Some 86 percent were rated highly satisfactory, integrating gender in analysis, program content, and monitoring and evaluation.

The total share of Bank lending that was gender informed rose from 54 percent to 95 percent between fiscal 2010 and fiscal 2014, reaching nearly

The Great Lakes Emergency SGBV and Women's Health Project is a regional health services project in Burundi, the Democratic Republic of Congo, and Rwanda. It helps provide integrated health and counseling services, legal aid, and economic opportunities to survivors of sexual and gender-based violence (SGBV). The number of women and girls expected to benefit from this project is more than 641,000, of whom half a million live in the Democratic Republic of Congo. © World Bank / Dominic Chavez (photographer). Permission required for reuse.

$38 billion in fiscal 2014. Ninety-three percent of operations in fragile and conflict-affected situations were gender informed in fiscal 2014, up from 62 percent in fiscal 2010. Similarly, 49 out of 54 operations (over 90 percent) in conflict-affected situations in Africa were gender informed in fiscal 2014.

Gender Integration. Gender integration in lending has deepened, with operations including gender-informed analysis, actions, and monitoring and evaluation.

. Gender-based violence (GBV) is a relatively new area of strategic focus for the World Bank. Before 2012, Bank projects that addressed it were typically subcomponents within a larger project, or financed primarily by trust funds. Since 2012, the number of such investments has been rising, and an increasing number of projects and development policy lending operations have a GBV focus. Going forward, the World Bank will scale up commitments on this front as part of a broader effort toward gender equality.

Economic and Legal Empowerment. Gender equality in the world of work is at the forefront of World Bank efforts to address inequality as a whole. A companion to the 2013 *World Development Report* on jobs, *Gender at Work*, highlighted priority areas for action. *Gender at Work* noted that since women face multiple constraints on employment that start early and extend throughout their lives, progressive, broad-based, and coordinated policy action is needed to close gender gaps. Common constraints include lack of mobility, time, and skills; exposure to violence; and the absence of basic legal rights. Addressing these, it argued, promises huge gains in productivity that will significantly advance efforts to end poverty and boost shared prosperity.

In 2013, the Bank launched two new open databases: enGENDER IMPACT, a repository of impact evaluations with key findings gathered from Bank and partner projects; and ADePT Gender, which houses a growing volume of gender data and produces quick, standardized analytical reports, including cross-country labor force statistics.

In May 2014, the World Bank Group launched a major new study, "Voice and Agency: Empowering Women and Girls for Shared Prosperity," focusing on the broad benefits of, and costly constraints to, the ability of women and girls to exercise control over key aspects of their own lives. It distilled vast data and hundreds of studies to shed new light on these constraints worldwide, from epidemic levels of gender-based violence to biased laws and norms that prevent them from owning property, working, and making decisions about their own lives. While highlighting gaps, the report equally reviewed promising policies and interventions and identified priority areas where further research and more and better data and evidence are needed.

IFC and Gender

IFC coordinates its gender efforts through the Gender Cross-Cutting Solution Area with the World Bank Group. IFC advances the Bank Group's goals of ending poverty and increasing shared prosperity by investing in and advising the private sector. One key development challenge is the inequality of economic opportunities for men and women. By working to eliminate gender barriers in the private sector, IFC enables companies and economies to improve their performance. When men and women alike are allowed to pursue employment, entrepreneurship, and leadership, societies can better realize their growth potential.

In fiscal 2014, women made up 24 percent of all IFC board nominees, compared with 19 percent in fiscal 2013. Out of IFC's 719 active advisory services projects, 201 had a dedicated gender component at the end of June 2014, which is 28 percent of the overall advisory services project portfolio; and IFC's investments in access to finance for women entrepreneurs continued to grow. By June 2014, $830 million had been invested in 25 commercial banks as part of IFC's Banking on Women program and an additional $430 million had been mobilized.

In addition, various recent IFC operations have helped women across the world access financial and extension services and increase their contribution to production value chains. For instance, in the postconflict north of Sri Lanka, IFC-supported programs help some 5,700 women gain access to financial services. In Mongolia, IFC completed gender diagnostics for XacBank and Khan Bank. And in Bangladesh, 2,000 women farmers were trained through the Women in Seed Entrepreneurship initiative.

To highlight the importance of providing quality employment opportunities for women in the private sector, IFC released the *Investing in Women's Employment: Good for Business, Good for Development* report at the 2013 Annual Meetings of the IMF and the World Bank Group. The report shows how investing in women's employment has enhanced productivity, improved staff retention, and increased access to talent for companies from diverse regions and sectors. It presents specific examples of how initiatives tailored to women—such as training, child care support, health services, and alternative work arrangements—can enhance business performance as well as improve working conditions for both women and men.

MIGA and Gender

MIGA believes that women have a crucial role to play in achieving sound economic growth and poverty reduction. Recognizing that women are often prevented from realizing their economic potential because of gender inequity, MIGA is committed to supporting business activities and projects that create opportunities for women.

General Services Department (*See also* Enabling Services.) The World Bank Group's General Services Department (GSD) provides a wide range of shared corporate services that are essential to the Bank Group's effective functioning. GSD supports and strengthens the Bank Group's primary mission by providing integrated services to make the work environment safe, comfortable, and functional. This unit is responsible for the design and maintenance of office space; procurement of goods and services; translation and interpretation; security; travel and shipping support; printing and graphic design; and mail, messenger, and food services. IFC and MIGA handle some of these responsibilities through their own offices for facilities management and administration.

Global Agriculture and Food Security Program

The Global Agriculture and Food Security Program (GAFSP) is a multilateral mechanism that supports country-led agriculture and food security plans and helps promote investments in smallholder farmers. The Group of 20 Summit in September 2009 asked the World Bank to prepare a multilateral mechanism to help implement pledges to long-term food security made at the L'Aquila Summit in July 2009. This mechanism is intended to fill the financing gaps in national and regional agriculture and food security strategies. The overall objective is to improve incomes and food and nutrition security in low-income countries by boosting agricultural productivity.

➲ http://www.gafspfund.org

Global and Regional Partnership Programs

Global and regional partnership programs are development programs that are organized outside the Bank's regular country operations at a cross-country level. They are thematic in focus and involve other partners (for example, bilateral donors, international organizations, civil society organizations such as foundations, or the private sector) in their structure. They generally involve external funding committed at the program level.

The Bank plays a number of roles in these programs and may be a donor, trustee, or both, as well as house and manage the secretariat where relevant, implement the activities at the country level, or provide other forms of collaborative support.

Global Development Learning Network

Global Development Learning Network (GDLN) is a partnership of over 120 recognized global institutions (affiliates) in some 80 countries. The affiliates are as diverse as the Korean Development Institute, the Kenya School of Government–eLearning and Development Institute, the Energy and Resource Institute in India, and the Instituto Tecnológico de Monterrey in Mexico. Collectively, affiliates put on more than 1,000 learning sessions a year that range from training courses and informal brainstorming sessions to multicountry dialogues and virtual conferences. GDLN learning specialists in these organizations collaborate in designing customized learning solutions for clients.

➲ http://gdln.org

Global Economic Prospects The World Bank's twice-yearly Global Economic Prospects examines growth trends for the global economy and how they affect developing countries. The reports include three-year forecasts for the global economy and long-term global scenarios that look 10 years into the future. Topical annexes in this online publication cover financial markets, trade, commodities, and inflation.

➲ http://www.worldbank.org/gep

Global Environment Facility The Global Environment Facility (GEF) is a partnership for international cooperation in which 183 countries work together with international institutions, civil society organizations, and the private sector to address global environmental issues.

Since 1991, the GEF has provided $12.5 billion in grants and leveraged $58 billion in co-financing for 3,690 projects in 165 developing countries. For 23 years, developed and developing countries alike have provided these funds to support activities related to biodiversity, climate change, international waters, land degradation, and chemicals and waste in the context of development projects and programs.

Through its Small Grants Programme (SGP) the GEF has made more than 20,000 grants to civil society and community-based organizations for a total of $1 billion.

➲ http://www.thegef.org

Global Facility for Disaster Reduction and Recovery (*See also* Social, Urban, Rural, and Resilience Global Practice.) Established in 2006, the Global Facility for Disaster Reduction and Recovery (GFDRR) is a partnership of 41 countries and 8 international organizations committed to helping developing countries reduce their vulnerability to natural hazards and adapt to climate change. The partnership's mission is to mainstream disaster risk reduction (DRR) and climate change adaptation (CCA) in country development strategies by supporting a country-led and managed

implementation of the Hyogo Framework for Action (HFA). GFDRR's Partnership Charter, revised in April 2010, sets its original mission, rationale, and governance structure.

GFDRR has three main business lines to achieve its development objectives at the global, regional, and country levels:

- Track I: Global and Regional Partnerships
- Track II: Mainstreaming Disaster Risk Reduction (DRR) in Development
- Track III: Sustainable Recovery

Six initiatives that complement the three tracks and Climate Change Adaptation (CCA) programs are:

- The Economics of Disaster Risk Reduction
- GFDRR Labs
- Disaster Risk Financing & Insurance
- Strengthening Weather and Climate Information and Decision-Support Systems (WCIDS)
- Capacity Development
- Gender

➲ https://www.gfdrr.org/about_gfdrr

Global Financial Development Report *Global Financial Development Report* (GFDR) is a new World Bank series that provides a unique contribution to financial sector policy debates, building on novel data, surveys, research, and wide-ranging country experience, with emphasis on emerging market and developing economies. Each report provides in-depth analysis and policy recommendations on a specific and important aspect of financial development. It also tracks financial systems in more than 200 economies before and during the global financial crisis.

An accompanying website contains extensive datasets, research papers, and other background materials, as well as interactive features. The report and website are of interest to and relevant for policy makers; staff of central banks, ministries of finance, and financial regulation agencies; nongovernmental organizations and donors; academics and other researchers and analysts; and members of the finance and development community.

⮑ **www.worldbank.org/financialdevelopment**

Global Fund to Fight AIDS, Tuberculosis, and Malaria The Global Fund to Fight AIDS, Tuberculosis and Malaria (GFATM) is the response by global leaders in 2002 when it was recognized that the devastation to families, societies, and economies caused by these three pandemics was considered a global emergency. Through Global Fund–supported programs, more than 6 million people are receiving lifesaving antiretroviral therapy as of the end of 2013. Diagnosis and treatment for tuberculosis have reached 11.2 million people, and 360 million insecticide-treated nets have been distributed to families to protect them from malaria. Thanks to these programs, and the efforts of many partners, total mortality from AIDS, tuberculosis, and malaria has decreased by 40 percent since 2000.

⮑ **http://www.theglobalfund.org/en/about/diseases**

Global Infrastructure Facility In 2014, the WBG announced that it planned to design a new mechanism (a global infrastructure facility) to mobilize resources and leverage them more effectively to support infrastructure investment in emerging markets and developing economies, including by strengthening the supporting policy and regulatory environment and project quality.

The development of the facility reflects several factors:

- With decreased fiscal space and significant demands on government budgets, the public sector alone cannot be expected to finance the significant (and growing) infrastructure needs.

- Private-sector investors with appropriately long-term investment horizons report a shortage of financially viable infrastructure projects in which to invest.

- With limited public and private resources, it is essential that governments increase the impact on job creation, growth, and development of the scarce resources allocated to infrastructure.

Against this backdrop, the WBG is working on an integrated platform that brings together upstream and downstream support for infrastructure, one that seeks to make better use of scarce WBG resources to leverage additional financing for infrastructure and more actively seeks partnerships with other multilateral and national development banks.

Global Monitoring Report The World Bank monitors how the world is doing in implementing the policies and actions for achieving the Millennium Development Goals (MDGs) and related development outcomes. The Global Monitoring Reports, produced jointly with the IMF, are a framework for accountability in global development policy. Published since 2004, this annual publication offers priorities for policy responses by both developing countries and the international community.

⮑ **http://www.worldbank.org/gmr**

Global Partnership for Education Global Partnership for Education (GPE), launched in 2002, aims to help low-income countries meet the education Millennium Development Goals (MDGs) and the Education for All (EFA) goals. The Global Partnership for Education is a platform for collaboration at the global and country levels. Through the GPE compact, developing countries commit to design and implement sound education plans while donor partners commit to align and harmonize additional support around these plans. Funding is channeled through existing bilateral and multilateral channels and through the GPE fund, which supports countries with insufficient resources to prepare and implement their education sector plans.

⮑ **http://www.globalpartnership.org**

Global Practices (*See also* Cross-Cutting Solution Areas.) In 2013, the World Bank Group (WBG) adopted a new strategy for achieving two ambitious goals: eradicating extreme poverty by reducing the number of people living on less than $1.25 a day to 3 percent by 2030 and boosting shared prosperity by fostering the income growth of the bottom 40 percent in every country. That strategy leverages the strengths of Bank Group institutions and their unique ability to partner with the public and private sectors to deliver customized development solutions backed by finance, world-class knowledge, and convening services.

Underpinning the strategy are the 14 Global Practices and 5 Cross-Cutting Solution Areas (CCSAs) that, in concert with the Bank Group regions, will pool their expertise to address client countries' most pressing developmental challenges and ultimately enable the Bank Group to meet its goals. The Global Practices are Agriculture; Education; Energy and Extractives; Environment and Natural Resources; Finance and Markets; Governance; Health, Nutrition, and Population; Macroeconomics and Fiscal Management; Poverty; Social, Urban, Rural, and Resilience; Social Protection and Labor; Trade and Competitiveness; Transport and ICT; and Water.

Agriculture

Because so many of the poor living in rural areas rely on farming, ending extreme poverty cannot be achieved without more and better investment in agriculture, food security, and nutrition. The World Bank Group is the largest provider of development finance for agriculture in the world and is uniquely positioned to support "farm-to-fork" integrated solutions through its combination of IBRD/IDA's policy, productivity, and smallholder focus and IFC's support for the agribusiness sector.

Education

Education is a powerful driver of development and one of the strongest instruments for reducing poverty, raising incomes, promoting economic growth and shared prosperity, and improving health, gender equality, peace, and stability. It is also central to the development strategies of all World Bank Group clients. The mandate of the Education Global Practice is building effective educational systems, creating and deploying global knowledge, and developing the capacity to deliver results, including through strategic partnerships.

Energy and Extractives

Providing reliable electricity to the unserved and inadequately served people of the world is central to efforts to eradicate extreme poverty and create a shared prosperity. The Energy and Extractive Industries Global Practice delivers comprehensive energy and extractive industry solutions through environmentally and socially sustainable approaches. It also houses financial solution experts specialized in guarantee structuring and execution, project finance, and market capital mobilization.

Environment and Natural Resources

Sustainable environment and natural resources management is at the heart of the World Bank Group's poverty reduction and inclusive green growth agenda. If managed carefully, productive natural assets such as forests and oceans represent engines for economic growth and important safety nets for the poor, who depend on natural resources for their food and livelihoods. The Environment and Natural Resources Global Practice has three broad functions: providing clients the lending and other services needed to support sustainable natural resources management, pollution management, climate change action, and policy reforms; working closely with other actors to mainstream environmental considerations into their policies, strategies, and operations; and providing technical input to other sectors to implement the Bank Group's environmental policies and ensure that development interventions do no harm.

Finance and Markets

Resilient, efficient, and transparent financial systems are essential to promoting a strong economy, ending extreme poverty, and building shared prosperity. By maintaining a healthy financial system, an economy can mobilize the capital it needs for investments in development priorities—infrastructure, industry, and social services—and in its people. The Finance and Markets Global Practice delivers tailored development solutions with WBG financial knowledge and convening services. The practice implements comprehensive solutions that integrate World Bank services (loans, credits, and risk management products) and IFC services (advisories and investments in private sector firms).

Governance

Governance is defined as the traditions and institutions by which authority in a country is exercised for the common good. Systems of governance that are transparent, responsive, participatory, and accountable ensure that benefits and services are delivered to the citizens that need them most, especially the poor and marginalized. Open and accountable public institutions help build citizens' trust in government and support for development policies and outcomes. The Governance Global Practice brings together professionals in procurement, financial management, taxation, public management, regulatory policy, open and accountable government, citizen engagement, digital governance, law and development, anticorruption, and social accountability to develop innovative, integrated solutions to pernicious institutional problems.

Health, Nutrition, and Population

High child, maternal, and adult mortality and widespread malnutrition and persistently high fertility—along with other health, nutrition, and population challenges—remain primary constraints to development in many countries. The Health, Nutrition, and Population Global Practice aims to accelerate progress toward universal health coverage so that by 2030 no one will be tipped into or kept in poverty because of expenditures on health care, and the poorest 40 percent of the population will have access to the quality health, nutrition, and population services they need.

Macroeconomics and Fiscal Management

The Macroeconomics and Fiscal Management Global Practice is the home of the World Bank Group's family of country economists and macroeconomic experts, providing integrative development strategies, policy-based lending, macrodata, global perspectives, real-time policy analysis, country risk assessments, and innovative projection tools. This practice delivers solutions based on global best practices, transformational financing, and cutting-edge knowledge and analytical tools.

Poverty

Despite progress in poverty reduction and human welfare in the past decade, extreme poverty and inequality persist at unacceptably high levels in many parts of the world. To eliminate extreme poverty and expand shared prosperity, clients will need to address several critical development challenges, including reaching the least well-off, sustaining welfare gains, and making progress on increasing access to opportunities for the most disadvantaged. The Poverty Global Practice delivers advice and knowledge on policies and multisectoral solutions, policy monitoring and evaluation, capacity building, innovative data collection and measurement systems, and global leadership on poverty and shared prosperity.

Social, Urban, Rural, and Resilience

The Social, Urban, Rural, and Resilience Global Practice works with clients to build inclusive resilient, sustainable, and prosperous territories, cities, villages, and communities. Among the practice's important service areas are social sustainability, disaster risk management, community-driven development, land tenure policy and administration, urban planning and land use management, social inclusion, violence and conflict prevention, tourism, and cultural heritage.

Social Protection and Labor

Well-designed modern social protection systems are proven to be both effective and efficient at lowering current and future poverty and to be flexible enough to buffer both systemic and specific shocks. The World Bank Group is the largest provider of development finance and solutions for social protection, working with high-income, middle-income, and low-income countries to develop country-specific solutions to social protection challenges. The Social Protection and Labor Global Practice delivers operational approaches and evidence-based solutions to help individuals and families manage risk, cope with chronic and transitional poverty, and access better livelihoods and jobs.

Trade and Competitiveness

Jobs are at the heart of the World Bank Group's dual goals of ending extreme poverty and boosting shared prosperity. With 90 percent of jobs created by the private sector, new solutions to support firm growth, higher productivity, innovation, and competitiveness are critical. The Trade and Competitiveness Global Practice mobilizes expertise, operational know-how, and financial resources in support of countries that tackle these growth challenges. The practice partners with governments, the private sector, donor agencies, and civil society to improve the business and trade environment, promote competitiveness across key industries, and encourage productive and responsible investments.

Transport and ICT

By facilitating the movement of people, goods, and information, the Transport and Information and Communication Technology (ICT) Global Practice

enables economic and social development, food security, and access to jobs and health and education services. Transport is also at the heart of the climate change solution, as it is one of the largest energy users and emitters of greenhouse gases. The Transport and Global Practice provides clients with infrastructure and policies for improving connectivity and competitiveness, linking people to markets and social services, increasing climate resilience, and reducing the carbon footprint.

Water

Sustainable access to water supply and sanitation, irrigation, energy, and many other economic, social, and environmental services is vital for poverty reduction and economic growth. Access to water sources, along with better and more equitable management of those resources, will benefit the poor through improved health, greater access to electricity, higher school attendance, more jobs, and increased food security. The Water Global Practice works to ensure that water is a reliable foundation for poverty reduction and broad prosperity through the delivery of public water "goods" coupled with private initiatives that add value to water services throughout the water cycle.

Global Practices Chief Economist (*See also* Global Practices.) The Global Practices Chief Economist is the principal economic adviser to the Global Practices Vice Presidents and works closely with the regional Chief Economists and the World Bank's Chief Economist. The Global Practices:

• Set and drive the strategic direction of their practice based on country and regional demands and global priorities

• Promote the flow of knowledge and expertise across the World Bank Group to deliver client solutions

- Coordinate with Regional Vice Presidencies and country management units to join global expertise with local knowledge

- Hold responsibility and are accountable for the technical quality of projects

Global Public Goods Public goods are defined as those goods that are both nonrival and nonexcludable. Global public goods have a spatial dimension and so include only those issues that are transborder in nature. In its strategy for addressing global public goods, the World Bank identifies five areas of global public goods for its engagement. These goods include the following:

- The environmental commons (including biodiversity and the prevention of climate change)

- Prevention of communicable diseases (including HIV/AIDS, tuberculosis, malaria, and avian influenza)

- International trade

- International financial architecture

- Global knowledge for development

⤷ http://go.worldbank.org/JKZLIHR2B0

Global Secondment Program (*See* Employment Opportunities at the World Bank Group.)

Goals, World Bank Group The World Bank Group has established ambitious but achievable goals to anchor its overarching mission and to galvanize international and national efforts in this endeavor. Accordingly, the institution will strive to end extreme poverty at the global level within a generation and promote what may be called "shared prosperity": a sustainable increase in the well-being of the poorer segments of society. This second goal reflects the fact that all countries aspire to rapid and sustained increases in living standards

for all of their citizens, not just the already privileged.

These two goals and their respective indicators can be summarized as follows:

- *End extreme poverty.* Ensure that the percentage of people living on less than $1.25 a day is no more than 3 percent globally by 2030.

- *Boost shared prosperity.* Foster income growth of the bottom 40 percent of the population in every country.

Ending extreme poverty within a generation and promoting shared prosperity must be achieved in such a way as to be sustainable over time and across generations. This requires promoting environmental, social, and fiscal sustainability. The aim must be for sustained social inclusion and for limiting the size of economic debt inherited by future generations.

The goals articulated here are not solely for the World Bank Group to achieve but rather are goals that the Bank Group hopes are consistent with those of its 188 member countries. The goals will guide the World Bank Group's strategy as it continues its transformation into a "Solutions Bank" by influencing what the organization does and how and by helping it become more selective and focused in its activities. The goals are well aligned with the overall objectives of the Millennium Development Goals process and reiterate the Bank Group's unwavering commitment to support it and to help shape the Post-2015 Development Agenda.

A "Solutions World Bank Group"
The adoption of the new goals has led to a radical restructuring of the way the World Bank Group conducts its business and to a new form of problem-solving engagement: one that moves definitively from a focus on individual projects to a development solutions culture grounded in widely disseminated knowledge and evidence of what

works and how to deliver it. The new structure—which leverages the expertise of the World Bank, IFC, and MIGA—will enable the Bank Group to deliver customized solutions to its clients that integrate knowledge and financial services and encompass the complete cycle from policy design through implementation to evaluation of results.

Meeting the Goals
Meeting the goals demands deepening partnerships across the development spectrum. Successfully overcoming the toughest development challenges requires concerted action at all levels. It will build on existing collaborative relationships and development partnerships to address key development issues in a way that no single agency or country can. It will also step back where others have clear comparative advantage and will actively support leadership roles for partner organizations.

Meeting the goals also means that the Bank Group will need to work together as one: collaboration across the Bank Group will be increased systematically, and planning and budgeting processes will be better coordinated. The Bank Group will increase the number of joint projects and review its portfolio of products and services to improve synergies and eliminate overlap.

While the challenges are great, the opportunity is historic. Achieving the goals depends on each member government and the international community as a whole demonstrating the political will to focus on the poor and disadvantaged and to act in partnership with the private sector and civil society. Effective global action requires that all countries and multilateral institutions demonstrate a renewed capacity to collaborate on doing what it takes to end poverty and build shared prosperity.

Governance (*See also* Global Practices.) One of the 14 new World Bank Group Global Practices, Governance utilizes a problem-driven, diagnostic approach, combining global comparative knowledge

of reform successes and failures with keen understanding of the institutional challenges and opportunities of developing countries.

World Bank Group and Governance
The WBG aims to build inclusive, open, and accountable institutions in client countries by providing operational support and expert advice focusing on three aspects of a well-managed public sector:

• Sustainable management of public resources that enhances policies and institutions for collecting domestic revenues; strengthens the composition, management, and reporting of public spending; efficiently manages public investments, procurement, and state-owned enterprises; and builds accountability through audit and legislative scrutiny

• Effective performance and delivery arrangements that boost results, harness innovations in public management, and deliver services in fragile and conflict-affected states

• Open and accountable governance that supports transparency, participation, and collaboration through access to information and through the disclosure and use of open data; supports basic rights and entitlements; provides access to basic services; empowers citizens by promoting and establishing mechanisms for inclusive and robust participation of nongovernmental actors; and builds social accountability through enhanced demand-side scrutiny of public institutions and legal and judicial reform

To this end, the new Governance Global Practice looks to expand governance support to others, such as those working on, for example, health or education, and in many country contexts, including fragile situations; to provide assistance in the spending reviews in a range of sectors, including the security sector and in fragile contexts; to address governance regulatory systems and private sector service delivery;

Geo-tagging for Good Governance makes innovative use of geo-tagging for improved transparency and effectiveness in procurement and project management. Geo-tagging was successfully tested by Philippine financial management and procurement officials in a number of reforestation projects. The story received the top Science of Delivery Award, an award for the Fragile and Conflict-Affected Situations December 2013 Procurement in Complex Situations. © World Bank / Dominic Chavez (photographer). Permission required for reuse.

to ensure that advice is realistic in light of political and bureaucratic constraints; and to enhance the capacity of governmental and nongovernmental actors for increased openness, collaboration, and accountability.

World Bank and Governance

To assist governments in their efforts to improve transparency, accountability, and service delivery, the World Bank's work on governance and public sector management has two main focus areas. It helps strengthen public sector management systems, including the management of public finances and human resources, as well as the procurement of goods and services. The World Bank's governance work goes beyond the executive branch, central government, and formal state institutions. It also seeks to improve the broader environment in which the public sector operates, by supporting institutions for public accountability, such as parliaments, offices of the ombudsman, media, civil society organizations, academia, and citizens and by tracking improvements through measures of the rule of law and trust in government institutions.

To meet these goals, the World Bank works with governments, businesses, citizens and civil society, media, parliaments, supreme audit institutions, and other actors to strengthen public management systems and improve the broader governance environment. The World Bank also supports the use of information and communication technologies to help enhance citizen participation, mediate and enable citizen engagement, and improve the reach and efficiency of public services. These efforts foster public accountability and openness, reduce corruption, build and enhance trust and ownership, and strengthen the delivery of critical services.

Green Bonds Both the World Bank and IFC offer Green Bonds to support climate-related projects.

The World Bank Green Bond raises funds from fixed-income investors to support World Bank lending for eligible projects that seek to mitigate climate change or help affected people adapt to it. The product was designed in partnership with Skandinaviska Enskilda Banken (SEB) to respond to specific investor demand for a triple-A rated fixed-income product that supports projects that address the climate challenge. Since 2008, the World Bank has issued more than $6 billion in Green Bonds through 65 transactions and 17 currencies. Green Bonds are an opportunity to invest in climate solutions through a high-quality credit fixed-income product.

The IFC Green Bond program supports one of IFC's strategic priorities: to develop and promote innovative financial products that attract greater investments to climate-related projects. To date, IFC medium-term Green Bonds have raised more than $2 billion. The proceeds of the bonds are set aside in a separate account for investing exclusively in renewable energy or energy-efficient projects and other climate-friendly investments in developing countries. IFC's bonds go to fund its climate-related business, which is a growing area of strategic importance for the Corporation.

⮑　http://tinyurl.com/WBG012

Guarantees
World Bank Guarantees

Bank guarantees help member countries mobilize private financing for development purposes. All Bank guarantees are partial so that risks are shared between the Bank and private financiers. The Bank's objective is to cover risks that it is in a unique position to bear, given its experience in developing countries and its relationships with governments. Bank guarantees are provided as Development Policy Financing or Investment Project Financing.

By covering government performance risks that the market is not able to absorb or mitigate, the World Bank's guarantee mobilizes new sources of financing at reduced financing costs and extended maturities, thereby enabling commercial and private lenders and investors to invest in projects in developing countries. Guarantees can mitigate a variety of critical sovereign risks and effectively attract long-term private investment and commercial financing in sectors such as power, water, transport, telecommunications, oil and gas, and mining. Guarantees can also enhance private sector interest in participating in privatizations and public-private partnerships. It can also help governments access the financial markets.

The Bank's presence in transactions is seen by investors as a stabilizing factor because of the World Bank's long-term relationship with the countries and policy support it provides to the governments. The World Bank guarantees help catalyze the private financing needed in emerging countries, which leads to greater job and income opportunities for people and therefore contributes to the achievement of the Millennium Development Goals' overall challenge of reducing poverty.

MIGA Guarantees

MIGA provides political risk insurance (guarantees) for projects in a broad range of sectors in developing member countries, covering all regions of the world. MIGA can help investors and lenders deal with these risks by insuring eligible projects against losses relating to

- Currency inconvertibility and transfer restriction
- Expropriation
- War, terrorism, and civil disturbance
- Breach of contract
- Nonhonoring of financial obligations

MIGA guarantees offer much more than just the assurance that losses will be recovered. The insurance also benefits investors and lenders by:

- *Deterring harmful actions.* MIGA's status as a member of the World Bank Group and its relationship with shareholder governments provide additional leverage in protecting investments.

- *Resolving disputes.* MIGA intervenes at the first sign of trouble to resolve potential investment disputes before they reach claim status, thereby helping to maintain investments and keep revenues flowing.

- *Accessing funding.* MIGA's guarantees can help investors obtain project finance from banks and equity partners.

- *Lowering borrowing costs.* MIGA-guaranteed loans may help reduce risk-capital ratings of projects.

- *Increasing tenors.* The Agency can provide insurance coverage for up to 15 years (in some cases 20), which may increase the tenor of loans available to investors.

- *Providing extensive country knowledge.* MIGA applies decades of experience, global reach, and knowledge of developing countries to each transaction.

- *Providing environmental and social expertise.* MIGA helps investors and lenders ensure that projects comply with what are considered to be the world's best social and environmental safeguards.

⮞ http://www.miga.org/investmentguarantees/index.cfm

H

Health, Nutrition, and Population (*See also* Global Practices.) One of 14 new World Bank Group Global Practices, Health, Nutrition, and Population focuses on access to quality, affordable health, nutrition and population services and products.

World Bank Group and Health, Nutrition, and Population

Access to quality, affordable health, nutrition, and population services and products is central to ending extreme poverty and boosting shared prosperity. Poor health and high out-of-pocket expenditures for health care are among the leading causes of poverty. Promoting health-wise investments in all sectors is indispensable to fostering healthy societies. Investing in health pays off: 11 percent of recent economic growth in developing countries is due to mortality reductions. Moreover, 24 percent of the growth in full income—which includes national income accounts and the value of additional life years between 2000 and 2011 resulted from improved life expectancy.

The goal of the Health, Nutrition, and Population (HNP) Global Practice is to end preventable deaths and disability through universal health coverage so that by 2030 no one will be tipped into or kept in poverty due to expenditures on health and to ensure that the poorest 40 percent of the population will have access to essential services for their health. The HNP Global Practice is working with governments, the private sector, and civil society, together with other development partners, to improve access to quality, affordable health services, medicines, and related products; to establish systems for fair and sustainable financing of health; to scale up and strengthen frontline and facility-based health services; and to harness the potential of other sectors necessary for improvements in HNP outcomes, such as agriculture, transport, social protection, gender, education, and fiscal policy and taxation. This collaboration includes working with countries to identify a combination of public and private sector solutions that contribute to ending poverty through better health outcomes.

World Bank and Health, Nutrition, and Population

Through the International Development Association (IDA), the World Bank's fund for the poorest countries, the World Bank has helped save lives and improve the health of millions of people in developing countries. From 2003 to 2013, IDA:

- Provided more than 117 million people with access to basic packages of health, nutrition, or reproductive health services

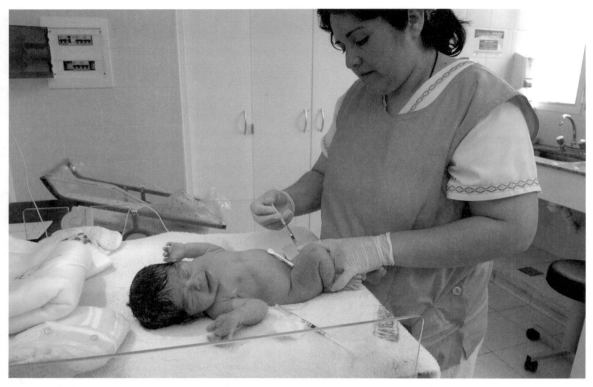

The Provincial Public Health Insurance Development Project extends the support of the Provincial Maternal and Child Health Investment Project, which introduced a system of incentives based on enhancing transparency and accountability of health care financing at national and provincial levels. The program improved the health conditions of 1.89 million uninsured mothers and children in Argentina by guaranteeing the delivery of a predefined health services package. © World Bank / Nahuel Berger (photographer). Permission required for reuse.

- Trained more than 2.6 million health personnel
- Constructed, renovated, or equipped more than 10,000 health facilities
- Immunized nearly 600 million children
- Provided more than 194 million pregnant women with antenatal care during a visit to a health care provider
- Ensured that more than 29 million births were attended by skilled health personnel
- Ensured that more than 210 million pregnant or lactating women, adolescent girls, or children under age five were reached by basic nutrition services
- Purchased or distributed more than 149 million long-lasting, insecticide-treated malaria bed nets
- Purchased or distributed more than 386 million condoms
- Provided more than 7.6 million people with tuberculosis treatment
- Ensured that more than 1.3 million adults and children received antiretroviral combination therapy

IFC and Health, Nutrition, and Population

By investing in the health sector, IFC is helping to expand access to high-quality care for lower- and middle-income people. Through its advisory and investment services, IFC supports efficient and effective companies whose activities make important contributions to the health and well-being of people in developing countries.

As part of its global agenda, IFC leverages its knowledge and understanding of private health care to work more closely with providers based in developed economies who are looking to expand their investments into underserved developing countries. Its strategy is to encourage and provide financing for the expansion of these global providers into new markets to build capacity and increase access to services. Developing country companies also benefit from global knowledge and expertise.

IFC's investments have supported a variety of private sector health services in developing countries: hospitals in Sub-Saharan Africa; regional diagnostic and outpatient services in Europe and Central Asia; an eye hospital, dental services, and outpatient facilities in East Asia and the Pacific; medical education, laboratories, and health technology in Latin America and the Caribbean; health insurance and hospitals in the Middle East and North Africa; and diagnostic laboratories and hospitals in South Asia.

MIGA and Health, Nutrition, and Population

MIGA's support to health services has included a pharmaceutical company in Afghanistan, an international dialysis center in Bosnia and Herzegovina, and diagnostic centers in Romania.

Heavily Indebted Poor Countries Heavily Indebted Poor Countries (HIPC) are a group of developing countries with high levels of poverty and debt that are eligible for special assistance from the World Bank and the International Monetary Fund. The HIPC Initiative, launched by the World Bank and the IMF in 1996, is the first international response to provide comprehensive debt relief to the world's poorest, most heavily indebted countries. The HIPC Initiative currently identifies 39 countries, most of them in Sub-Saharan Africa, as potentially eligible to receive debt relief.

➲ http://www.imf.org/external/np/exr/facts/hipc.htm

High-Income Countries (*See also* Classification of Countries.) The World Bank Group classifies high-income economies as those countries with a gross national income per capita of $12,746 or more.

➲ http://tinyurl.com/WBG013

HIV and AIDS The World Bank pioneered global human immunodeficiency virus (HIV) and acquired immune deficiency syndrome (AIDS) financing early in the emergency and remains committed to achieving Millennium Development Goal 6, to halt by 2015 and begin to reverse the spread of HIV and AIDS, through prevention, care, treatment, and mitigation services for those affected by HIV and AIDS.

The World Bank helps define the global response to HIV and AIDS and contributes to the achievement of the 2015 Millennium Development Goals. As a co-sponsor of the Joint United Nations Program on HIV/AIDS (UNAIDS), the Bank embraces the vision "Zero new HIV infections. Zero discrimination. Zero AIDS-related deaths." However, it also brings to the AIDS response its unique cross-sectoral expertise.

The World Bank offers to countries financing and specialized technical support and knowledge for effective prevention of new HIV infections, care and treatment for people living with HIV/AIDS, and alleviation of social and economic consequences for affected communities.

Upon request from national governments (and as part of the World Bank Country Partnership Strategies developed with the countries), the Bank provides financing (grants, credits, and loans) for HIV/AIDS programs. Financing can be provided through stand-alone projects or (more typically) integrated with broader health sector financing; it can also be provided through results-based financing for health systems strengthening or through financing for projects including infrastructure, transport, or urban development.

Since 1989, World Bank financing for HIV and AIDS has totaled more than $5 billion. As of fiscal 13, the World Bank's active portfolio for HIV/AIDS stands at $1.5 billion.

The World Bank also helps countries do "better for less" through actionable analytical work and technical assistance, helping countries improve the implementation, efficiency, effectiveness, and sustainability of their own national AIDS responses. The Bank supports analytical work to help countries maximize their HIV resource allocations and identify what to invest in: allocative efficiency, effectiveness studies, financing and sustainability studies, and/or national strategic planning. The Bank also supports countries in their efforts to understand how to better deliver HIV services and to attain the quality standards and coverage levels targeted in their national strategic plans. The Bank works with stakeholders to improve evidence related to HIV prevention and engages in key sectors such as education, transport, energy, and infrastructure.

↪ http://www.worldbank.org/en/topic/hivandaids

Honda, Keiko Keiko Honda is the Executive Vice President and Chief Executive Officer of MIGA. Previously, Honda was the first woman senior partner in Asia at McKinsey & Company. Prior to joining McKinsey, Honda worked for Bain & Company and Lehman Brothers. Honda also served as a visiting associate professor at Hitotsubashi University's business school and as a lecturer at Chuo University's business school. She has served on a number of Japanese government committees under several administrations, including the Council of Regulatory Reform. She was the vice chair of the Committee on the Promotion of Economic Partnership Agreements and Free Trade Agreements

for Keizai Doyukai, the Japanese association of corporate executives. Honda has authored and co-authored several books, including *M&A and Alliance Strategy* and *Turnaround*.

Honda holds a bachelor's degree in consumer economics from Ochanomizu University and an MBA from the University of Pennsylvania's Wharton School, where she was selected as a Fulbright Scholar.

Human Resources (*See also* Enabling Services.) The World Bank and IFC each have Human Resource (HR) Vice Presidencies that work in close partnership with their respective business units and senior management, at headquarters and in country offices. Collectively, their role is to develop and implement HR policies and strategies that enable the Bank Group to attract and retain a diverse, high-quality, mobile, and productive workforce to deliver on its mission.

HR work covers a wide range of issues, from global HR strategies, policies, and programs that support the business objectives at the corporate level to strategic staffing, decentralization, organizational development, career development, compensation, performance management, and exit management at the unit level. In addition, the Office of Diversity Programs provides guidance on institutional- and unit-level diversity and inclusion strategies across HR processes, and the Health Services Department serves the staff and management of the Bank Group by promoting good health and by contributing to a healthy work environment.

Human Rights Human rights embody value commitments that are not uniformly interpreted. Furthermore, the concept of universality underpinning the international human rights framework is a complex one that must be assessed in progressive terms and interpreted according to its current legal, political, and historical context. In recent years, the World Bank Group has placed new emphasis on understanding the relationship between human rights and development. There is a growing body of research from development experts that shows the links between human rights and development, and many development partners are increasingly integrating human rights into their programs.

Human Rights and Development

The World Bank Group contributes to the realization of human rights in different areas, for example, improving poor people's access to health, education, food, and water; promoting the participation of indigenous peoples in decision making and the accountability of governments to their citizens; supporting justice and regulatory reforms, fighting corruption, and increasing the transparency of governments; and expanding economic opportunities in the private sector for entrepreneurs and businesses large and small.

Through the Nordic Trust Fund program, Bank Group staff members are developing a more informed view on how human rights relate to the institution's core work and mission of promoting economic growth and poverty reduction. This internal knowledge and learning program supports activities that:

- Capture and make available knowledge about how human rights relate to the Bank Group's analytical sector and thematic work

- Capture and make available knowledge about how human rights relate to the Bank Group's operational work, including strategy, planning, and implementation

- Increase awareness among staff and management of how the Bank Group's work and human rights are related and how human rights aspects can be applied to the Bank's work

Human Rights and Justice Institutions

It is now widely accepted that justice institutions are crucial for good governance and sustainable development and play an important role in promoting and protecting human rights. Recent *World Development Reports* have highlighted the role of justice—along with citizen security and economic opportunity—in breaking cycles of fragility and conflict.

Justice institutions are critical to the fair distribution of power and rights. They also underpin the forms and functions of other institutions that deliver public services and regulate access to resources. Clear, equitable rules and processes can facilitate effective and peaceful transitional change and can create the enabling conditions for a functioning social and economic net by challenging inequitable practices. At the same time, there is still limited understanding of how equitable justice systems emerge and thus how they can be supported or promoted. While recent experience in advancing legal and judicial reform has generated some partial successes and lessons learned, there is a growing understanding of the limitations of existing approaches.

In recognition of how well-functioning justice systems empower countries to combat extreme poverty and economic inequality, the World Bank's Justice for the Poor (J4P) program engages with justice reform as a cross-cutting issue in the practice of development. Grounded in evidence-based approaches focused on the perspective of the poor and marginalized, the program aims to improve the delivery of justice services and to support sustainable and equitable development processes that manage grievance and conflict stresses effectively.

J4P works in countries across East Asia and the Pacific (Indonesia, Papua New Guinea, Solomon Islands, Timor-Leste, and Vanuatu), as well as in Africa (Kenya, Nigeria, and Sierra Leone). The program focuses on access to justice, equity in service delivery, and land and natural resource governance, with attention to gender and development effectiveness in all of its projects.

Nordic Trust Fund
⟳ http://go.worldbank.org/PKPTI6FU40

World Bank and Human Rights
⟳ http://go.worldbank.org/WA4KU9E940

Hydropower In some countries, only 9 percent of people have access to electricity. It is estimated that by 2025, 2.4 billion people will live in countries without enough water to meet needs. Energy and water security are key to lifting people out of poverty and boosting prosperity.

The World Bank Group is firmly committed to the responsible development of hydropower projects of all sizes and types—run of the river, pumped storage, and reservoir—including off-grid projects meeting decentralized rural needs.

The Bank Group supports interventions and demand-management approaches to address and integrate energy consumption and water resource issues in ways that maximize benefits and minimize risks. This support arises from the recognition that hydropower is not only a vital renewable energy resource, but for many countries, it is the only renewable energy that has the potential to expand access to electricity to large populations. Yet it remains underdeveloped in many countries, especially in Africa, where less than 10 percent of hydropower potential has been tapped.

When designed properly, hydropower projects can deliver benefits far beyond energy and water security. They often lead to investments in roads, social infrastructure, communications, and skills building to support local or regional economic development. They can also provide power generation for industrial, manufacturing, and commercial operations that create jobs.

The intent in such projects is to recognize the potential synergies and efficiencies available when hydropower infrastructure is considered within the broader landscape of development and poverty reduction. Multipurpose hydropower dams can support adaptation to increasingly extreme weather conditions by strengthening a country's ability to regulate and store water and thereby resist flood and drought shocks. By having the World Bank Group cover the investment risk, countries can secure investment from the private sector to realize their energy and water security projects. Perceived high risk has traditionally inhibited private sector investment in infrastructure in many countries.

The Bank Group also helps client governments strengthen their capacity for early incorporation of environmental and social dimensions in hydropower projects, including consultations, benefit sharing, and inclusion of indigenous peoples. The Bank Group supports the Hydropower Sustainability Assessment Protocol, an enhanced sustainability assessment tool used to measure and guide performance in the hydropower sector, launched in Brazil in 2011.

Since the 2003 Water Resources Strategy, which states that the Bank would re-engage in hydraulic infrastructure, the World Bank (which includes the IBRD/IDA, GEF, and Recipient Executed Activities) has approved about 100 projects related to hydropower (fiscal 2003–13), for a total of $5.7 billion in financing. The World Bank portfolio since 2003 shows:

- 48 percent of projects were for green-field investments
- 27 percent supported rehabilitation
- 25 percent were for technical assistance and preparatory studies

Of the green-field and rehabilitation projects: 36 percent were storage hydro; 31 percent, run-of-river; and 30 percent, programs for small-scale development (including off-grid micro hydro). The remaining 3 percent of projects were pumped storage.

During this period, the Bank Group also facilitated 21 carbon market transactions around hydropower to offset emissions from other technologies. Of these, approximately 60 percent were for run-of-river projects. IFC has approved 42 hydropower projects totaling $1.3 billion over the last decade.

⟳ http://www.worldbank.org/en/topic/hydropower

I

IBRD (*See* International Bank for Reconstruction and Development.)

ICSID (*See* International Centre for Settlement of Investment Disputes.)

IDA (*See* International Development Association.)

IEG (*See* Independent Evaluation Group.)

IFC (*See* International Finance Corporation.)

IMF (*See* International Monetary Fund.)

Impact Evaluation An impact evaluation assesses changes in the well-being of individuals, households, communities, or firms that can be attributed to a particular project, program, or policy. The central impact evaluation question is what would have happened to those recipients if they had not received the intervention.

Impact evaluation is aimed at providing feedback to help improve the design of programs and policies. In addition to providing for improved accountability, impact evaluations are a tool for dynamic learning, allowing policy makers to improve ongoing programs and ultimately better allocate funds across programs.

⮕ http://go.worldbank.org/2DHMCRFFT2

Independent Evaluation Group The Independent Evaluation Group (IEG) is an independent unit within the World Bank Group that assesses the relevance and impact of the Bank Group's work to reduce poverty and improve people's lives in a sustainable manner. It reports directly to the Executive Directors. IEG's goals are to contribute to the objective basis for assessing results, to provide accountability in the achievement of development objectives, and to share learning gained from experience. IEG makes its findings available to the broader development community and the public at large.

⮕ http://ieg.worldbankgroup.org

Indigenous Peoples The World Bank aims to promote indigenous peoples' development in a manner that ensures that the development process fosters full respect for the dignity, human rights, and uniqueness of indigenous peoples.

The World Bank seeks to position excluded groups, such as indigenous peoples, at the center of the development agenda. Doing so includes the following:

• Strengthening the policy and institutional frameworks affecting indigenous peoples and their relations with other members of society

- Supporting indigenous peoples' capacity for self-development based on their own views and priorities, including cultural heritage and knowledge

- Demonstrating the important role that indigenous peoples can play in the management of fragile ecosystems and biodiversity conservation and in climate change adaptation

- Disseminating experience and lessons learned from such indigenous development initiatives to national governments and the international donor community

In recent years, the World Bank has engaged directly with indigenous leaders and their representative Indigenous Peoples Organizations (IPOs). The Bank participates each year in a number of high-level international Indigenous Peoples' forums, including the UN Permanent Forum on Indigenous Issues (UNPFII) in New York.

Indigenous peoples are disproportionally vulnerable to the impacts of climate change, given that they often live in environmentally sensitive areas (such as the Arctic region, tropical forests, mountains, and deserts) and frequently depend primarily on surrounding biodiversity for subsistence as well as cultural survival. As a result, indigenous peoples hold traditional knowledge that may be critical to climate change adaptation. The Bank aims to build on indigenous peoples' knowledge when assisting countries in developing strategies to adapt to changing environmental patterns and conditions.

➲ http://www.worldbank.org/en/topic/indigenouspeoples

Information and Communication Technologies
The Information and Communication Technologies (ICT) sector strategy, adopted in 2012, helps developing countries use information and communication technologies to transform the delivery of public services, drive innovations and productivity gains, and improve competitiveness. The strategy reflects rapid changes in the sector over the past decade, including a dramatic increase in use of mobile phones and the Internet, a sharp drop in the prices of computing and mobile Internet devices, and the increasing prevalence of social media.

Under this strategy, the World Bank, IFC, and MIGA focus on three priority areas:

- **Transformation.** Making development more open and accountable and improving service delivery, for instance, by facilitating citizen feedback to governments and service providers.

- **Connectivity.** Scaling up affordable access to broadband, including for women, disabled citizens, disadvantaged communities, and people living in remote and rural areas.

- **Innovation.** Developing competitive IT-based service industries and fostering ICT innovation across the economy with a focus on job creation, especially for women and youth.

➲ http://www.worldbank.org/en/topic/ict

Information and Technology Solutions (*See also* Enabling Services.) Information and Technology Solutions (ITS) enables the World Bank Group to achieve its mission of ending extreme poverty and boosting shared prosperity in a sustainable manner by delivering transformative information and technologies to its staff working in more than 130 client countries. ITS services are broad and include establishing the infrastructure to reach and connect staff members and development stakeholders; providing the devices and agile technology and information applications to facilitate the science of delivery through decentralized services; creating and maintaining tools to integrate information across the Bank Group, the clients it serves, and the countries where it operates; and delivering the computing power staff members need to analyze development challenges and identify solutions. The ITS business model combines services tailored to specific WBG business needs and shared services that provide infrastructure, applications, and platforms for the entire Bank Group.

InfoShop The InfoShop is a public retail bookstore and resource center that offers public access to information on World Bank Group projects and programs. Through the events program, it is also a forum for dialogue and debate on development issues.

The InfoShop is open to the public and carries all World Bank Group publications and books from more than 700 other publishers on topics related to development economics. Gift items,

The InfoShop is located at 1176 Pennsylvania Ave. NW, Washington, D.C., 20004. © World Bank. Permission required for reuse.

world music on CDs, souvenirs, and maps are also available.

⤵ http://www.worldbankgroup.org/infoshop

Infrastructure (*See also* Energy and Extractives; Environment and Natural Resources; Transport and ICT; Social, Urban, Rural, and Resilience; Water.)

World Bank Group and Infrastructure

The updated World Bank Group Infrastructure Strategy fiscal 2012–15 lays out the framework for transforming the Bank Group's engagement in infrastructure. It looks at what is required—in terms of partnership, knowledge, advice, and projects—for infrastructure to accelerate growth and even shift client countries toward a more sustainable development trajectory. It also supports a new vision of who will finance infrastructure solutions. The new strategy rests on three principal pillars:

- *Core Engagement.* The Bank Group will increase its support for access to basic infrastructure services and growth. Access to electricity, improved water services and sanitation, all season roads, telecommunication, and Internet services are still key constraints in many low-income countries, for some population segments in middle-income countries, and in fragile states. This support represents the bedrock of the Bank Group's involvement in infrastructure and will continue to do so going forward. But more effectiveness is needed to enhance the delivery of infrastructure services to the poor and to mainstream gender and governance in projects.

- *Transformational Engagement.* The Bank Group will scale up its engagement in tackling the more systemic development challenges. This will require reaching beyond the line ministries and other traditional partners. It will require repositioning the Bank Group in global forums to lead the infrastructure debate. It will require facilitating knowledge transfer between clients instead of merely generating it. It will require new types of projects, both large and small, which optimize spatial, green, inclusive, and co-benefits. In Sub-Saharan Africa, for instance, this will involve more emphasis on regional projects that connect countries with power grids, broadband, transportation corridors, and large-scale renewable energy. In East Asia, it will involve partnering with city mayors, the private sector, civil society, regional organizations, and other donors to optimize low-carbon growth in urban settings.

• *Mobilization of Private Capital.* The Bank Group will leverage its capital more systematically by mobilizing other sources of financing, including the private sector and other multilateral development banks, with the view of increasing the financing envelope for infrastructure.

World Bank and Infrastructure

The World Bank's infrastructure engagement includes activities in the energy, information and communication technologies, water, and transport sectors. Infrastructure, however, is more than the sum of these individual sectors; finding solutions to modern development challenges requires tackling the complexity and interconnectivity among sectors:

• *Energy.* Access to environmentally and socially sustainable energy is essential to reducing poverty. While millions of people around the world have benefited from Bank Group energy financing, more than 1.3 billion people are still without access to electricity, almost all of whom live in developing countries. Since 2000, for the poorest

countries—many of them in Africa—Bank Group support has helped build, and make more reliable, almost 8 gigawatts of electricity.

• *Information and communication technology (ICT).* Technological progress is a strong driver of economic growth. ICT infrastructure in particular has attracted much investment and generated significant fiscal revenues and employment opportunities in developing countries. The World Bank Group has supported more than 100 developing countries in reforming their telecommunications and ICT sectors, helping spur the investment and modernization that in turn accelerate economic growth and poverty reduction.

• *Transport.* Transport is crucial for economic growth and trade, both of which are highly dependent on the conveyance of people and goods. Virtually no production or consumption can take place unless people, raw materials, commodities, fuel, and finished products can be moved to and from different locations.

• *Water.* Efficient water services (water supply and sanitation, irrigation and drainage, energy, environmental services) promote growth and development, but water is finite, and access to services is not guaranteed if they are not managed properly. Managing water and land in a more integrated way is critical to ensuring access to clean drinking water, reducing water pollution, protecting biodiversity, controlling flooding, and increasing food security.

IFC and Infrastructure

IFC supports innovative, high-impact, private infrastructure projects that can be widely replicated. It helps increase access to power, transport, and water by financing infrastructure projects and advising client governments on public-private partnerships. IFC mitigates risk and leverages specialized financial structuring and other capabilities. IFC also helps increase access to power, transport, and water by financing infrastructure projects and advising client governments on public-private partnerships. The Corporation mitigates risk and leverages specialized financial structuring and other capabilities. In fiscal 2014, IFC's new commitments in this sector totaled about $2.4 billion, or about 14 percent of commitments for IFC's own account.

MIGA and Infrastructure

MIGA's political risk insurance can play a pivotal role in helping companies attract funds for large, capital-intensive investments. In fiscal 2014, MIGA issued $1.4 billion in guarantees to support infrastructure projects, accounting for 45 percent of MIGA's new issuance.

MIGA has a comparative advantage in supporting complex infrastructure investments, particularly for cash-intensive investments that involve municipal governments, and in securing financing at better rates and for longer periods. Infrastructure development is an important priority for MIGA, given the estimated infrastructure gap of $1 trillion in low- and middle-income countries and the growing demand for infrastructure to deal with the rapidly growing urban centers and underserved rural populations in developing countries.

MIGA's strategy builds on its market strengths: encouraging investments in the more difficult, frontier markets, as well as supporting investments at the subsovereign level, which often involves inexperienced and therefore riskier partners.

Integrity Vice Presidency (*See also* Enabling Services.) The Integrity Vice Presidency (INT) is an independent unit within the World Bank Group that has the unique function of investigating and pursuing sanctions related to allegations of fraud and corruption in Bank Group–financed activities. As an integral part of the Bank Group's overall governance and anticorruption strategy, INT performs a preventive function as well, working closely with other World Bank units and external stakeholders to mitigate risks through advice, training, and outreach efforts. Where the Bank Group's own staff members may be implicated in such misconduct, INT also investigates and acts in relation to those allegations.

Intelligent Transport Systems Intelligent Transport Systems (ITS) is an emerging field that leverages information and communication technologies to gather, organize, analyze, use, and share transport data for the efficient and effective operation of transport systems. Information gathered through ITS can be used to inform the development of transport networks, and the ability of ITS to process real-time data makes it useful in managing day-to-day transport operations, matching supply and demand, and responding to emergency situations.

ITS systems have become more popular over the past 10 years, including in many developing countries where ITS has contributed to mitigating challenges such as traffic congestion. There are, however, many more challenges that could benefit from the application of ITS.

Internal Audit The Internal Audit (IAD) Vice Presidency is an independent and objective assurance and advisory function designed to add value to the World Bank Group (WBG) by improving the operations of the WBG organizations. It assists the Bank Group in accomplishing its objectives by bringing a systematic and disciplined approach to evaluating and improving the effectiveness of the organization's risk management, control, and governance processes. IAD's reports provide a high-level overview of its activities' for senior management and the Audit Committee. Its "Quarterly Activity Report" is also publicly disclosed, under the Bank's Access to Information Policy.

Internal Justice System (*See also* Enabling Services.) The Council for Internal Justice comprises Bank Group staff members involved in matters relating to internal workplace governance, including employment disputes, ethical queries, and cases of alleged misconduct. The council's principal responsibilities are as follows:

- Identifying trends, current issues, and potential gaps in services relating to internal workplace governance

- Preparing training, communication, and events to expand awareness of the Internal Justice System

- Administering surveys on internal governance issues

- Ensuring consistency in the monitoring and evaluation of Internal Justice System offices

- Reviewing and discussing annual reports of the Internal Justice System offices

International Bank for Reconstruction and Development (*See also* World Bank; World Bank Group.) One of the five World Bank Group agencies, the International Bank for Reconstruction and Development (IBRD) is also one of two agencies that make up the World Bank (the other is IDA). IBRD aims to reduce poverty in middle-income countries and creditworthy poorer countries by promoting sustainable development through loans, guarantees, risk management products, and analytical and advisory services. Established in 1944 as the original institution of the World Bank Group, IBRD is structured like a cooperative that is owned and operated for the benefit of its 188 member countries.

IBRD raises most of its funds on the world's financial markets and has become one of the most established borrowers since issuing its first bond in 1947. The income that IBRD has generated over the years has allowed it to fund development activities and to ensure its financial strength, which enables it to borrow at low cost and offers clients good borrowing terms.

⮑ http://www.worldbank.org/ibrd

International Centre for Settlement of Investment Disputes (*See also* World Bank; World Bank Group.) The International Centre for Settlement of Investment Disputes (ICSID) is an autonomous international institution established under the Convention on the Settlement of Investment Disputes between States and Nationals of Other States with more than 140 member states. The convention sets forth ICSID's mandate, organization and core functions. The primary purpose of ICSID is to provide facilities for conciliation and arbitration of international investment disputes. ICSID is one of the five institutions that make up the World Bank Group.

⮑ http://www.worldbank.org/icsid

International Development Association (*See also* World Bank; World Bank Group.) One of the five World Bank Group entities, the International Development Association (IDA) is one of two organizations that make up the World Bank (the other is IBRD). Established in 1960, IDA aims to reduce poverty in the poorest countries by providing loans and guarantees for programs that boost economic growth, reduce inequalities, and improve people's living conditions.

IDA is one of the largest sources of assistance for the world's 82 poorest countries, 40 of which are in Africa. It is the single-largest source of donor funds for basic social services in these countries. IDA-financed operations deliver positive change for 2.5 billion people, the majority of whom survive on less than $2 a day.

IDA lends money on concessional terms. This means that IDA charges little or no interest and repayments are stretched over 25–40 years, including a 5- to 10-year grace period. IDA also provides grants to countries at risk of debt distress. IDA provides guarantees to help attract private financing. In addition, IDA provides significant levels of debt relief through the Heavily Indebted Poor Countries Initiative and the Multilateral Debt Relief Initiative.

Since its inception, IDA has supported activities in 108 countries. Annual commitments have increased steadily and averaged about $16 billion over the past three years, with about 50 percent of that going to Africa. In fiscal 2014, IDA commitments rose to a record $22.2 billion from $16.3 billion in the previous fiscal year.

⤳ http://www.worldbank.org/ida

International Development Association Resource Allocation Index The World Bank's IDA Resource Allocation Index is based on the results of the annual Country Policy and Institutional Assessment (CPIA) exercise that covers the IDA-eligible countries.

The CPIA rates countries against a set of 16 criteria grouped in four clusters: economic management, structural policies, policies for social inclusion and equity, and public sector management and institutions. The criteria are focused on balancing the capture of the key factors that foster growth and poverty reduction, with the need to avoid undue burden on the assessment process.

⤳ http://www.worldbank.org/ida/IRAI-2011.html

International Finance Corporation (*See also* World Bank Group.) The International Finance Corporation (IFC), one of the five institutions that make up the World Bank Group, is the largest global development institution focused exclusively on the private sector in developing countries. Established in 1956, IFC is owned by 184 member countries, a group that collectively determines its policies. With work in more than 100 developing countries, IFC helps companies and financial institutions in emerging markets create jobs, generate tax revenues, improve corporate governance and environmental performance, and contribute to their local communities.

IFC has five strategic priorities:

- Strengthening the focus on frontier markets

- Addressing climate change and ensuring environmental and social sustainability

- Addressing constraints to private sector growth in infrastructure, health, education, and the food-supply chain

- Developing local financial markets

- Building long-term client relationships in emerging markets

⤳ http://www.ifc.org

International Monetary Fund The International Monetary Fund (IMF) is an organization with 188 member countries, working to foster global monetary cooperation, secure financial stability, facilitate international trade, promote high employment and sustainable economic growth, and reduce poverty around the world. It is a specialized agency of the United Nations but has its own charter, governing structure, and finances. Its members are represented through a quota system broadly based on their relative size in the global economy.

The IMF works to foster global growth and economic stability. It provides policy advice and financing to members in economic difficulties and also works with developing nations to help them achieve macroeconomic stability and reduce poverty. Through its economic surveillance, the IMF keeps track of the economic health of its member countries, alerting them to risks on the horizon and providing policy advice. It also lends to countries in difficulty and provides technical assistance and training to help countries improve economic management.

⮑ https://www.imf.org

Internships World Bank Group internships offer highly motivated and successful individuals an opportunity to improve their skills while working in a diverse environment. The Bank Group typically seeks candidates in the following fields: economics, finance, human development (public health, education, nutrition, population), social sciences (anthropology, sociology), agriculture, environment, and private sector development, as well as other related fields. Candidates can apply for summer and winter internship positions.

IFC Internships
⮑ http://tinyurl.com/WBG078

World Bank Internships
⮑ http://www.worldbank.org/jobs

Investment Climate The World Bank Group helps governments implement reforms to improve their business environments and encourage and retain investment, thus fostering competitive markets, growth, and job creation. Funding is provided by IFC, the World Bank, and MIGA, along with donor partners working through the multidonor platform of Facility for Investment Climate Advisory Services.

Advisory work is organized under two main areas of practice: regulatory simplification and investment generation. In both practice areas, the focus is on improving the policies, laws, and regulations that affect domestic and foreign investors and influence their decisions to invest.

Support is provided to implement reforms that reduce unnecessary costs and risks faced by firms, strengthen fair competition, and promote investment. Specific areas include business taxation, business regulation, insolvency, trade logistics, alternative dispute resolution, investment policy and promotion, industry-based programs, the development of special economic zones, and public-private dialogue. Assistance is also available for a range of short-term projects designed to address specific issues highlighted by the Doing Business indicators. In addition, the World Bank offers technical assistance through its loan products and analytic and advisory services, which conduct economic and sector analyses.

⮑ https://www.wbginvestmentclimate.org

Investment Services (*See also* Products and Services.) IFC's investment services provide a broad suite of financial products—including loans, equity, trade finance, structured finance, and syndications—designed to promote worthy enterprises and encourage entrepreneurship. IFC continues to develop new financial products that enable companies to manage risk and broaden their access to foreign and domestic capital markets.

iSimulate iSimulate is a platform that facilitates collaborative economic simulations across the Internet. iSimulate allows users to run simulations on a variety of economic models, without the need to install any specific software on their computer. iSimulate hosts some of the World Bank's experimental global macromodels, all of which are 100 percent free to use. iSimulate users can connect with each other via virtual working groups and use automatically configured group blogs as publishing tools to disseminate their work to the world.

⟳ http://isimulate.worldbank.org

J·K

Jobs (*See also* Cross-Cutting Solution Areas.)

World Bank Group and Jobs

One of five new Cross-Cutting Solution Areas, Jobs is the cornerstone of economic and social development. Access to jobs and increasing wages is critical for the World Bank Group's mission of reducing poverty. Good, steady jobs and living wages will help the world end extreme poverty by 2030 and build more inclusive societies.

Nothing drives poverty reduction as much as access to jobs and increasing wages, World Bank research shows. The *World Development Report 2013* calls jobs a cornerstone for development that connects living standards, productivity, and social cohesion—all critical for achieving inclusive growth.

Keeping people in growing nations employed will be a challenge, however. The International Labour Organization estimates that more than 400 million more jobs must be created worldwide between 2012 and 2022 to keep unemployment from rising.

World Bank and Jobs

The World Bank works with client countries to give poor people—especially women and young people—better access to the labor market. It supports employment training initiatives, credit services, small business development, and other labor-related programs in dozens of countries. The Bank is also working with clients to reform and strengthen labor protection laws.

Underpinning such projects is a large body of analytical work on jobs and employment that guides World Bank programs. Such research covers labor market developments, wage inequality, job creation strategies, and much more. The Bank's work to expand job markets and opportunities takes many shapes and forms. As an example, the Bank is financing a $30 million, six-year program in Niger that focuses on vocational training to try to reduce youth unemployment. The program seeks to promote entrepreneurship by targeting 11,000 people ages 15 to 25.

A recent World Bank initiative, the Jobs Knowledge Platform, mobilizes a broad range of institutions and advocates brainstorming on how to create and improve jobs worldwide. The platform offers videos, blogs, research, data, information on a range of labor-related topics, and a jobs database.

In fiscal 2014, the World Bank's labor-related lending totaled $218 million. From fiscal 2011 to fiscal 2013, the Bank supported 1.5 million new labor

The Employment Generation Program for the Poorest (EGPP) Project provides short-term employment on community subprojects to enable households to better cope with vulnerability in Bangladesh. The EGPP has provided a secure and regular source of income to more than 700,000 of the poorest people; more than 33 percent of them are women. © World Bank / Scott Wallace (photographer). Permission required for reuse.

market program beneficiaries, half of whom were female.

IFC and Jobs

IFC believes the private sector—which accounts for 9 out of every 10 jobs—is critical to creating more and better jobs. As the world's largest global development institution focused on the private sector, IFC works with private businesses in more than 100 countries to foster the right kind of job growth. IFC works to ensure that jobs are created for both men and women—including youth—and that these jobs are sustainable and productive; that they offer fair pay and good working conditions; and that they provide opportunities to advance. In 2013, IFC clients directly supported about 2.6 million jobs.

IFC also works with financial institutions to increase lending to micro, small, and medium enterprises—which in turn employ more than 100 million people. But direct jobs are only a small part of the story. For example, IFC estimates that across value chains, every direct job may lead to as many as 20 indirect jobs.

MIGA and Jobs

MIGA's support for private sector investments helps encourage growth and job creation in developing countries. The Agency works in a number of sectors, including agribusiness, infrastructure, manufacturing, power, services, and transportation.

⮑ https://www.jobsknowledge.org

Journals For more information, please see the individual entries for each of the following journals:

- World Bank Economic Review
- World Bank Research Observer

Kim, Jim Yong (*See* Presidents of the World Bank Group.)

Knowledge Sharing (*See also* World Bank Group Publications.)

Knowledge sharing at the World Bank Group has evolved over time. From an early emphasis on capturing and organizing knowledge, the focus is now on enabling knowledge to be freely modified, adapted, and used as an essential tool for reaching the twin goals of ending extreme poverty and boosting shared prosperity.

In 2014 the World Bank Group underwent a historic institutional change that entailed the creation of Global Practices and Cross-Cutting Solution Areas. This change will encourage and support knowledge flows across the Bank Group, enabling client countries to more readily benefit from the collective accumulation of experience and knowledge.

L

Labor (*See also* Social Protection and Labor.) According to the International Labour Organization (ILO), the world will need more than 600 million more jobs in the next 10 years to avoid a further increase in unemployment. In regions such as Africa and South Asia, countries face particular challenges as a growing number of youth are entering the labor market. Creating new jobs is not the sole concern of government, however. Policy makers are also focused on low rates of participation in the labor market and high poverty rates among those who participate and have a job.

Labor policies and programs can help improve labor market participation and address the high poverty rates. Labor regulations and insurance programs protect workers from risks and, if well-designed, can facilitate labor market transitions and thereby allow individuals to engage in higher-risk, higher-return activities. Active labor market programs such as training, job search assistance, or support to self-employment can also help workers acquire the skills they need and connect them to jobs.

The World Bank Group works with countries to design and implement labor regulations, income protections, and active labor market programs that can be extended to a majority of the labor force.

The Bank Group also helps countries develop the right solutions for their unique social and economic circumstances, with a focus on expanding social protection and insurance coverage while also maintaining or providing incentives to create jobs.

From 1998 to 2012, the Bank Group supported job creation and worker protection activities in 99 countries, with total lending reaching $7.3 billion (comprising $5.6 billion through IBRD lending, $1.7 billion through IDA lending, and $47 million in grants). Programs included unemployment benefits, public works, employment services, training, support to self-employment and entrepreneurship, and access to credit. During 1998–2012, the two largest regional borrowers for labor market support were Europe and Central Asia and Latin America and the Caribbean.

⟳ http://www.worldbank.org/en/topic/socialprotectionlabor

LAC (*See* Latin America and Caribbean.)

Latin America and the Caribbean
World Bank Group in Latin America and the Caribbean

Steady growth and sound economic policies have improved the lives of millions in the Latin America and the Caribbean (LAC) region over the past decade.

93

LATIN AMERICA AND THE CARIBBEAN REGION SNAPSHOT

581.4 million	Total population
1.2 percent	Population growth
$9,070	Gross national income per capita
5.5 percent	Population living below $1.25 per day
74 years	Life expectancy at birth
92.2 percent	Adult (15+) literacy rate

This region includes the following countries:*

Antigua and Barbuda
Argentina
Belize
Plurinational State of Bolivia
Brazil
Chile
Colombia
Costa Rica
Cuba
Dominica
Dominican Republic
Ecuador
El Salvador
Grenada
Guatemala
Guyana
Haiti
Honduras
Jamaica
Mexico
Nicaragua
Panama
Paraguay
Peru
St. Kitts and Nevis
St. Lucia
St. Vincent and the Grenadines
Suriname
Trinidad and Tobago
Uruguay
República Bolivariana de Venezuela

*Regions are defined for analytical and operational purposes and may differ from common geographic usage. Variances also exist across the five World Bank Group institutions.

Member Countries by WBG Institution

🔁 www.worldbank.org/en/about/leadership/members#1

The poverty rate dropped from 42 percent in 2000 to 25 percent in 2012, while the ranks of the middle class increased from 22 to 34 percent in those same years. For the first time ever, the number of people belonging to the middle class now surpasses the number of poor, a sign that the LAC region is moving toward becoming middle class.

The World Bank in Latin America and the Caribbean

In line with the World Bank Group's overall strategy centered on eliminating extreme poverty by 2030 and boosting shared prosperity, the World Bank's work in the region addresses the following core areas of shared prosperity, increased productivity, state efficiency, inclusive green growth, and disaster resilience.

Shared Prosperity. Despite impressive recent gains—a growing middle class and fewer poor—Latin America and the Caribbean remains a very unequal region, with some 82 million people living on less than $2.50 per day. In addition, while the middle class accounts for 34 percent of the region's total population, 38 percent of Latin Americans remain vulnerable to falling back into poverty. Perhaps more worrisome is the fact that inequality reduction may be stagnating. Addressing the inequality gap and creating opportunities for all is at the top of the Bank's regional agenda.

Increased Productivity. The region's extraordinary recent growth and ability to weather the 2008–09 global recession contrast sharply with its lagging productivity. Logistics costs are high, infrastructure is decaying, and education lacks quality. Logistics in LAC cost two to four times more than in countries of the Organisation for Economic Co-operation and Development and the Asian Tigers (Hong Kong, China; Singapore; the Republic of Korea; and Taiwan, China). While the share of Latin Americans with higher education rose from 9.5 to 14.2 percent in 1990–2009, the Asian Tiger economies went from 10 to 20 percent over the same period.

State Efficiency. Access to quality public services remains a challenge. Citizens have a diminished confidence in the state's capacity to provide efficient services, with many opting out if they can afford it. About 7 percent of the population does not have access to safe water and 20 percent of Latin Americans still lack access to sanitation. Citizen security is a development challenge for many countries, especially small ones, and governments are eager to develop an integrated response to growing crime and violence. The World Bank has been supporting these efforts through financing as well as high-level knowledge exchanges.

Inclusive and Green Growth. Latin America and the Caribbean has served as a global showcase for some of the most innovative environmentally friendly practices. Accounting for only 6 percent of global greenhouse emissions, the region has the lowest carbon-intensive energy matrix of the developing world. It has also adopted payment schemes for preserving the environment. But the economic bonanza of recent years has led to exploding urbanization: more than 80 percent of the region's population now lives in cities. The Bank's green growth agenda recognizes the paramount importance of the issue to the region's development and for preserving natural resources for future generations.

Disaster Resilience. Naturally prone to hazards, LAC is home to 9 of the top 20 countries exposed to disasters, which cost governments about $2 billion annually. Countries have become more disaster savvy and are increasing their focus on prevention. The Bank provides tools and mechanisms to boost resilience, including cutting-edge instruments such as catastrophic risk insurance.

IFC in Latin America and the Caribbean

IFC supports private sector projects throughout the region, with a focus on several objectives:

- *Promoting inclusive growth.* IFC is working to increase access to finance, basic goods and services, and infrastructure.

- *Strengthening competitiveness and innovation.* IFC is helping to address bottlenecks in infrastructure through public-private partnerships, improving the investment climate, expanding vocational and tertiary education, and supporting new sectors such as mobile banking.

- *Facilitating regional and global integration.* IFC is helping to improve legal frameworks for trade logistics, integrate regional financial markets, increase South-South initiatives, and strengthen energy networks and transportation. Sustainable growth and competitiveness depend on integration.

- *Helping the region cope with climate change through mitigation and adaptation.* Mitigation activities pertain to renewable energy, cleaner production, and land use, while adaptation focuses on wastewater treatment, disaster insurance, and zoning codes.

In fiscal 2014, IFC invested more than $5.1 billion in LAC, including about $1 billion mobilized from other financial institutions. IFC's clients supplied water to 7.5 million people and provided education to 1.1 million students. Also, in the financial sector, they provided 12.7 million loans to micro, small, and medium enterprises.

MIGA in Latin America and the Caribbean

Recent guarantees issued by MIGA for companies investing in Latin America and the Caribbean supported a range of sectors, including wind power and agribusiness in Nicaragua, wind power in Honduras, transportation in Panama, banking in Bolivia and Colombia, and financial services in El Salvador.

Data Resources on Latin America and the Caribbean

➲ http://data.worldbank.org/region/LAC

Research on Latin America and the Caribbean

➲ http://www.worldbank.org/en/region/lac/research

Leadership, Learning, and Innovation Vice Presidency (*See also* World Bank Institute.) The new Leadership, Learning, and Innovation Vice Presidency (LLI) is working to help the World Bank Group accelerate the achievement of its goals of ending poverty and boosting shared prosperity. By supporting the new Global Practices and Regional Vice Presidencies in practitioner learning, collaborative leadership, and surfacing innovative solutions. It translates global knowledge into effective practitioner learning that is aligned with the competencies and needs of Bank Group clients; strengthens leadership and coalition-building skills to help clients identify intractable problems and the corresponding multistakeholder solutions; and scans and helps scale innovative solutions to assist clients in tackling their thorniest problems.

Legal (*See also* Enabling Services.) The World Bank, IFC, and MIGA have separate legal Vice Presidential Units, each headed by the institution's own general counsel. Each of these units provides legal services for its respective institution and helps ensure that all activities comport with the institution's charter, policies, and rules. The focus includes legal and judicial reform in developing countries.

Local Currency Finance (*See also* Products and Services.) To avoid risks from exchange-rate volatility, companies with revenues in local currency should generally borrow in the same currency.

By matching the currency denomination of assets and liabilities, companies can concentrate on their core business rather than worry about how unstable exchange rates will affect profitability. The Bank provides local currency loans and provides guarantees to local currency commercial loans.

IFC provides local currency debt financing in four ways:

- Loans from IFC denominated in local currency

- Risk management swaps that allow clients to hedge existing or new foreign currency–denominated liabilities back into local currency

- Credit enhancement structures that allow clients to borrow in local currency from other sources

- Credit lines from local financial institutions

IFC has also made local currency financing a priority to help develop local capital markets. Companies that receive financing in the same currency as their revenues are more creditworthy clients for IFC.

Lower-Middle-Income Countries (*See also* Classification of Countries.) The World Bank Group classifies lower-middle-income economies as having a per capita gross national income of $1,026 to $4,035.
➲ http://tinyurl.com/WBG013

Low-Income Countries (*See also* Classification of Countries.) The World Bank Group classifies low-income economies as having a per capita gross national income of $1,045 or less.
➲ http://tinyurl.com/WBG013

M

Macroeconomics and Fiscal Management (*See also* Global Practices.) One of 14 new World Bank Group Global Practices, Macroeconomics and Fiscal Management provides integrative development strategies, policy-based lending, macro data, global perspectives, real-time policy analysis, country risk assessments, and innovative projection tools.

World Bank Group and Macroeconomics and Fiscal Management

In 2014, developing countries are confronting a slow and uneven recovery from the global financial crisis; tremendous ongoing shifts in the patterns of resource, goods, and capital flows; and growing pressures to improve competitiveness. They seek to identify macropolicy frameworks that create the conditions for more rapid, more inclusive, and more sustainable growth. Some elements of those frameworks are not new—sound fiscal policy, efforts to mitigate macrovulnerabilities and promote resilience, and targeted growth strategies that identify and then build on comparative advantage, among others.

Other strategies are the subject of ongoing debates and innovations: inflation targets, capital controls, structural fiscal deficits, macrofinancial regulation, and publicly owned sources of credit—all

fields in which much rethinking is taking place in the practice of macroeconomic policy. The search for new forms of internally consistent, long-term macroeconomic frameworks is ongoing and will dominate the profession—and the radar screens of policy makers—for many years.

As the only global institution with activities spanning all segments of the economy, the World Bank Group plays a unique role in identifying and supporting long-term macroeconomic policy frameworks directed toward promoting poverty-reducing growth. No other multilateral institution has a deeper understanding of the microeconomic foundations of macroeconomic policy. Because it operates across all sectors along the development spectrum, the WBG can advise on the links between sector-specific challenges (such as teacher salaries or electricity subsidies) and growth sustainability, through the fiscal impact of spending on education or power.

Moreover, the WBG is the only global institution that can deliver integrated diagnostics, strategies, and solutions for all developing countries, including fragile situations and small states. It is as applicable to resource-rich poor countries as it is to up-and-coming emerging economies dealing with "middle-income traps."

The Turkey Sustaining Shared Growth Development Policy Loan supports the country's goal of continued socially and environmentally sustainable shared growth by improving business climate, enhancing transparency, boosting labor force participation, widening access to finance and deepening Turkey's infrastructure reforms. © World Bank / Simone D. McCourtie (photographer). Permission required for reuse.

The WBG has a large and expanding menu of financial and analytical products and services in these areas, including fiscal and debt policy and sustainability; growth analytics and diversification opportunities; natural resource management; and subnational and spatial dimensions of growth, fiscal, and debt policy. This practice is responsible for 20 percent of recent World Bank commitments over the past two years. Almost all this financing is underpinned by cross-sectoral and structural policy programs that contribute to the long-term development of countries.

The Macroeconomics and Fiscal Management Global Practice is responsible for delivering analytical tools, training, and capacity building in the areas of fiscal management, macroeconomics, growth, and debt for Bank staff members and clients, as well as timely policy advice to support the following lines of work:

- Designing macrofiscal frameworks aligned with the goals of reducing extreme poverty and boosting sharing prosperity and grounded in economic, social, and environmental sustainability

- Fiscal and debt policy and sustainability, including on the effectiveness, efficiency, level, and composition of government spending

- Growth analytics and policies for starting, sustaining, and boosting growth

- Analyzing the impact of external shocks and developments on growth and the government fiscal position, including, for example, terms of trade, global crises, and longer-term issues such as population aging

In addition, the global practice contributes to the integration of policies for growth, poverty reduction, and shared prosperity.

IFC and MIGA contribute their expertise in matters relating to the private sector, particularly in supporting the growth of private businesses, trade, and environmental and social sustainability.

Managing Directors (*See also* Organizational Structure.) The President of the World Bank Group delegates some of his or her oversight responsibility to the Managing Directors, each of whom oversees several organizational units. The President relies on them to oversee the strategic direction and day-to-day operations of the organization. Currently there are two Managing Directors for the Bank Group: one who also serves as Chief Operating Officer and the other who serves as Chief Financial Officer.

McCloy, John J. (*See* Presidents of the World Bank Group.)

McNamara, Robert (*See* Presidents of the World Bank Group.)

Membership The organizations that make up the World Bank Group are owned by the governments of member nations, which have the ultimate decision-making power within the organizations on all matters, including policy, financial, and membership issues. Member countries govern the World Bank Group through the Boards of Governors and the Boards of Executive Directors. These bodies make all major decisions for the organizations.

To become a member of the Bank, under the IBRD Articles of Agreement, a country must first join the International Monetary Fund (IMF). Membership in IDA, IFC, and MIGA are conditional on membership in IBRD. In each of these cases, member countries buy shares in the institution, thereby helping build the institution's capital and borrowing power. This arrangement is known as capital subscriptions. Member countries also sign the founding document of each institution: the Articles of Agreement for IBRD, IDA, and IFC and the MIGA Convention.

In tandem with the IMF, and in consultation with other WBG staff members, the Corporate Secretariat Vice Presidency coordinates the process for new membership and maintains the information relating to the status of membership, which includes the membership lists.

As of June 2014, IBRD had 188 members, IDA had 173, IFC had 184, MIGA had 180, and ICSID had 150.
⮕ http://www.worldbank.org/en/about/leadership/members

MENA (*See* Middle East and North Africa.)

Meyer, Eugene (*See* Presidents of the World Bank Group.)

Microfinance
World Bank Group and Microfinance
There are an estimated 2.5 billion financially excluded adults today, with almost 80 percent of those living on less than $2 per day and having no accounts at formal financial institutions. This exclusion undermines the World Bank Group's goals of eradicating extreme poverty by 2030 and increasing the share of income held by the bottom 40 percent of the population.

The World Bank's Global Financial Inclusion Database (Global Findex) reports that three-quarters of the world's poor lack a bank account because of poverty, costs, travel distances, and the often burdensome requirements involved in opening an account. Only 25 percent of adults earning less than $2 a day have saved money at a formal financial institution. Being "unbanked" is linked to income inequality: the richest 20 percent of adults in developing countries are more than twice as likely to have a formal account. Microfinance—that is, financial services for underprivileged and low-income clients—is a way to fill that unmet need.

Over the past few decades, different types of financial services providers for poor people have emerged to offer new possibilities: nongovernmental organizations, cooperatives, community-based development institutions like self-help groups and credit unions, commercial and state banks, insurance and credit card companies, telecommunications and wire services, post offices, and other points of sale.

World Bank and Microfinance
Within the World Bank Group, different institutions work together toward responsible financial inclusion. In line with President Jim Yong Kim's vision of achieving universal access to finance by 2020, the World Bank works with governments and regulators on providing policy advice, data and diagnostics, technical assistance for legal and regulatory reforms, institutional development, risk sharing, and financing.

The World Bank supports increased access to a range of financial products and services through several avenues: policy and regulatory reforms for micro and SME finance; the development of sound and efficient financial infrastructure for payments, supply chain finance, credit information, and collateral frameworks; innovations to reach poorer households, including through government-to-person payments linked to financial accounts; and responsible finance, through financial capability and consumer protection. The World Bank also partners with countries to support national strategies for financial inclusion and provides data, technical assistance, financing, and capacity building to support the implementation and sustainability of these strategies.

The Consultative Group to Assist the Poor (CGAP) develops innovative solutions for financial inclusion through practical research and active engagement with financial service providers, policy makers, and funders. Established in 1995 and housed at the World Bank, CGAP combines a pragmatic approach to market development with an evidence-based advocacy platform to advance poor people's access to finance. Its global network of members includes more than 30 development agencies, private foundations, and national governments that share a common vision of improving the lives of poor people with better access to finance.

CGAP projects cover a wide range of topics on financial inclusion and microfinance. Focus areas include developing new business models for mobile banking and promoting effective policy frameworks for branchless banking. CGAP also leads an innovative global program to understand how safety nets, livelihoods, and microfinance can be sequenced to create pathways for the poorest to move out of extreme poverty.

IFC and Microfinance

Microfinance constitutes one of the most important tools IFC possesses to achieve its ambitious targets over the coming years. IFC is the World Bank Group's lead investor in microfinance and works with more than 100 institutions in over 60 countries, effectively providing a combination of investment and advisory services to a range of financial intermediaries. In fiscal 2013, IFC committed $402 million in 51 projects with microfinance institutions. IFC's cumulative investment portfolio in microfinance exceeds $3 billion, with outstanding commitments of $1.45 billion. In fiscal 2013, IFC's advisory services in microfinance came to $66.2 million, representing advisory assistance for 73 projects.

IFC also helps improve financial inclusion by improving financial infrastructure. It takes an active role in advising microfinance institutions and building or strengthening comprehensive and robust credit reporting systems such as credit bureaus, which are critical to avoiding overindebtedness and supporting responsible lending practices. Through its Global Credit Reporting Program, IFC has created or significantly improved credit reporting systems in more than 30 countries and advocated for relevant laws in 33 countries.

IFC's focus is on creating and supporting commercially viable microfinance institutions that can attract the private capital needed to scale up and respond to unmet demand. IFC is playing an important role by demonstrating the business case for commercial microfinance and promoting it as an asset class to private institutional investors. Since pioneering commercial microfinance in the early 1990s, IFC has continued to lead innovation in microfinance, using developments in technology, financial products, and policy to help financial institutions reach a greater number of people in a more cost-effective way.

MIGA and Microfinance

MIGA's support for microfinance projects is aligned with the World Bank Group's microfinance strategy, which includes improving the supply of microfinance in large but underserved markets, enhancing deposit capacity by assisting microfinance institutions in savings mobilization, building capacity, creating and shaping markets, and fostering innovation. The agency has supported a number of microfinance projects in various countries, including Afghanistan, Bolivia, Georgia, and Pakistan.

IFC and Microfinance
⮑ http://tinyurl.com/WBG016

The Consultative Group to Assist the Poor
⮑ http://www.cgap.org

The Global Financial Inclusion (Global Findex) Database

⮑ http://go.worldbank.org/1F2V9ZK8C0

The New Microfinance Handbook: A Financial Market System Perspective

⮑ http://tinyurl.com/WBG082

World Bank and Microfinance

⮑ http://www.worldbank.org/microfinance

Middle East and North Africa

World Bank Group in the Middle East and North Africa

In response to the changing political climate in the region, the World Bank Group's framework for engagement in the Middle East and North Africa (MENA) region builds on the demands of the Arab Spring and the reforms under way. The framework is based on four main pillars: creating jobs, strengthening governance, increasing social and economic inclusion, and accelerating sustainable growth. These are complemented by cross-cutting themes of gender, regional integration, and fostering a competitive private sector.

Given the challenges facing MENA, the Bank Group is scaling up its support in finance, knowledge, and convening power. This effort will involve a focus on partnership with Arab partners, traditional donors, the United Nations, and the International Monetary Fund. The Bank Group has committed to mainstreaming citizen engagement and collaboration with civil society. It will also harness knowledge and finances to allow more transformational engagements that foster greater resilience and more inclusive growth.

The World Bank Group continues to promote partnerships with bilateral and multilateral donors, regional development banks, Islamic financial institutions, and emerging-country donors. Less traditional partnerships are just as crucial: one of the sharp lessons of the recent political awakening has been the urgent need to reach out more consistently and consult across a wide spectrum of society, including civil society, academics, and the private sector.

World Bank in the Middle East and North Africa

World Bank lending increased from $1.5 billion in fiscal 2012 to $2.8 billion in fiscal 2014 despite challenges in the region. The Bank has also mobilized extensive resources to support countries neighboring Syria and has focused a great deal of attention on its analytical work related to the region. It has published a number of studies that address themes central to the region's political transitions, including studies on accelerating high-speed Internet access, the costs imposed by "restricted lands" on the Palestinian economy, the effects of the Syrian conflict on Lebanon, health systems in MENA, the regional reforms needed to stimulate growth and the jobs that come with it, gender equality in the region, and proposals for removing the obstacles that have produced one of the world's lowest rates of female participation in the labor force despite gains in female access to higher education.

IFC in the Middle East and North Africa

IFC helps address the economic issues facing MENA by supporting the region's private sector, working to create jobs, and promoting sustainable growth. High levels of unemployment and a weak investment climate remain major hurdles for development in MENA—where IFC commitments totaled nearly $2.2 billion in fiscal 2014, including $470 million mobilized from other investors.

IFC's focus in the region is on improving the investment climate, supporting public-private partnerships, and fostering private sector participation in education. In 2013, IFC's clients provided 2.3 million loans to micro, small, and medium enterprises in the region, totaling $14.1 billion. They also enabled 28.3 million phone connections and supplied water to 1.8 million customers.

MIDDLE EAST AND NORTH AFRICA REGION SNAPSHOT

339.6 million   Total population

1.7 percent   Population growth

$3,450   Gross national income per capita

2.4 percent   Population living below $1.25 per day

71 years   Life expectancy at birth

77.7 percent   Adult (15+) literacy rate

This region includes the following countries:*

Algeria
Djibouti
Arab Republic of Egypt
Islamic Republic of Iran
Iraq
Jordan
Lebanon
Libya
Morocco
Syrian Arab Republic
Tunisia
Republic of Yemen

*Regions are defined for analytical and operational purposes and may differ from common geographic usage. Variances also exist across the five World Bank Group institutions.

Member Countries by WBG Institution
⟳ www.worldbank.org/en/about/leadership/members#1

MIGA in the Middle East and North Africa
Recent guarantees issued by MIGA for companies investing in MENA support a range of sectors, including manufacturing, telecommunications, oil and gas, services, and infrastructure.

Data Resources on the Middle East and North Africa
⟳ http://data.worldbank.org/region/MENA

Research on the Middle East and North Africa
⟳ http://www.worldbank.org/en/region/mena/research

Middle-Income Countries (*See also* Classification of Countries.) The World Bank Group classifies middle income countries as having a per capita gross national income of $1,046–12,746.

⊃ http://tinyurl.com/WBG083

MIGA (*See* Multilateral Investment Guarantee Agency.)

Migration Migration of people across international borders affects economic growth and social welfare in both sending and receiving countries. Around the world, the money that migrants send home (remittances) is more than twice as large as foreign aid. For many countries, remittances are the largest source of foreign exchange. The World Bank Group has placed new emphasis on understanding the importance of migration and remittances to both economic and human development.

Research shows that migration brings strong economic gains. In developing countries, remittances frequently lead to more investment in education and greater entrepreneurship; they have a positive effect on learning and health, savings, and macroeconomic stability; and they also appear to contribute to reducing poverty and social inequality. But migration can also have disruptive effects, such as the "brain drain"—that is, the massive migration of highly skilled professionals, especially from small low-income countries. Issues also arise in rich countries because of illegal immigration, social welfare of migrants, and security concerns.

To generate and synthesize knowledge on migration issues, the World Bank Group initiated the Global Knowledge Partnership on Migration and Development (KNOMAD). This effort is aimed at creating a menu of policy choices based on multidisciplinary knowledge and evidence and at providing technical assistance and capacity building to both sending and receiving countries.

KNOMAD oversees implementation of pilot projects, evaluation of migration policies, and data collection. Launched in 2013, the partnership is being supported with funding from the Swiss Agency for Development and Cooperation and the German Federal Ministry of Economic Cooperation and Development.

The World Bank Group is closely involved in global partnerships to develop policy coherence on the treatment of migration, including active participation in the Global Migration Group and the Global Forum on Migration and Development. The Bank Group is also supporting efforts to reflect migration issues in the Post-2015 Development Agenda.

KNOMAD

⊃ http://www.knomad.org

Migration

⊃ http://worldbank.org/migration

Millennium Development Goals (*See also* Post-2015 Development Agenda.) The Millennium Development Goals (MDGs) identify—and quantify—specific gains in improving the lives of the world's poor people. The aim of the MDGs is to reduce poverty while improving health, education, and the environment. These goals were endorsed by 189 countries at the September 2000 United Nations (UN) Millennium Assembly in New York. They help focus the efforts of the World Bank Group, other multilateral organizations, governments, and other partners in the development community on significant, measurable improvements in the lives of poor people in developing countries.

The MDGs grew out of the agreements and resolutions that have resulted from world conferences organized by the United Nations in the past 15 to 25 years. Each goal is to be achieved by 2015, with progress measured by comparison with 1990

MILLENNIUM DEVELOPMENT GOALS (MDGS)

Goals and Targets from the Millennium Declaration

Goal 1 Eradicate Extreme Poverty and Hunger

TARGET 1 Halve, between 1990 and 2015, the proportion of people whose income is less than $1 a day

TARGET 2 Halve, between 1990 and 2015, the proportion of people who suffer from hunger

Goal 2 Achieve Universal Primary Education

TARGET 3 Ensure that by 2015, children everywhere, boys and girls alike, will be able to complete a full course of primary schooling

Goal 3 Promote Gender Equality and Empower Women

TARGET 4 Eliminate gender disparity in primary and secondary education, preferably by 2005, and at all levels of education no later than 2015

Goal 4 Reduce Child Mortality

TARGET 5 Reduce by two-thirds, between 1990 and 2015, the under-five mortality rate

Goal 5 Improve Maternal Health

TARGET 6 Reduce by three-quarters, between 1990 and 2015, the maternal mortality ratio

Goal 6 Combat HIV/AIDS, Malaria, and Other Diseases

TARGET 7 Have halted by 2015 and begun to reverse the spread of HIV/AIDS

TARGET 8 Have halted by 2015 and begun to reverse the incidence of malaria and other major diseases

Goal 7 Ensure Environmental Sustainability

TARGET 9 Integrate the principles of sustainable development into country policies and programs and reverse the loss of environmental resources

TARGET 10 Halve by 2015 the proportion of people without sustainable access to safe drinking water and basic sanitation

TARGET 11 Have achieved a significant improvement by 2020 in the lives of at least 100 million slum dwellers

Goal 8 Develop a Global Partnership for Development

TARGET 12 Develop further an open, rule-based, predictable, nondiscriminatory trading and financial system (including a commitment to good governance, development, and poverty reduction, nationally and internationally)

TARGET 13 Address the special needs of the least developed countries (including tariff- and quota-free access for exports of the least developed countries; enhanced debt relief for heavily indebted

(continued next page)

poor countries and cancellation of official bilateral debt; and more generous official development assistance for countries committed to reducing poverty)

TARGET 14 Address the special needs of landlocked countries and small island developing states (through the Programme of Action for the Sustainable Development of Small Island Developing States and the outcome of the 22nd special session of the General Assembly)

TARGET 15 Deal comprehensively with the debt problems of developing countries through national and international measures to make debt sustainable in the long term

TARGET 16 In cooperation with developing countries, develop and implement strategies for decent and productive work for youth

TARGET 17 In cooperation with pharmaceutical companies, provide access to affordable, essential drugs in developing countries

TARGET 18 In cooperation with the private sector, make available the benefits of new technologies, especially information and communication

Note: The Millennium Development Goals and targets come from the Millennium Declaration signed by 189 countries, including 147 heads of state, in September 2000. The goals and targets are related and should be seen as a whole. They represent a partnership of countries determined, as the declaration states, "to create an environment—at the national and global levels alike—which is conducive to development and the elimination of poverty."

➲ http://mdgs.un.org/unsd/mdg/host.aspx?Content=indicators/officiallist.htm

levels. Although the goals are sometimes numbered, the numbers are not intended to indicate any differences in priority or urgency. The goals establish yardsticks for measuring results, not just for the developing countries but also for the high-income countries that help fund development programs and for the multilateral institutions that work with countries to implement those programs. The first seven goals are mutually reinforcing and are directed at reducing poverty in all its forms. The last goal—to develop a global partnership for development—is directed at the means for reaching the first seven.

Many of the poorest countries will need assistance if the MDGs are to be achieved, and countries that are both poor and heavily indebted will need further help to reduce their debt burdens. But providing assistance is not limited to providing financial aid. Developing countries may also benefit if trade

barriers are lowered and therefore permit a freer exchange of goods and services.

Achieving the goals is an enormous challenge. Partnerships between the Bank Group, the UN Development Group (UNDG), and other organizations, as well as between donors and developing countries, are the only way to ensure coordinated and complementary efforts. The UNDG consists of the many UN programs, funds, and agencies engaged in development assistance and related activities. The Bank Group participates in the UNDG and supports its framework for greater coherence and cooperation in UN development operations.

Since 2004, the World Bank—in partnership with the International Monetary Fund (IMF)—has published the annual *Global Monitoring Report*, which tracks the performance of donor countries, developing countries, and international financial institutions in delivering on their commitments to support achievement of the MDGs. The report reviews key developments in the previous year, discusses priority emerging issues, and assesses performance.

In 2010, the World Bank launched the eAtlas of the Millennium Development Goals. This online data visualization tool allows users to map the indicators that measure progress on the MDGs. Features include worldwide mapping, timeline graphing, ranking tables, and the exporting and sharing of graphics.

For the Bank Group, as for other agencies, the challenge of implementing the MDGs provides a starting point for all operations.

⮑ http://www.worldbank.org/mdgs

Monterrey Consensus The Monterrey Consensus emerged out of a meeting of the International Conference on Financing for Development in Monterrey, Mexico, in March 2002. With more than 50 heads of state in attendance, along with representatives of the World Bank, the International Monetary Fund, and the World Trade Organization, a new partnership for global development was conceived.

The Monterrey Consensus is a landmark framework for global development partnership in which the developed and developing countries agreed to take joint actions for poverty reduction. The Monterrey Consensus is distinguished by its recognition of both the need for developing countries to take responsibility for their own poverty reduction and the necessity for rich nations to support this endeavor with more open trade and increased financial aid.

Multilateral Debt Relief Initiative The Multilateral Debt Relief Initiative provides for 100 percent relief on eligible debt from three multilateral institutions to a group of low-income countries. The initiative is intended to help them advance toward the United Nations' Millennium Development Goals, which are focused on halving poverty by 2015.

⮑ https://www.imf.org/external/np/exr/facts/mdri.htm

Multilateral Investment Guarantee Agency The Multilateral Investment Guarantee Agency (MIGA) is one of the five organizations included in the World Bank Group. Its mission is to promote foreign direct investment into developing countries by providing risk insurance (guarantees) and credit enhancement and thereby to help support economic growth, reduce poverty, and improve people's lives.

MIGA's operational strategy attracts investors and private insurers into difficult operating environments. MIGA focuses on insuring investments in the areas where it can make the greatest difference:

• Countries eligible for assistance from IDA

• Fragile and conflict-affected environments

• Complex projects that can be transformational, especially in infrastructure and extractive industries

• Middle-income countries where the Agency can have impact

MIGA has comparative advantages in all of these areas—from its unique package of products and ability to restore the business community's confidence to its ongoing collaboration with the public and private insurance market to increase the amount of insurance available to investors.

As a multilateral development agency, MIGA supports only investments that are developmentally sound and meet high social and environmental standards. MIGA applies a comprehensive set of social and environmental performance standards to all projects and offers extensive expertise in working with investors to ensure compliance to these standards.

MIGA offers coverage for five noncommercial risks. Coverages may be purchased individually or in combination:

- **Currency inconvertibility and transfer restriction.** This coverage protects against losses arising from an investor's inability to legally convert local currency (capital, interest, principal, profits, royalties, and other remittances) into hard currency (dollar, euro, or yen) or to transfer hard currency outside the host country where such a situation results from a government action or failure to act.

- **Expropriation.** This coverage protects against losses arising from certain government actions that may reduce or eliminate ownership of, control over, or rights to the insured investment.

- **War, terrorism, and civil disturbance.** This coverage protects against loss from, damage to, or the destruction or disappearance of tangible assets or total business interruption caused by politically motivated acts of war or civil disturbance in the country, including revolution, insurrection, coups d'état, sabotage, and terrorism.

- **Breach of contract.** This coverage protects against losses arising from the government's breach or repudiation of a contract with the investor (for example, a concession or a power purchase agreement).

- **Nonhonoring of financial obligations.** This coverage protects against losses resulting from a failure of a sovereign, subsovereign, or state-owned enterprise to make a payment when due under an unconditional financial payment obligation or guarantee related to an eligible investment.

⮌ http://tinyurl.com/WBG017

N·O

Noncommercial Risks (*See* Multilateral Investment Guarantee Agency; Products and Services.)

Nongovernmental Organizations (*See also* Civil Society Organizations.) Nongovernmental organizations (NGOs), including community-based organizations, are important to the World Bank Group because of the skills and resources they bring to emergency relief and development activities. NGOs also foster participatory development processes. Nongovernmental organizations involved in development projects are usually one of three types: support (for example, fiscal, technical, medical, or educational), advocacy (for example, environment, legal, or special interest), or representative.

⊃ http://www.worldbank.org/afr/ik/guidelines/ngoguides.pdf

Open Access (*See also* Open Data; Open Development; Open Knowledge Repository; Publications.) In 2012, the World Bank announced the implementation of a new Open Access Policy for its research outputs and knowledge products. The new policy built on earlier efforts to increase access to information at the World Bank and to make its research as widely available as possible.

The centerpiece of the policy was the creation of the Open Knowledge Repository (OKR), launched in April 2012, the official open access repository of the World Bank. The OKR contains more than 16,000 research and knowledge products from thousands of works including published books, editions of the World Development Report, Policy Research Working Papers, Economic and Sector Work studies, journal articles, World Bank Group annual reports, and independent evaluation studies.

In support of the new policy, the World Bank adopted the Creative Commons Attribution (CC BY) copyright license for content formally published by the Bank. This license—the most accommodating of all licenses offered by Creative Commons—allows users to use, reuse, share, build upon, and distribute the Bank's formally published work, even commercially, as long as proper attribution is given. World Bank content published by third-party publishers is available in the OKR under the more restrictive Creative Commons licenses.

While much of the Bank's research outputs and knowledge products were available for free on the institution's website and other channels, the new Open Access Policy marked a significant shift in how Bank content is used, reused, disseminated and shared.

Open Access Policy
⮑ http://tinyurl.com/WB0060

Open Knowledge Repository
⮑ www.openknowledge.worldbank.org

Open Data (*See also* Open Development.) In 2010, the World Bank Group launched its Open Data Initiative, which provides free and open access to data about development in countries around the globe. More than 160 data sets are published in the Data Catalog, from general socioeconomic data collections to more specialized data including commodity prices, gender statistics, migration data, debt statistics, education data, and data on the World Bank's finances, projects, and operations, as well as survey-level micro data. The data include more than 8,000 indicators, many that go back 50 years, and are available in Arabic, Chinese, English, French, and Spanish, with selected data available in a further 18 languages. The DataBank tool makes it possible for users to interactively search, filter, and visualize these data and save and share the results.

In addition to publishing data, the World Bank Group has sought out new engagement with data users. Since 2010, the institution has run two mobile application competitions: Apps for Development and Apps for Climate that challenged the developer community to create tools, applications, and analyses using World Bank data that aim to improve user's understanding of development issues. The Bank also regularly hosts developer events such as data dives that bring together software experts and development professionals to tackle real world problems. The Bank has also developed its own suite of mobile apps for iOS and Android that make it easier than ever to find and visualizr data on subjects including

poverty, education, health, jobs, climate change, and development in general.

Since launching the Open Data Initiative, the World Bank has been recognized as a leading donor in the area of aid transparency and has seen a more than 10-fold increase in the number of online visits from users including government staff and policy makers, researchers, journalists, software developers and civil society organizations who can now use these data to inform their work. The Data Helpdesk offers support to hundreds of these data users every month and hosts a growing knowledge base of frequently asked questions.

Apps for Climate Competition
⮑ http://tinyurl.com/WBG076

Apps for Development Competition
⮑ http://tinyurl.com/WBG077

DataBank
⮑ http://databank.worldbank.org/data/home.aspx

Data Help Desk
⮑ https://datahelpdesk.worldbank.org

Data Mobile Applications
⮑ http://apps.worldbank.org

Open Data Initiative
⮑ http://data.worldbank.org

Open Development (*See also* Knowledge; Open Access; Open Data.) As part of its modernization, the World Bank Group has actively worked to make its operations, data, research, and knowledge products more open, transparent, and accessible through a variety of tools, programs, and policies. Open development is about making information and data freely available and searchable, encouraging feedback, information-sharing, and accountability. The Bank Group opened its data, knowledge, and research to foster innovation and increase transparency in development, aid flows, and finances.

The Open Development portal offers links to "open solution" sites, such as the World Bank's Policy on Access to Information, the Open Knowledge Repository, Doing Business, and the World Development Report; to data sources, such as the Open Data portal, World Development Indicators, and World Governance Indicators; to knowledge resources, such as World Bank research, World Bank experts, and Knowledge in Development Notes; and to Open Knowledge platforms on specific development topics like jobs, urbanization, nutrition, fragility and conflict, and violence.

Data and Knowledge

The Bank Group collects a wealth of data and knowledge about its member countries and their economies and on complex development topics. Opening up Bank Group data and development knowledge allows a more robust picture of development to emerge and allows for innovation and solutions for development.

Open Data Initiative

In April 2010, the World Bank Group announced that its thousands of comprehensive sets of data on development would be made open and freely available to the public. At the same time, it challenged the global community to use the data to create new applications and solutions to help poor people in the developing world. The data are accessible in Arabic, Chinese, English, French, and Spanish. Other initiatives followed including:

- *ADePT* is a tool that automates the economic analysis of survey data, dramatically reducing the time required for the production of analytical reports, minimizing human error, and allowing easy introduction of new techniques to a wide audience of policy practitioners.

- *Climate Change Knowledge Portal* was launched to create a hub for climate information.

- *Mapping for Results* shows maps for all 142 IBRD and IDA countries; more than 30,000 project locations are mapped and geographic locations depicted for 1,600 active Bank projects.

- *Microdata Library* offers access to raw data from more than 700 household surveys and sources was opened.

- *Open Data Portal* provides free, open, and easy access to the Bank's comprehensive data sets on development, available in Arabic, Chinese, French, English, and Spanish.

- *Open Data Readiness Assessment Tool* was developed by the World Bank's Open Government Data Working Group for governments and agencies to evaluate, design, and implement an Open Data Initiative.

- *WITS data tool* provides access to international trade and tariff data.

Open Knowledge

- *Open Access policy* allows free and unrestricted access to tens of thousands of Bank publications with free and unrestricted use under the Creative Commons Attribution License.

- *Open Knowledge Repository* is the online home for all the World Bank Group's research outputs and knowledge products.

- *South-South knowledge exchanges* allow developing countries to share knowledge globally.

- *Georesults* is an ICT-enabled platform to capture, track and share project results, which uses interactive mapping technologies, before and after pictures, videos and local stories to explore results on the ground.

- **The E-institute** is a new open learning platform that allows cutting-edge global knowledge to be accessible via e-learning courses.

Open Operations and Results

The World Bank has freely shared information on its own operations and data on finances and projects. This information promotes better monitoring of project results and impact on people, enhances transparency, and strengthens country dialogue and civic engagement.

- **Operations Portal** offers project-level information, including project locations, financial details, procurement information, and official project documents.

- **Corporate Scorecard** provides an online snapshot of the Bank's overall performance and provides users with easy access to indicators, longer time series, and more detailed data.

- **World Bank's Independent Evaluation Group** publishes project performance evaluations.

- **World Bank Finances site** offers a high-level financial view of Bank resources available to countries in a social, interactive format.

- **Open Budgets program** aims to strengthen budget transparency and encourage public participation. This is supported by BOOST, a data platform that consolidates and visualizes spending data with other data sources to explore links between spending and outputs, currently in use in 40 countries.

- **AidFlows website** shares information on the location of projects and how much development aid— both from the Bank and from donors—is provided and received around the world.

- **Access to Information Policy**, under which the Bank released 40,000 documents to the public on its Documents and Reports site. Documents and Reports contains more than 145,000 publicly available World Bank documents that enable sharing the institution's extensive knowledge base and implementing its access to information policy.

Partnerships for Openness and Transparency

In 2011, the Bank continued to integrate the governance and anti-corruption agenda into all of its work, across countries, sectors, and projects. The Bank is tracking aid flows to present a more complete picture of what money is being committed to development and where it is being spent. It is also partnering with others to encourage greater openness in development projects, aid, and in government.

- **Global Partnership for Social Accountability** supports efforts to strengthen accountability in public service delivery and awards grants to help civil society strengthen their programs in this area.

- **Open Aid Partnership** seeks to increase transparency through open data on aid flows and public service delivery. Malawi piloted this and mapped aid from 27 donors.

- The Bank is helping **signatories of the Open Government Partnership** achieve greater transparency and participation through mapping of public spending. It is also helping governments implement Access to Information legislation.

⮩ http://www.worldbank.org/open

Open Government Open government is defined by the following principles: transparency, citizen participation, and collaboration between governmental and nongovernmental actors.

The World Bank Group views openness as key to the more efficient operation of government and to the promotion of private sector growth and socially inclusive economic development. The World

Bank Group has been advancing open government globally and in countries, by supporting nations in disclosing and using open data, in establishing inclusive and robust mechanisms for citizen engagement, and in facilitating collaborative processes that bring together a wide range of stakeholders to solve complex governance challenges. Thematically, the World Bank Group has been fostering open government through programs such as Open Contracting, Open Budgeting, and the Open Private Sector Platform, while also supporting countries that have committed to furthering this agenda through their national action plans in the context of the Open Government Partnership.

Open Knowledge Repository The World Bank is the largest single source of development knowledge. The World Bank Open Knowledge Repository (OKR) is the World Bank's official open access repository for its research outputs and knowledge products. Through the OKR, the World Bank collects, disseminates, and permanently preserves its intellectual output in digital form. The OKR also increases the range of people who can discover and access Bank content—from governments and civil society organizations (CSOs), to students, the private sector, and the general public.

The OKR is built on DSpace and is interoperable with other repositories. It supports optimal discoverability and reusability of the content by complying with Dublin Core Metadata Initiative (DCMI) standards. All OKR metadata is exposed through the Open Archives Initiative Protocol for Metadata Harvesting (OAI-PMH) protocol.

By extending and improving access to World Bank research, the World Bank aims to encourage innovation and allow anyone in the world to use its knowledge to help improve the lives of those living in poverty. Since its launch in 2012, millions of publications have been downloaded from the OKR, and nearly half of its users are in developing countries.

The OKR contains thousands of research and knowledge products including:

- World Bank Group Annual Reports and Independent Evaluation Studies

- Books published by the World Bank Group including flagship publications, academic books, and practitioner volumes

- All editions of the *World Development Report* (*WDR*) plus recent *WDR* background papers

- Journal articles published in *World Bank Economic Review* (*WBER*) and *World Bank Research Observer* (*WBRO*), which are published by Oxford University Press on behalf of the World Bank

- Accepted manuscripts of Bank-authored journal articles from selected external publishers (after an embargo period, if applicable)

- Metadata and links to Bank-authored external journal articles

- Serial publications (typically data-intensive outlook reports)

- *Policy Research Working Papers* (PRWP)—a series of papers that disseminate findings of work in progress in order to encourage the exchange of ideas about development issues

- Economic and Sector Work (ESW) studies—a series of analytical reports prepared by Bank staff. ESWs gather and evaluate information about a country's economy and/or a specific sector

- *Knowledge Notes*, providing short briefs that capture lessons of experience from Bank operations and research

- The latest Country Opinion Surveys done in client countries for feedback on World Bank Group activities

- Selected translated titles

⟳ **https://openknowledge.worldbank.org**

Operational Manual (*See* Policies and Procedures.)

Operations Policy and Country Services (*See also* Enabling Services.) Operations Policy and Country Services (OPCS) supports World Bank Group operations from its unique position at the interface of the Board, Senior Management, and the operations complex. It works with Senior Management to support the Board in its policy-making role; it supports Senior Management and Bank Group teams with advice, reviews, and knowledge sharing on the country and sector strategies that provide the framework for operations; it coordinates the development and implementation of strategies for particular groups of countries; it provides upstream reviews and advice on areas central to Bank Group operations; and it spearheads the Bank Group's work on corporate and international priorities, including fragile situations, avian influenza, the harmonization and alignment agenda, and the results agenda.

Organisation for Economic Co-operation and Development The Organisation for Economic Co-operation and Development (OECD) promotes policies that will improve the economic and social well-being of people around the world. The OECD provides a forum in which governments can work together to share experiences and seek solutions to common problems. The OECD works with governments to understand what drives economic, social, and environmental change. It also measures productivity and global flows of trade and investment, analyzes and compares data to predict future trends, and sets international standards on a wide range of topics, from agriculture to the safety of chemicals.
↻ http://www.oecd.org

Organizational Structure (Refer to the following organizational charts for the World Bank, IFC, and MIGA.)

THE WORLD BANK ORGANIZATIONAL CHART

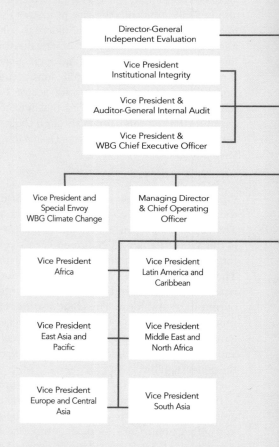

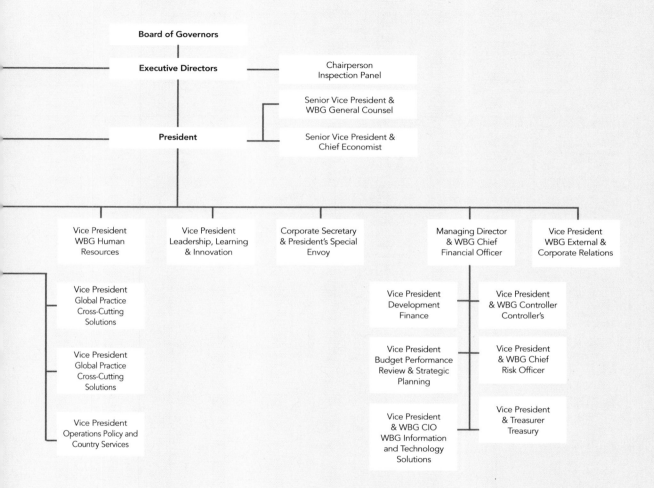

Board of Governors

Executive Directors — Chairperson
Inspection Panel

Senior Vice President &
WBG General Counsel

President — Senior Vice President &
Chief Economist

Vice President
WBG Human
Resources

Vice President
Leadership, Learning
& Innovation

Corporate Secretary
& President's Special
Envoy

Managing Director
& WBG Chief
Financial Officer

Vice President
WBG External &
Corporate Relations

Vice President
Global Practice
Cross-Cutting
Solutions

Vice President
Development
Finance

Vice President
& WBG Controller
Controller's

Vice President
Global Practice
Cross-Cutting
Solutions

Vice President
Budget Performance
Review & Strategic
Planning

Vice President
& WBG Chief
Risk Officer

Vice President
Operations Policy and
Country Services

Vice President
& WBG CIO
WBG Information
and Technology
Solutions

Vice President
& Treasurer
Treasury

IFC ORGANIZATIONAL CHART

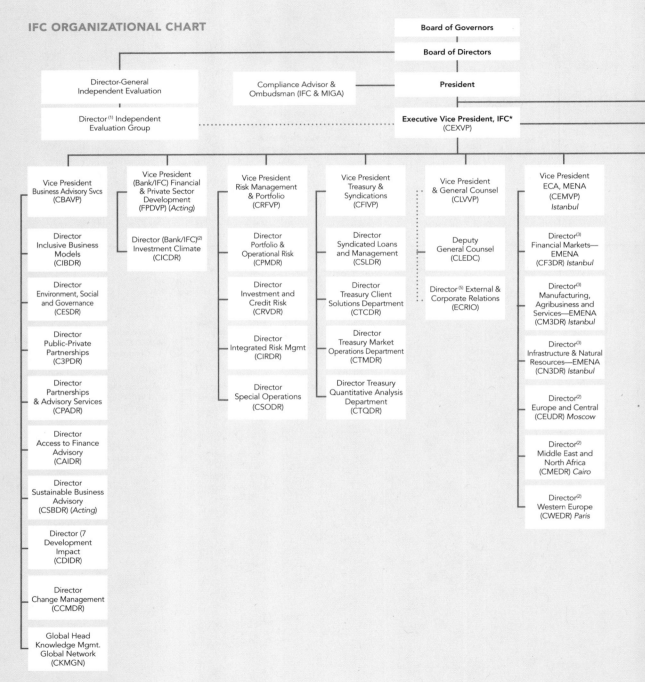

Board of Governors

Board of Directors

President

Executive Vice President, IFC*
(CEXVP)

Director-General
Independent Evaluation

Compliance Advisor &
Ombudsman (IFC & MIGA)

Director[1] Independent
Evaluation Group

Vice President
Business Advisory Svcs
(CBAVP)

Director
Inclusive Business
Models
(CIBDR)

Director
Environment, Social
and Governance
(CESDR)

Director
Public-Private
Partnerships
(C3PDR)

Director
Partnerships
& Advisory Services
(CPADR)

Director
Access to Finance
Advisory
(CAIDR)

Director
Sustainable Business
Advisory
(CSBDR) (Acting)

Director (7
Development
Impact
(CDIDR)

Director
Change Management
(CCMDR)

Global Head
Knowledge Mgmt.
Global Network
(CKMGN)

Vice President
(Bank/IFC) Financial
& Private Sector
Development
(FPDVP) (Acting)

Director (Bank/IFC)[2]
Investment Climate
(CICDR)

Vice President
Risk Management
& Portfolio
(CRFVP)

Director
Portfolio &
Operational Risk
(CPMDR)

Director
Investment and
Credit Risk
(CRVDR)

Director
Integrated Risk Mgmt
(CIRDR)

Director
Special Operations
(CSODR)

Vice President
Treasury &
Syndications
(CFIVP)

Director
Syndicated Loans
and Management
(CSLDR)

Director
Treasury Client
Solutions Department
(CTCDR)

Director
Treasury Market
Operations Department
(CTMDR)

Director Treasury
Quantitative Analysis
Department
(CTQDR)

Vice President
& General Counsel
(CLVVP)

Deputy
General Counsel
(CLEDC)

Director[5] External &
Corporate Relations
(ECRIO)

Vice President
ECA, MENA
(CEMVP)
Istanbul

Director[3]
Financial Markets—
EMENA
(CF3DR) Istanbul

Director[3]
Manufacturing,
Agribusiness and
Services—EMENA
(CM3DR) Istanbul

Director[3]
Infrastructure & Natural
Resources—EMENA
(CN3DR) Istanbul

Director[2]
Europe and Central
(CEUDR) Moscow

Director[2]
Middle East and
North Africa
(CMEDR) Cairo

Director[2]
Western Europe
(CWEDR) Paris

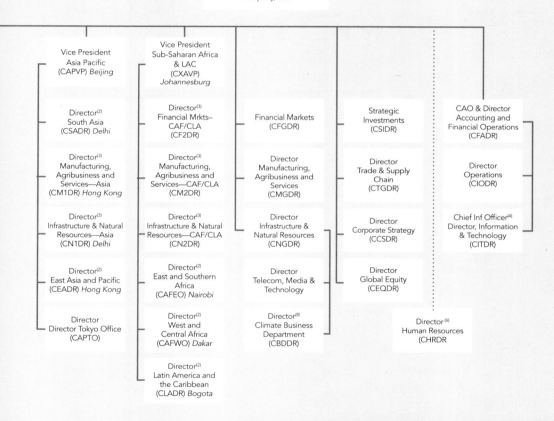

Corporate Secretary &
President's Special Envoy

Chief Executive Officer
IFC Asset Management
Company, LLC*

Vice President
Asia Pacific
(CAPVP) *Beijing*

Vice President
Sub-Saharan Africa
& LAC
(CXAVP)
Johannesburg

Director[2]
South Asia
(CSADR) *Delhi*

Director[3]
Financial Mrkts–
CAF/CLA
(CF2DR)

Financial Markets
(CFGDR)

Strategic
Investments
(CSIDR)

CAO & Director
Accounting and
Financial Operations
(CFADR)

Director[3]
Manufacturing,
Agribusiness and
Services—Asia
(CM1DR) *Hong Kong*

Director[3]
Manufacturing,
Agribusiness and
Services—CAF/CLA
(CM2DR)

Director
Manufacturing,
Agribusiness and
Services
(CMGDR)

Director
Trade & Supply
Chain
(CTGDR)

Director
Operations
(CIODR)

Director[3]
Infrastructure & Natural
Resources—Asia
(CN1DR) *Delhi*

Director[3]
Infrastructure & Natural
Resources—CAF/CLA
(CN2DR)

Director
Infrastructure &
Natural Resources
(CNGDR)

Director
Corporate Strategy
(CCSDR)

Chief Inf Officer[4]
Director, Information
& Technology
(CITDR)

Director[2]
East Asia and Pacific
(CEADR) *Hong Kong*

Director[2]
East and Southern
Africa
(CAFEO) *Nairobi*

Director
Telecom, Media &
Technology

Director
Global Equity
(CEQDR)

Director
Director Tokyo Office
(CAPTO)

Director[2]
West and
Central Africa
(CAFWO) *Dakar*

Director[8]
Climate Business
Department
(CBDDR)

Director[6]
Human Resources
(CHRDR

Director[2]
Latin America and
the Caribbean
(CLADR) *Bogota*

1) Reports to the Director-General, Independent Evaluation; to the EVP for administrative purposes
2) Dotted reporting line to Vice President, Business Advisory Services on advisory business activities
3) Also reports to the relevant Global Industry Directors (GIDs)
4) Reports to the WBG Chief Information Officer (ITS)
5) Reports to the WBG Vice President (ECR)
6) Reports to the WBG Vice President (HR)
7) Also reports to Global Industry Director (CMG)
8) Also reports to Vice President (CBAVP)

* EVP is chairperson of IFC AMC Board of Directors; AMC is a wholly owned subsidiary of IFC

MIGA ORGANIZATIONAL CHART

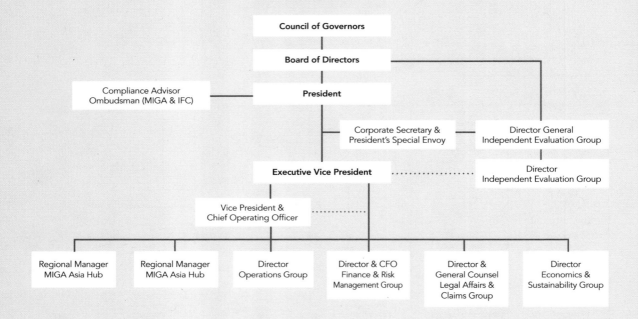

Council of Governors

Board of Directors

Compliance Advisor
Ombudsman (MIGA & IFC)

President

Corporate Secretary &
President's Special Envoy

Director General
Independent Evaluation Group

Executive Vice President

Director
Independent Evaluation Group

Vice President &
Chief Operating Officer

Regional Manager
MIGA Asia Hub

Regional Manager
MIGA Asia Hub

Director
Operations Group

Director & CFO
Finance & Risk
Management Group

Director &
General Counsel
Legal Affairs &
Claims Group

Director
Economics &
Sustainability Group

P

Pandemics A pandemic is a global disease outbreak that represents a top global catastrophic risk. Influenza (flu), for example, transmits readily and can spread rapidly. Every year, up to 500,000 people die from flu. In years when pandemic flu occurs, the toll can rise well into the millions. The 1918 pandemic flu, the most severe of the four flu pandemics in the past 100 years, infected up to 40 percent of some national populations and killed 50–100 million people. A severe pandemic would harm health, economies, and communities in all countries, but especially in poor and fragile states. Pandemic prevention requires robust public health systems (veterinary and human) that collaborate to stop contagion promptly.

The World Bank supports countries in their efforts to strengthen veterinary and human health systems, and the bridges between them, to prevent pandemics including communication and public awareness; coordination; building system capacity; pandemic planning at community, national, and international levels using whole-of-society approaches; and implementation assistance. This approach is in line with World Health Organization (WHO) and World Organisation for Animal Health (OIE) standards.

Since 2005, the World Bank has contributed to the international response to the avian and pandemic influenza threat through a multidimensional approach to disease control and prevention that encompasses human health, animal health, analytical and technical support, disaster risk management, and development communications. This was key to effective, integrated country-led programs.

In 2008, the WHO, OIE, and Food and Agriculture Organization (FAO), coordinated by the World Bank and United Nations System Influenza Coordinator (UNSIC), prepared a global strategy for using "One Health" approaches to reduce health risks at animal-human-environment interfaces. Ministers of health and agriculture from across the world have welcomed this strategy and urged that it be implemented. The World Bank continues to work with these partners and with countries to develop tools for assessing country systems in the veterinary and human public health areas, and the bridges between them.

When these systems meet international standards, they will work to prevent pandemics (such as flu), reduce the costs of ongoing and emerging health crises such as antimicrobial resistance, zoonotic diseases like rabies, and other diseases. In August 2014, the World Bank pledged $200 million to help contain the deadly Ebola virus by providing emergency assistance to Guinea, Liberia, and Sierra Leone to help the West African nations contain the deadly outbreak thath has killed more than 887 since the outbreak began in March 2014.

⮑ http://www.worldbank.org/en/topic/pandemics

Paris Declaration on Aid Effectiveness Beyond its principles of effective aid, the Paris Declaration (2005) lays out a practical, action-oriented road map for improving the quality of aid and its impact on development. It puts in place a series of specific implementation measures and establishes a monitoring system to assess progress and ensure that donors and recipients hold each other accountable for their commitments. The Paris Declaration outlines the following five fundamental principles for making aid more effective:

- *Ownership.* Developing countries set their own strategies for poverty reduction, improve their institutions, and tackle corruption.

- *Alignment.* Donor countries align behind these objectives and use local systems.

- *Harmonization.* Donor countries coordinate, simplify procedures, and share information to avoid duplication.

- *Results.* Developing countries and donors shift focus to development results and results get measured.

- *Mutual accountability.* Donors and partners are accountable for development results.

⮑ http://tinyurl.com/WBG019

Partnerships There are tens of thousands of donor-funded development projects worldwide, each governed by countless demands, guidelines, and procedures designed to protect the projects and ensure that aid gets to the poor. Experience shows that capacity in developing countries can be improved and strengthened quickly when donors better coordinate their activities and harmonize their procedures.

To that end, the World Bank Group works with other international institutions and donor agencies, civil society organizations, and professional and academic associations to improve the coordination of aid policies and practices in countries at both the regional and global levels.

The following are some of the global partnerships in which the World Bank Group participates:

The Carbon Fund. Works to develop viable, flexible market mechanisms to reduce greenhouse gas emissions under the Kyoto Protocol.

⮑ http://www.carbonfund.org

Consultative Group for International Agricultural Research (CGIAR). Created and promoted crop improvements in developing countries over the past 30 years through a network of research centers.

⮑ http://www.cgiar.org

Consultative Group to Assist the Poor (CGAP). Expands access to microfinance by the poor in developing countries through a consortium of 28 public and private development agencies.

⮑ www.cgap.org

Financial Sector Reform and Strengthening Initiative (FIRST). Provides flexible, practical assistance to developing countries to strengthen their financial systems and adopt international financial standards.

⮑ http://www.firstinitiative.org

Global Alliance for Vaccines and Immunization (GAVI). Seeks to protect public health worldwide through the widespread use of vaccines.

⮑ http://www.gavialliance.org

Global Development Learning Network (GDLN). Collaborates in the design of customized learning solutions for individuals and organizations working in development.

⮑ http://gdln.org

Global Environment Facility (GEF). Provides grants to developing countries to fund projects that benefit the global environment and promote sustainable livelihoods in local communities.

⮑ http://www.thegef.org/gef

The Global Forum on Law, Justice and Development (GFLJD). A permanent knowledge sharing and co-generation initiative based on a broad partnership of more than 150 development partners. The GFLJD convenes, connects, and facilitates collaboration among regional and international organizations, international financial institutions, governments, judiciaries, think tanks, academia, and civil society organizations with relevant research and practice in law and justice.

⮑ http://globalforumljd.org

Global Partnership on Output-Based Aid (GPOBA). Funds, designs, demonstrates, and documents output-based aid approaches to improve delivery of basic infrastructure and social services to the poor in developing countries.

⮑ https://www.gpoba.org

Global Water Partnership (GWP). Supports countries in the sustainable management of their water resources.

⮑ http://www.gwp.org

Harmonization for Health in Africa (HHA). Provides regional support to governments in Africa in strengthening their health systems.

⮑ http://www.hha-online.org

Haiti Reconstruction Fund (HRF). Mobilizes, coordinates, and allocates contributions from bilateral and other donors to finance high-priority projects, programs, and budget support to help finance postearthquake reconstruction.

⮑ http://www.haitireconstructionfund.org

Infodev. Works at the intersection of innovation, technology, and entrepreneurship to create opportunities for inclusive growth, job creation, and poverty reduction.

⮑ http://www.infodev.org

Joint United Nations Programme on HIV/AIDS. Advocates for global action on the HIV/AIDS epidemic and works with civil society, the business community, and the private sector.

⮑ http://tinyurl.com/WBG0039

Onchocerciasis Control Program (OCP). Successfully halted transmission of river blindness in 11 countries with a collective population of 35 million.

⮑ http://tinyurl.com/WBG0038

Roll Back Malaria. Coordinates the international fight against malaria, which kills more than 1 million people a year, most of them children in Africa.

⮑ http://www.rollbackmalaria.org

Stolen Asset Recovery Initiative (StAR). Works with developing countries and financial centers to prevent the laundering of the proceeds of corruption and to facilitate more systematic and timely return of stolen assets.

⮑ http://star.worldbank.org/star

Water and Sanitation Program (WSP). Works directly with client governments at the local and national level to support poor people in obtaining affordable, safe, and sustainable access to water and sanitation services.

⮑ http://www.wsp.org

Pensions The past decade has brought broad recognition of the importance of pension systems to the economic stability of nations and the security of their aging populations. For the past 10 years, the World Bank has taken a leading role in addressing this challenge through its support for pension reforms around the world.

International experience shows that there is no uniform model for pension reform. There are, however, clear principles that can provide useful guidance to policy makers as they develop appropriate solutions based on a country's culture, political system, economy, and labor force structure. The World Bank's general framework for pension reform urges policy makers to start with the following three steps:

- *Environment.* Assessment of the macroeconomic, social, and demographic environment (initial conditions and capacities)

- *Design.* Establishment of policy intervention objectives, selection and evaluation of the reform design architecture, and establishment of the parameters of the scheme using actuarial modeling and analysis

- *Performance.* Evaluation of the system(s) using generally accepted principles of pension design or reform developed from international best practices

These principles include the most relevant ones: accessibility (coverage), adequacy, and sustainability. Other principles are affordability, fairness, predictability, robustness, economic, and administrative efficiency. These principles are intended to help policy makers rule out bad policy choices, thereby freeing them to design pension systems that are consistent with international best practices while still having considerable latitude to craft solutions that are appropriate for their country's social preferences and country-specific conditions.

⮑ http://www.worldbank.org/en/topic/pensions

Policies and Procedures The World Bank Group has established policies and procedures to help ensure that its operations are economically, financially, socially, and environmentally sound. Each operation must follow these policies and procedures to ensure quality, integrity, and adherence to the Bank Group's mission, corporate priorities, and strategic goals. These policies and procedures—including rigorous safeguard policies on projects affecting, for example, women, the environment, and indigenous peoples—are codified in the World Bank Operational Manual. They are subject to extensive review while being formulated and to compliance monitoring after being approved.

Operational Manual

The World Bank Operational Manual deals with the Bank's core development objectives and goals and the instruments for pursuing them, in addition to the requirements applicable to Bank-financed lending operations. The manual contains all policies, procedures, and good practices that are meant to ensure that World Bank activities are economically, financially, socially, and environmentally sound.

The manual includes several different kinds of operational statements, including operational policies and Bank procedures. Operational policies are short, focused statements that follow from the Bank's Articles of Agreement and the general conditions and policies approved by the Board of Executive Directors. They establish the parameters for conducting operations, describe the circumstances in which exceptions to policy are admissible, and spell out who authorizes exceptions. Bank procedures explain how staff members carry out the operational policies by describing the procedures and documentation required to ensure consistency and quality across the Bank.

⮑ http://go.worldbank.org/DZDZ9038D0

Environmental and Social Standards

Environmental and social safeguard policies—listed under "Bank procedures" in the Operational Manual—help avoid, minimize, mitigate, and compensate for adverse environmental and social impacts in Bank-supported operations that result from the development process. These standards help ensure that environmental and social issues are thoroughly evaluated by Bank and borrower staff in the identification, preparation, and implementation of Bank-financed programs and projects. The effectiveness and positive development impact of these projects and programs have increased substantially as a result of attention to these policies. The safeguard policies also provide a platform for stakeholder participation in project design and are an important instrument for building ownership among local populations.

The Bank has 10 safeguard policies that cover the following issues: environmental assessment, natural habitats, pest management, involuntary resettlement, indigenous peoples, forests, cultural resources, dam safety, international waterways, and projects in disputed areas.

The Bank also has a policy to govern the use of borrower systems for environmental and social safeguards. Bank safeguards require screening of each proposed project to determine the potential environmental and social risks and opportunities and how to address those issues. The Bank classifies the proposed project into risk categories depending on the type, location, sensitivity, and scale of the project and the nature and magnitude of its potential environmental and social impact. This categorization influences the required risk management and mitigation measures for the proposed project. The borrower is responsible for any studies required by the safeguard policies, with general assistance

provided by Bank staff members. The Bank's Quality Assurance and Compliance Unit within the Bank's Operations Policy and Country Services (OPCS) Vice Presidency, jointly with the Environmental and International Law Practice Group of the Legal Vice Presidency, provides support to Bank teams that are dealing with environmental and social risks in Bank-supported operations.

Open Access (*See* Open Access.)

IFC, MIGA, and ICSID Policies

The policies and procedures of the World Bank Group also apply to IFC and to MIGA, with some specific variations in guidelines, as appropriate to their clients:

- IFC's Access to Information Policy and its environmental and social policy and standards

- MIGA's Access to Information Policy and its environmental and social policy and standards

- ICSID's policies as set forth in its basic documents, additional facility documents, and other documents

Bank Procedures
⮑ http://tinyurl.com/WBG0035

Environmental and Social Policy and Standards
⮑ http://www.ifc.org/disclosure

ICSID
⮑ http://tinyurl.com/WBG0034

MIGA's Standards
⮑ http://www.miga.org/policies

Open Data
⮑ http://data.worldbank.org

Open Development
⮑ http://www.worldbank.org/open

World Bank Operational Manual

⊃ http://tinyurl.com/WBG0037

Political Risk Guarantees (*See also* Products and Services.) Multinational enterprises and banks face a number of risks when conducting business overseas. Some of these risks can be removed or mitigated by conducting due diligence on the parties involved and on the economic viability of the proposed business. Other risks are harder for investors or lenders to predict. These include some commercial risks and some noncommercial—or political—risks. Guarantees offered by the Bank and MIGA (political risk insurance) are tools businesses can use to mitigate and manage risks arising from the adverse actions—or inactions—of governments. As a risk-mitigation tool, political risk guarantee contributes to a more stable environment for investments into developing countries and can unlock better access to finance.

⊃ http://tinyurl.com/WBG084

Post-2015 Development Agenda (*See also* Millennium Development Goals.) The eight Millennium Development Goals (MDGs)—which range from halving extreme poverty to halting the spread of HIV/AIDS and providing universal primary education—have been a milestone in global and national development efforts. The framework has helped galvanize development efforts and guide global and national development priorities. While three of the eight goals have been achieved, further efforts and a strong global partnership for development are needed to accelerate progress by the 2015 deadline and beyond. Those development priorities and strategies are referred to as the Post-2015 Development Agenda.

According to the United Nations, the achievement of the MDGs has been uneven among and within countries. While much work remains, more than a decade of experience in working toward the goals has shown that focused global development efforts can make a difference.

The United Nations is working in concert with governments, civil society, and other partners to build on the momentum generated by the MDGs and to craft an ambitious, yet realistic, Post-2015 Development Agenda.

To identify the work still remaining and propose a path toward accomplishing it, the UN High Level Panel on the Post-2015 Development Agenda released "A New Global Partnership: Eradicate Poverty and Transform Economies through Sustainable Development," a report that sets out a universal agenda for eradicating extreme poverty from the face of the earth by 2030 and delivering on the promise of sustainable development.

In the report, the panel calls for the new post-2015 goals to drive the five big transformative shifts summarized below:

- **Leave no one behind.** After 2015, the objective should move from reducing extreme poverty to ending it, in all its forms. No person—regardless of ethnicity, gender, geography, disability, race, or other status—should be denied universal human rights and basic economic opportunities.

- **Put sustainable development at the core.** The world must act now to halt the alarming pace of climate change and environmental degradation, which pose unprecedented threats to humanity. More social inclusion is essential. This is a universal challenge requiring structural change, with new solutions.

- **Transform economies for jobs and inclusive growth.** The panel calls for a quantum leap forward in economic opportunities and a profound economic transformation to end extreme poverty and improve livelihoods. This means a rapid shift to sustainable patterns of consumption and production—harnessing innovation, technology, and the potential of private business to create more value and drive sustainable and inclusive growth. Diversified economies, with equal opportunities for all, can unleash the dynamism that creates jobs and livelihoods, especially for young people and women.

- **Build peace and effective, open, and accountable institutions for all.** Freedom from fear, conflict, and violence is the fundamental human right and the essential foundation for building peaceful and prosperous societies. At the same time, people the world over expect their governments to be honest, accountable, and responsive to their needs. The panel calls for a fundamental shift—to recognize peace and good governance as core elements of well-being.

- **Forge a new global partnership.** Perhaps the most important transformative shift is toward a new spirit of solidarity, cooperation, and mutual accountability that must underpin the Post-2015 Agenda. A new partnership should be based on a common understanding of a shared humanity, underpinning mutual respect and mutual benefit in a shrinking world. This partnership should involve governments but also include others: people living in poverty, those with disabilities, women, civil society organizations, indigenous and local communities, traditionally marginalized groups, multilateral institutions, local and national government, the business community, academia, and private philanthropy.

The World Bank Group's goals—to end extreme poverty and to boost shared prosperity—are closely aligned with the Post-2015 Development Agenda. The "Financing for Development Post-2015" report analyzes how the Bank Group can best apply its financial expertise and resources to this next phase of development effort.

According to the report, the World Bank Group and its regional counterparts can add value through a combination of technical expertise; prudent risk management policies; application of clear standards to project design, execution, and

corporate governance; a long-term perspective; and cross-country experience. Multilateral development banks (MDBs) can bring financing partners into specific deals, for example, in the form of syndications or through cofinancing arrangements. Generally, the MDBs' stamp of approval and role of "honest broker" in disputes can help reassure investors and contribute to a project's viability, which in turn reduces the cost of engagement, including to private investors. MDBs can also contribute to extending maturities of private flows to finance productive investments.

A New Global Partnership: Eradicate Poverty and Transform Economies through Sustainable Development
- http://tinyurl.com/WBG0050

Financing for Development Post-2015
- http://tinyurl.com/WBG0052

Millennium Development Goals
- http://www.un.org/en/ecosoc/about/mdg.shtml

Post-2015 Development Agenda
- http://www.post2015hlp.org

United Nations
- http://tinyurl.com/WBG0051

PovcalNet PovcalNet is an interactive computational tool that allows users to replicate the calculations made by the World Bank's researchers in estimating the extent of absolute poverty in the world. PovcalNet was developed for the sole purpose of public replication of the World Bank's poverty measures for its widely used international poverty lines, including $1.25 a day and $2 a day.
- http://go.worldbank.org/36VJBJCT20

Poverty (*See also* Global Practices.) One of 14 new World Bank Group Global Practices, Poverty identifies key policies and multisectoral solutions that effectively reduce poverty and benefit the less well off.

World Bank Group and Poverty

The Bank Group works closely with governments to develop sound policies so that the poor and the less well-off in every country can improve their livelihoods and have access to social and infrastructure services and good jobs. In April 2013, the World Bank Group set two new goals: ending extreme poverty and boosting shared prosperity in a sustainable way. The first goal, to eradicate extreme poverty within a generation, includes a specific target: to decrease the global extreme poverty rate to no more than 3 percent by 2030. This is possible but challenging, and galvanizing efforts to fight against extreme poverty is critical, as many low-income countries and most fragile and conflict-affected states will face significant challenges in meeting this target.

The second goal, to boost shared prosperity, is measured by the growth in income among the bottom 40 percent of the income distribution in each country. This goal helps the World Bank Group focus on the welfare of the less well-off wherever they are and includes a strong emphasis on tackling persistent inequalities that keep people in poverty from generation to generation.

Despite progress in poverty reduction and human welfare in the past decade, extreme poverty and inequality persist at unacceptably high levels in many parts of the world. In order to tackle the last miles of extreme poverty and to boost shared prosperity, countries must address several critical development challenges. In particular, it will be necessary to improve upon historical growth trends, ensuring that growth benefits the poorest; to sustain past welfare gains in the face of slow global growth; and to promote equal access to opportunities for all.

The Poverty Global Practice works closely with country governments and across the World

The Pakistan Poverty Alleviation Fund empowers the targeted poor by increasing incomes, improving productive capacity, and providing access to services to achieve sustainable livelihoods. Since the Third Pakistan Poverty Alleviation Fund (PPAF III) in July 2009, approximately 10 million vulnerable and marginalized people have benefited from the program interventions, more than half of them women. © World Bank / Visual News Associates (photographer). Permission required for reuse.

Bank Group to create cutting-edge knowledge and expertise, to analyze data in order to better understand constraints to and opportunities for poverty reduction and shared prosperity, to ensure that a strong evidence base is a critical part of the development dialogue, and to help governments improve their capacity and accountability for results. The Poverty Global Practice works with country, regional, and global teams across all Global Practices to provide a more robust evidence base and sharpen the poverty reduction focus of WBG operations in a way that is reflected in the composition and effectiveness of programs.

The World Bank Group will continue to be a global leader in poverty reduction and shared prosperity and will use its global reach and convening capabilities to share ideas, knowledge, and lessons learned with client and partner countries, with the goal of working together to end poverty within a generation and improve the welfare of the less-well-off in every country.

IFC and Poverty

IFC assists in the fight against poverty by helping build the private sector in developing countries. It focuses many of its investment and advisory services on sectors that have the most direct effect on living standards, jobs, and economic growth, including financial services, infrastructure, information and communication technologies, small and medium enterprises, microfinance, health, and education. IFC's five strategic priorities all aim to reduce poverty and improve living standards:

• Strengthening the focus on frontier markets

• Addressing climate change and ensuring environmental and social sustainability

• Addressing constraints to private sector growth in infrastructure, health, education, and the food-supply chain

• Developing local financial markets

• Building long-term client relationships in emerging markets

MIGA and Poverty

MIGA promotes foreign direct investment in developing countries to help support economic-growth, reduce poverty, and improve people's lives. It focuses on insuring investments in the areas where it can make the greatest difference in development, including infrastructure, manufacturing, services, power, oil and gas, agribusiness, and banking.

President The World Bank Group President is selected by the Executive Directors. The President serves a term of five years, which may be renewed. There is no mandatory retirement age. In addition to chairing the meetings of the Boards of Directors, the President is responsible for the overall management of the World Bank Group. The Executive Vice

Presidents of IFC and MIGA report directly to the World Bank Group President, and the President serves as Chair of ICSID's Administrative Council. (ICSID operates as a secretariat whose Secretary-General is selected by the Administrative Council every six years.) Within IBRD and IDA, most organizational units report to the President and, through the President, to the Executive Directors.

The two exceptions are the Independent Evaluation Group and the Inspection Panel, which report directly to the Executive Directors. In addition, the President delegates some of his or her oversight responsibility to three Managing Directors, each of whom oversees several organizational units.

⟳ http://worldbank.org/president

Presidents of the World Bank Group
Eugene Meyer

Eugene Meyer was the first President of the World Bank Group. In 1946, Meyer laid the groundwork for lasting Bank business policies. His short but pivotal six-month presidency introduced issues that would define the institution in the next decades.

Meyer first began the task of building organization within the company. He recruited senior staff and professional personnel capable of analyzing loan proposals, built a research department needed to make decisions about loans and guarantees, and began defining loan policies. Meyer also set the mission of instilling confidence in the Bank on Wall Street.

His excellent reputation on Wall Street and his conservative approach served to allay fears and encourage those who looked to the Bank to play a major role in the postwar economic field. Investors welcomed his promise that the Bank would operate on sound investing principles. Meyer actively promoted changes in state legislation in the United States that would allow insurance companies, savings banks, and other bodies to purchase IBRD bonds. Meyer is also credited with helping to define the fundamental relationship between the World Bank and the United Nations.

John J. McCloy

John McCloy was the second President of the World Bank Group. From 1947 to 1949 McCloy took on the foundational tasks that included: starting up lending operations, strengthening staff, clarifying the respective roles of the Executive Directors and the President, and reinforcing the relationship between the Bank and the United Nations and between the Bank and the United States.

During McCloy's tenure, the Bank started to borrow in the capital market. McCloy realized that the main problem of the Bank's earliest days would not be to find borrowers, but to find lenders offering funding at reasonable rates. McCloy was well known and trusted in financial circles. His election signaled that the Bank was not to be a charitable or a political agency, but was to be a financially sound lending institution, following criteria that were acceptable to Wall Street.

McCloy's term also marked a point where the Bank defined its basic policies and operational procedures, made its first loans for reconstruction and for development, filled out its management team, and doubled its staff in size. Perhaps most important, McCloy settled the issue of the division of responsibilities between the President and the Board of Executive Directors. The establishment of the executive autonomy of the President, the emphasis that investment decisions would be made on economic rather than political grounds, and the close link between the President and the U.S. Executive

Director were important factors in bolstering the confidence of the U.S. securities market.

Eugene R. Black

Eugene Black was the third President of the World Bank Group. From 1949 to 1962, Black led the institution from its tentative beginnings to broad recognition as an important, well-functioning, effective, and profitable development institution. He assembled a growing international staff that brought experience and imagination to tackle the demands of an expanding membership. Lending increased rapidly and covered virtually all sectors relevant to economic progress, including infrastructure, industry, agriculture, and education.

Black spent much time on the task of promoting the credit of the Bank and its access to the U.S. capital market. While gaining the trust of its creditors, the Bank was establishing its reputation in the developing countries as the gatekeeper of the international financial markets. Black came to personify access to those markets and to the people who controlled them. Establishing the Bank's reputation as a financially sound institution with an impeccable credit record was Black's most important achievement.

To identify the appropriate national economic context of project investments, Black put strong emphasis on the need for carefully prepared national development plans. This emphasis on well-informed economic planning led to the Bank's early foray into the field of technical assistance. Technical assistance activities grew in number, as member countries recognized the Bank's expertise in a wide field of economic activity. As the Bank's experience with economic development grew, the limitations inherent in the conventional banking concept became more evident, and the need to broaden the scope of the institution became clear. In response to the changing needs of the membership, two major affiliates were created: IFC and IDA.

The creation of IFC and IDA complemented the original International Bank for Reconstruction and Development, and the Bank could now assist all its members regardless of their income level and capacity for servicing debt. The three affiliates signaled the transformation of the World Bank into a serious development institution.

George Woods

George Woods was the fourth President of the World Bank Group. From 1963 to 1968, Woods oversaw the evolution of the Bank into a development institution by redirecting its focus and resources to the analysis of development and the support of more relevant economic activities.

Woods emphasized the importance of IDA and pushed for an increase in the Bank's level of activity. He envisioned the global role of the Bank as an institution that could help correct the disparity between rich and poor. Woods oversaw the evolution of the Bank from a primarily conservative financial institution to a development institution by redirecting its focus and resources to the analysis of development and the support of more relevant economic activities. Under Woods, the Bank analyzed the factors that hindered growth in developing countries.

During his tenure, the horizons of Bank lending expanded, economic analysis took a central role, IFC was strengthened, and aid coordination (through the rapid expansion of consultative groups) allowed more effective use of donor resources. Woods recognized that the developing countries' needs could not be satisfied solely by the Bank and IFC

and that private foreign investment was essential. But many foreign investors were hesitant to become involved in some countries for fear of government expropriation of assets or other acts that discouraged private investments. Woods embraced a proposal by the Bank's general counsel, to establish a facility that could resolve investment disputes. In October 1966, the International Centre for Settlement of Investment Disputes (ICSID) was established, which provided much-needed assurance for foreign private investors. His successors would further elaborate the scope of the Bank's activities in its global position.

Robert McNamara

Robert McNamara was the fifth President of the World Bank Group. From 1968 to 1981, McNamara brought with him the firm belief that the problems of the developing world could be solved. He believed that success depended only on clear analysis of the problems and determination in applying the appropriate remedies.

The Bank Group that McNamara joined in 1968 had been completely transformed by the time he left 13 years later. McNamara developed an elaborate system of numerical reporting tables that provided complete pictures of the lending program and country needs. One of his first actions upon taking office was to request a list from his managers of all the projects that should be undertaken, regardless of the financial, political, or economic constraints. He used this list as the basis of his first five-year lending plan, and in September 1968 he proposed that the Bank double the volume of lending during the next five years.

The proposed increase in the Bank Group's activities required a rapid expansion in the number and diversity of staff members. Between 1968 and

1973, the professional staff increased 125 percent. The strengthening of the research staff stimulated interaction with the academic community and allowed the Bank to claim a role as an intellectual leader in development matters. McNamara also decided that the Bank's organizational structure required an overhaul. With an expanding volume of business, the system of large centralized projects and geographical departments had become unwieldy and bureaucratic; a major reorganization of the Bank Group took place in 1972.

McNamara expanded the geographical range of the Bank's lending, and the Bank became actively engaged in all countries that needed help. During his tenure, lending for education increased three-fold. McNamara also launched an attack on urban poverty and attempted to raise the productivity of the poor. He urged governments to meet the "basic human needs" of their populations. McNamara's determination to assist those in "absolute poverty" remained the motivation driving his presidential tenure.

Alden W. Clausen

Alden Clausen was the sixth President of the World Bank Group. From 1981 to 1986, Clausen presided over the Bank Group in difficult times. When Clausen assumed the presidency, the international economy was deep into one of the worst recessions of the post–

World War II era. The institution had to respond to profound changes in the international economy and in the views of the U.S. President and Congress.

Clausen advocated for increased structural and sectoral lending and expanded aid coordination, including consortia, consultative groups, and close collaboration with the IMF. Clausen's fundamental commitment to free markets, private flows of capital, and international cooperation, together

with his commercial banker's knowledge of finance, inspired innovations in investment guarantees and cofinancing with commercial banks. Clausen recognized that private investment was constrained by investors' inability to manage the political risks associated with investments in developing countries. Accordingly, Clausen revived an idea developed earlier in the Bank to form an investment insurance agency, and thus plans for the Multilateral Investments Guarantee Agency (MIGA) began in 1986. (MIGA came into existence in 1988.)

The Bank, in response to borrower demands, also accelerated the pace of disbursements in a program created in coordination with other development banks and aid agencies. The Bank Group urged developing countries to complete projects as quickly as possible and to provide the basis for long-term growth. Clausen took an active role in presenting the Bank Group's purpose to the news media, business gatherings, and development organizations, a move that may have ultimately improved his successors' relations with the U.S. government.

Barber B. Conable

Barber Conable was the seventh President of the World Bank Group. From 1986 to 1991, Conable was noted for the major reorganization of the Bank he directed in 1987 and the emphasis on poverty reduction as a central mission of the Bank Group. Conable was the

first career politician to be appointed President of the Bank Group and the only one without substantial Wall Street experience. His extensive political skills made him an effective spokesman for the institution, persuasively advancing the Bank's reform agenda.

Conable publicly advocated increasing the Bank Group's attention to environmental problems, promoting programs to curtail population growth, and advancing the role of women in development. His focus on environmental protection as an important goal culminated in the Bank Group joining with the United Nations Development Programme and the United Nations Environment Programme to establish the Global Environment Facility in 1991.

The ongoing developing world debt crisis was an issue that faced Conable when he came to the Bank Group. The U.S.-sponsored Baker Plan was implemented to alleviate developing country debt, primarily by urging financial institutions and commercial lenders to lend new monies to countries engaged in acceptable structural reforms. By 1987, Conable conceded that the adjustment process and the resumption of growth were proceeding more slowly than was acceptable, and he announced that the Bank Group (together with the IMF) would assemble special debt-restructuring packages to reduce existing debt and supplement new lending. By the end of Conable's tenure, five countries had debt and debt-service reduction plans in effect, and the Bank Group was effectively aligned with the U.S. government on the debt crisis.

Lewis T. Preston

Lewis Preston was the eighth President of the World Bank Group. Serving from 1991 to 1995, the distinguished commercial banker created a client-oriented vision for the Bank Group as it celebrated its 50th anniversary. He declared that alleviating poverty would be the Bank Group's overarching objective and said that applications for loans would be judged on a nation's social justice record as well as on its economic efficiency.

Preston emphasized the quality of lending over the quantity of lending. He led the institution through one of its most turbulent eras.

Preston's chief objectives were to make the Bank more flexible, more cost-effective, and more responsive to prevailing social concerns. He stated that the key to success for the World Bank Group depended on its ability to respond to the changes in the world and to execute its administrative role accordingly. With Preston's concern with the efficacy of the institution's operations, he strengthened social sector lending.

Preston made a clear link between poverty and environmental degradation. Preston's predecessor instituted measures to improve the Bank Group's performance in the environmental field, including the establishment of an Environment Department to oversee the Bank Group's work. An effort that came to fruition during Preston's tenure was the Global Environment Facility (GEF), a cooperative program among the World Bank Group, the United Nations Development Programme (UNDP), and the United Nations Environment Programme (UNEP). The GEF agreement was formalized in 1991, and the first grant for environmental projects was made in December of that year.

Preston instituted a further reorganization of the Bank Group's structure, designed to streamline the management structure and simplify the budgeting process. He created the Business Innovation and Simplification Committee to simplify and improve the Bank Group's business processes and established large new units in the areas of human resources, environmentally sustainable development, and the promotion of the private sector.

James D. Wolfensohn

James Wolfensohn was the ninth President of the World Bank Group. From 1995 to 2005, the "Renaissance Banker" focused the spotlight back on the Bank Group's true purpose—fighting global poverty and helping the world's poor forge better lives.

Under his leadership, the Bank Group implemented a range of significant reforms to help achieve its mission and broke ground in several major areas, including corruption, debt relief, disabilities, the environment, and gender.

In his 10 years as President, Wolfensohn traveled to more than 120 countries to better understand the challenges facing the Bank Group's 184 member countries. In addition to visiting development projects, he met with government clients and representatives from business, labor, media, nongovernmental organizations, religious and women's groups, students, and teachers. Wolfensohn drew attention to the importance of involving young people and the need to expand the development dialogue to include civil society, indigenous peoples, faith-based groups, and other stakeholders.

During Wolfensohn's leadership, the World Bank Group redoubled its efforts to monitor and combat corruption, give voice to clients living in poor communities, and magnify the return on development investments. Further, the Bank Group became the largest external financier of primary education, basic health, HIV/AIDS programs, the environment, and biodiversity.

Wolfensohn helped forge strategic partnerships around culture and peace, faith and development, and communications technology, including the Global Distance Learning Network and Development Gateway. Internally, he transformed the World Bank Group by greatly increasing decentralization, bringing the institution forward technologically, and turning it into a far more open and transparent organization.

Paul D. Wolfowitz

Paul Wolfowitz was the 10th President of the World Bank Group. From 2005 to 2007, Wolfowitz placed the poorest people of Africa at the forefront of his agenda. On his frequent visits to the region, he stressed that Africa could fulfill its promise as a

"continent of hope," if the international community supported its leaders in confronting key development challenges.

By focusing the Bank Group on those development challenges—good governance, effective safeguards against corruption, sound infrastructure, greater trade opportunities, and protection of the environment—he ensured the Bank's strong and continuing support to the region.

In 2007, Wolfowitz announced the creation of the Stolen Assets Recovery Initiative, or StAR, through which the Bank would work with the UN and other agencies to help developing countries recover looted assets. Wolfowitz worked with the world's leading economies to secure an agreement for 100 percent debt relief for the world's most indebted nations. He introduced a strengthened governance and anticorruption policy at the Bank Group following a consultation process that gathered advice and opinions from thousands of experts and representatives of civil society, parliaments, and the private sector in dozens of countries.

Robert B. Zoellick

Robert Zoellick was the 11th President of the World Bank Group. From 2007 to 2012, Zoellick recapitalized the Bank Group and expanded financing for the poorest countries following the food, fuel, and financial crises of recent years. He modernized the Bank Group by making it more accountable, flexible, fast-moving, and transparent on good governance and anticorruption.

Zoellick declared that the world needed "new geopolitics for a multi-polar economy, where all are fairly represented in associations for the many, not clubs for the few." His remarks were applauded by activist groups who long campaigned for a greater voice and platform for developing countries in the institutions that oversee the world economy. Zoellick increased representation of developing countries in governance and staffing and encouraged developing countries to set their own priorities rather than having them dictated by the Bank Group. His record was also marked by an increased role for the private sector through IFC, which under his leadership recruited sovereign wealth funds and pension funds to invest in poor countries, especially in Africa.

During Zoellick's tenure, the Bank Group's capital stock expanded; lending volumes increased to member countries; and the shareholding, Executive Board, and voting structure were transformed to boost the control of developing and emerging economies in the Bank's governance.

Jim Yong Kim

Jim Yong Kim became the 12th President of the World Bank Group on July 1, 2012. A physician and anthropologist, Kim has dedicated himself to international development for more than two decades, helping to improve the lives of underserved populations worldwide.

Kim comes to the Bank after serving as President of Dartmouth College.

As President of Dartmouth, Kim earned praise for reducing a financial deficit without cutting any academic programs. He founded the Dartmouth Center for Health Care Delivery Science, a multidisciplinary institute dedicated to developing new models of health care delivery and achieving better health outcomes at lower costs.

Before assuming the Dartmouth presidency, Kim held professorships and chaired departments at Harvard Medical School, the Harvard School of Public Health, and Brigham and Women's Hospital, Boston. He also served as Director of Harvard's François-Xavier Bagnoud Center for Health and Human Rights.

In 1987, Kim cofounded Partners in Health, a Boston-based nonprofit organization working in poor communities on four continents. Challenging previous conventional wisdom that drug-resistant tuberculosis and HIV/AIDS could not be treated in developing countries, PIH successfully tackled these diseases by integrating large-scale treatment programs into community-based primary care.

As Director of the World Health Organization's HIV/AIDS Department, Kim led the "3 by 5" initiative, the first-ever global goal for AIDS treatment, which sought to treat 3 million new HIV/AIDS patients in developing countries with antiretroviral drugs by 2005. Launched in September 2003, the ambitious program ultimately reached its goal by 2007.

Kim's work has earned him wide recognition. He was awarded a MacArthur "Genius" Fellowship (2003), was named one of America's "25 Best Leaders" by U.S. News & World Report (2005), and was selected as one of Time magazine's "100 Most Influential People in the World" (2006).

⮑ http://tinyurl.com/WBG085

Preston, Lewis T. (*See* Presidents of the World Bank Group.)

Private Sector Development The World Bank Group places major emphasis on the role of the private sector in spurring economic growth and reducing poverty, with two of its institutions, IFC and MIGA, focusing specifically on private enterprises. In addition, a joint World Bank–IFC Vice Presidency takes the lead on many aspects of private sector development. The Bank Group institutions provide research and advisory services on corporate governance, corporate social responsibility, investment climate diagnostics and reform, private participation in infrastructure, privatization transactions, and microenterprise and small business development.

Procurement The procurement policies and procedures in Bank Group–financed projects are explained in "Guidelines: Procurement of Goods, Works and Non-Consulting Services under IBRD Loans, IDA Credits and Grants by World Bank Borrowers" and "Guidelines: Selection and Employment of Consultants under IBRD Loans and IDA Credits and Grants by World Bank Borrowers." IFC uses the World Bank Group's vendor guidelines for procurement.

➲ http://go.worldbank.org/9KQZWXNOI0

Procurement Opportunities Every year, investment projects financed by the World Bank Group generate billions of dollars in opportunities for contractors and suppliers of goods and services. The responsibility for the procurement of goods, works, and services—and therefore for the award and administration of contracts—rests with the borrower. The Bank Group, for its part, is required by its Articles of Agreement to ensure that the proceeds of the loan are used only for the purposes for which the loan was granted, with due attention to considerations of economy and efficiency and without regard to political or other considerations. The Procurement Policy and Services Group of the World Bank Group is responsible for procurement policy formulation and interpretation.

The World Bank Group is currently preparing and advancing a proposed new framework on procurement, which will seek to make the Bank Group's procurement policies as modern and effective as possible.

➲ http://worldbank.org/procure

Products and Services (*See also* Financial Products and Services.) All World Bank Group products and services are designed to support governments in reducing poverty and boosting shared prosperity.

World Bank Products and Services
The following services are designed to share the best knowledge available to achieve development results:

- *Technical assistance.* The World Bank Group's professional technical advice supports legal, policy, management, governance, and other reforms needed for a country's development goals. Its wide-ranging knowledge and skills are used to help countries build accountable, efficient public sector institutions to sustain development in ways that will benefit their citizens over the long term. Bank Group staff members offer advice and support governments in the preparation of documents such as draft legislation, institutional development plans, country-level strategies, and implementation action plans. The Bank Group can also assist governments in shaping or putting new policies and programs in place.

- *Reimbursable advisory services.* At client request, the Bank Group provides reimbursable advisory services, which can be used when the Bank Group cannot fully fund an activity within the existing budget. This can include traditional knowledge and advisory work as well as convening services. Subject to appropriate safeguards and risk management, the Bank Group may provide technical assistance for project-related preparation and implementation support services—except for advice directly related to engineering or final design.

- *Economic and sector work.* In collaboration with country clients and development partners, Bank Group country staff members gather and evaluate information (data, policies, and statistics) about the existing economy, government institutions, or social services systems. These data provide a starting point for policy and strategic discussions with borrowers and enhance a country's capacity and knowledge. Studies and analytical reports support clients in planning and implementing effective development programs and projects.

- **Donor aid coordination.** The World Bank Group acts on occasion as a coordinator for organized regular interaction among donors (governments, aid agencies, humanitarian groups, foundations, development banks). Activities range from simple information sharing and brainstorming, to cofinancing a particular project, to joint strategic programming in a country or region. Activities also include the preparation of donor coordination events, such as consultative group meetings (joint meetings of partners) focused on a particular issue or country.

- **Research and analysis.** The World Bank Group seeks to increase understanding of development policies and programs by providing intellectual leadership and analytical services to the institution and the development community. It focuses on research and knowledge creation, global monitoring and projections, international statistics, statistical capacity building, and results monitoring.

⟳ http://www.worldbank.org/en/about/what-we-do

IFC's Products and Services

IFC provides investment, advice, and asset management. These are mutually reinforcing services, delivering financing and global expertise to clients in developing countries. Together, they give IFC a special advantage in helping the private sector create opportunities. IFC's investment and advice can be tailored to a client's specific needs, and in ways that add value. The ability to attract other investors brings additional benefits, introducing IFC's clients to new sources of capital and better ways of doing business.

IFC's products and services are offered under its three business lines: investment services, advisory services, and asset management:

- Through its investment services, IFC provides a broad suite of financial products and services— including loans, syndicated loans, equity finance, trade finance, structured finance, risk management products, local currency financing, and private equity and investment funds—designed to promote sustainable development in emerging economies and help reduce poverty.

- Through its advisory services, IFC offers advice, problem solving, and training to companies, industries, and governments, all aimed at helping private sector enterprises overcome obstacles to growth. Access to finance, investment climate, sustainable business, and public-private partnerships are the focus of IFC's advisory services.

- The IFC Asset Management Company, a wholly owned subsidiary of IFC, mobilizes and manages third-party capital funds for investment in developing and frontier markets.

⟳ http://tinyurl.com/WBG074

MIGA's Products and Services

MIGA provides political risk insurance (guarantees) and credit enhancement products to private sector investors and lenders. MIGA's guarantees protect investments against noncommercial risks and can help investors obtain access to funding sources with improved financial terms and conditions. Projects supported by MIGA create jobs; provide water, electricity, and other basic infrastructure; strengthen financial systems; generate tax revenues; transfer skills and technological know-how; and help countries tap natural resources in an environmentally sustainable way. MIGA also conducts research and shares knowledge as part of its mandate to support foreign direct investment into emerging markets.

⟳ http://www.miga.org/index.cfm

Program-for-Results In 2012, the World Bank introduced a new lending instrument, Program-for Results (PforR). PforR supports government programs and links the disbursement of funds directly to the delivery of defined results with a special focus on strengthening institutions. With PforR, disbursements are linked to the achievement of tangible and verifiable results. The focus is on results as well as on how the results are achieved. PforR provides assurance that Bank financing is used appropriately and that the environmental and social impacts of the program are adequately addressed.

⤳ http://worldbank.org/p4r

Project Cycle
World Bank's Project Cycle
The project cycle is the framework used by the World Bank to design, prepare, implement, and supervise projects. In practice, the World Bank and the borrowing country work closely throughout the project cycle, although they have different roles and responsibilities. Generally, the duration of the project cycle is long by commercial standards. It is not uncommon for a project to last more than four years, from the time it is identified until the time it is completed. The World Bank project cycle includes six stages: identification, preparation, appraisal, negotiation/approval, implementation, and evaluation.

IFC's Project Cycle
The project cycle illustrates the stages a business investment goes through as it becomes an IFC-financed project. There is no standard application form for IFC financing. A company or entrepreneur, foreign or domestic, seeking to establish a new venture or expand an existing enterprise can approach IFC directly. This is best done by reading how to apply for financing and by submitting an investment proposal. Stages of the IFC project cycle include

business development, early review, appraisal (due diligence), investment review, negotiations, public notification, board review and approval, commitment, disbursement of funds, project supervision and development outcome tracking, evaluation, and closing.

MIGA's Project Cycle
MIGA's underwriting process begins when a client submits a preliminary application. The application is free, confidential, and short, and can be done online. On receipt of an application, MIGA will assign an underwriter to review it to determine whether the project meets eligibility criteria. MIGA will then contact the client to discuss the project.

At this point, the underwriter discusses preliminary pricing with the client, the potential size of the guarantee, and the MIGA covers that are most appropriate for the investment. MIGA also works with the client to identify environmental and social impact assessments that must be undertaken.

⤳ http://tinyurl.com/WBG086

Publications, World Bank Group (*See also* Open Access Policy; Open Knowledge Repository; World Bank eLibrary.) To support its mission, the World Bank Group, in partnership with groups across the Bank, publishes and disseminates a large selection of research and knowledge products. World Bank Group Publications produces authoritative reports such as the World Development Report and Doing Business that feature research from some of the world's top development economists and practitioners.

The Bank Group's publications portfolio includes:

- Major flagship reports to provide policy makers with in-depth analysis on key development topics

- Handbooks to train and aid practitioners

- Scholarly books that contribute to the development debate in universities and think tanks

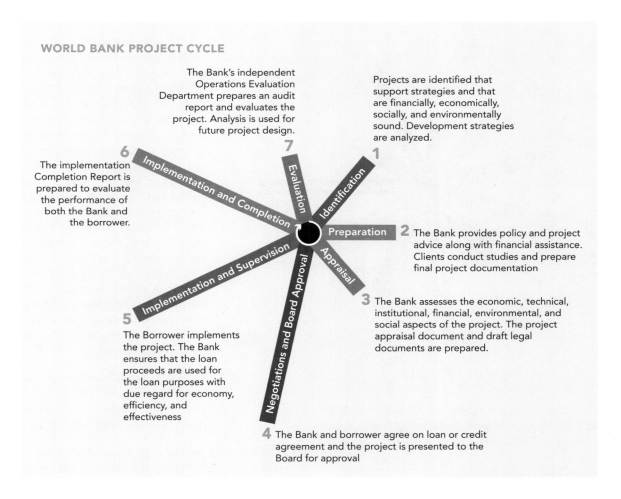

WORLD BANK PROJECT CYCLE

The Bank's independent Operations Evaluation Department prepares an audit report and evaluates the project. Analysis is used for future project design.

Projects are identified that support strategies and that are financially, economically, socially, and environmentally sound. Development strategies are analyzed.

The implementation Completion Report is prepared to evaluate the performance of both the Bank and the borrower.

The Bank provides policy and project advice along with financial assistance. Clients conduct studies and prepare final project documentation

The Borrower implements the project. The Bank ensures that the loan proceeds are used for the loan purposes with due regard for economy, efficiency, and effectiveness

The Bank assesses the economic, technical, institutional, financial, environmental, and social aspects of the project. The project appraisal document and draft legal documents are prepared.

The Bank and borrower agree on loan or credit agreement and the project is presented to the Board for approval

6 — Implementation and Completion
7 — Evaluation
1 — Identification
Preparation
2
Appraisal
3
Negotiations and Board Approval
Implementation and Supervision
5
4

- Outreach publications aimed at general audiences interested in international development

World Bank Group publications cover a broad range of economic and social issues, including development policy, finance, health, education, environment, trade, poverty, climate change, and globalization. In addition to print resources, World Bank Group online resources offer access to the most reliable research on economic and social development to millions of users around the world. The World Bank eLibrary, an online collection of nearly 9,000 formal publications, includes books, reports, journals, and policy research working papers, as well as all new titles as they are published.

World Bank Group publications are available for free in numerous online locations including the Open Knowledge Repository, websites of the World Bank Group, through Google Books, and on social readings sites, allowing a vast global community to freely access, read, and share Bank titles. They are also disseminated through commercial channels,

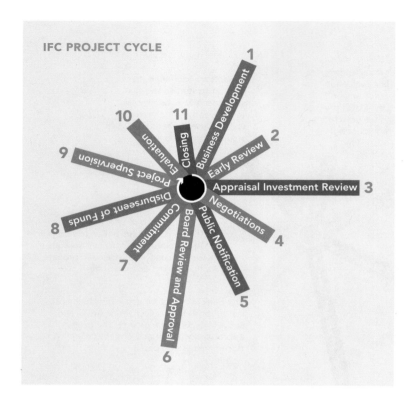

IFC PROJECT CYCLE

1. Business Development
2. Early Review
3. Appraisal Investment Review
4. Negotiations
5. Public Notification
6. Board Review and Approval
7. Commitment
8. Disbursement of Funds
9. Project Supervision
10. Evaluation
11. Closing

including through Amazon and Apple iTunes stores and for an array of devices including tablets, smart phones, and e-readers.

Open Knowledge Repository
↻ https://openknowledge.worldbank.org

World Bank eLibrary
↻ https://elibrary.worldbank.org

World Bank Group Publications
↻ http://www.worldbank.org/reference

Public-Private Infrastructure Advisory Facility
(*See also* Public-Private Partnerships; Infrastructure.) The Public-Private Infrastructure Advisory Facility (PPIAF) was created in 1999 to act as a catalyst to

increase private sector participation in emerging markets. It provides technical assistance to governments to support the creation of a sound enabling environment for the provision of basic infrastructure services by the private sector. A sound business enabling environment consists of strong institutions, legal systems and rule of law, high standards of public and corporate governance, transparency, competition, protection of investments, enforcement of laws, and dispute resolution mechanisms.

Governments are the main generators of private sector projects, but there are obstacles that impede private sector participation. PPIAF assists in removing some of these obstacles by supporting:

- Policy formulation, as public authorities decide between public and private provision of infrastructure services

- The selection of the best mode of delivery of infrastructure services and the risk allocation between the public and the private sectors

- Building capacity in public authorities to design public-private partnership projects, manage the award process and the service delivery, and partner with private investors

- Adequate consultation with beneficiaries to share project objectives

- Legislation and institutional reforms to ensure the sustainability of the investments and the protection of property and contractual rights

• Support for the negotiations of contracts to ensure adequate risk allocation between public and private parties

PPIAF is a multidonor technical assistance facility, financed by 17 multilateral and bilateral donors: Asian Development Bank, Australia, Austria, Canada, European Bank for Reconstruction and Development, France, Germany, International Finance Corporation, Italy, Japan, Millennium Challenge Corporation, Netherlands, Sweden, Switzerland, United Kingdom, United States, and the World Bank. PPIAF funds are untied and grants are provided on a demand-driven basis.

PPIAF is governed by a Program Council composed of its donors. An independent technical advisory panel reviews PPIAF activities and provides strategic advice to the Program Council.

The Project Management Unit manages day-to-day operations. To facilitate outreach and monitoring of its technical assistance activities, the project management unit maintains field offices in Nairobi and Dubai.

Public-Private Partnerships (*See also* Cross-Cutting Solution Areas.) One of five new Cross-Cutting Solution Areas, Public-Private Partnerships enhance the reach and quality of basic service provision.

There is no broad international consensus on what constitutes a PPP. In general, PPP refers to arrangements, typically medium to long term, between the public and the private sectors whereby some of the services that fall under the responsibility of the public sector are provided by the private sector, with clear agreement on shared objectives for delivery of public infrastructure or services. PPPs typically do not include service contracts or turnkey construction contracts, which are categorized as public procurement projects, or the privatization of utilities where there is a limited ongoing role for the public sector.

In some jurisdictions, and in particular countries that follow the tradition of the Code Napoleon, a distinction is made between public contracts such as concessions, where the private party is providing a service directly to the public and taking end-user risk, and PPPs, where the private party is delivering a service to a public party in the form of a bulk supply, such as a build-operate-transfer (BOT) project for a water treatment plant or the management of existing facilities (for example, hospital facilities) against a fee.

In other countries, specific sectors are carved out from the definition, particularly those sectors that are effectively regulated or where there is extensive private sector initiative, such as in telecommunications. In some countries, arrangements involving more limited risk transfer, such as management contracts, are excluded from the definition for institutional reasons because the authorities prefer that they fall under traditional procurement processes for goods and services.

PPPs in Infrastructure

Public-private partnerships in infrastructure can enable the development or improvement of energy, water, transport, and telecommunications and information technology through the participation of private and government entities. Where governments are facing aging infrastructure and require more efficient services, a partnership with the private sector can help foster new solutions, including clean technology.

PPPs combine the skills and resources of both the public and the private sectors in new ways through the sharing of risks and responsibilities. This arrangement allows governments to benefit from the expertise of the private sector and focus instead on policy, planning, and regulation by delegating day-to-day operations.

Achieving a successful partnership requires a careful analysis of the long-term development objectives and risk allocation. In addition, the legal

The Ouarzazate I Concentrated Solar Power (CSP) Project partially funds the construction of a concentrated solar power plant which supports the first phase of an ambitious Moroccan plan to expand the country's reliance on its domestic renewable energy sources. Morocco aims to increase the share of renewable energy in its energy mix to 42 percent by 2020. © World Bank / Dana Smillie (photographer). Permission required for reuse.

framework must adequately support this new model of service delivery and be able to monitor and regulate the outputs and services provided. A well-drafted PPP agreement is informed by both the laws of the country and international best practices to delineate risks and responsibilities clearly.

World Bank Group and PPPs

The World Bank Group provides support to client countries in their development of programs and projects for public-private partnerships through a number of different tools and mechanisms. It helps governments improve the enabling environments for PPPs and pursue sector reforms through technical assistance and, as part of broader sector support, through facilities that promote the development of PPPs. The World Bank Group also offers a number of knowledge management tools and collaborates on other initiatives that foster public-private partnerships. The Infrastructure Resource Center

for Contracts, Laws, and Regulations, for example, gives a general introduction to PPPs, offers practical tools for the development of the legal enabling environment and regulation of PPPs, and provides sample and annotated contracts from various structures in private sector participation in infrastructure.

World Bank and PPPs

In addition to technical assistance and sector support, the Bank has provided innovative guarantee support for PPP projects, particularly in infrastructure, often in collaboration with IFC and MIGA.

IFC and PPPs

IFC's advisory services in public-private partnerships help national and municipal governments partner with the private sector to improve basic services, such as education, electricity, health, sanitation, and roads, as well as tackle today's most pressing issues like climate change and food security.

IFC has a number of financing mechanisms for supporting PPP projects, whether in their early stages, through lending to and equity participation in private sector operators in projects, through infrastructure funds and facilities supporting projects, and through guarantees.

As of June 2014, IFC had an active portfolio of 118 PPP advisory projects in more than 50 countries, valued at about $152 million. IFC helped governments sign 10 PPP contracts, including 6 in IDA countries. These partnerships are expected to improve access to infrastructure and health services for more than 1.6 million people and mobilize $306 million in private investment.

MIGA and PPPs

The private sector has an enormous role to play in helping countries keep their commitments to their citizens, whether on its own or in tandem with governments through public-private partnerships. Here, MIGA makes a significant contribution, by catalyzing foreign direct investment that supports economic growth, reduces poverty, and improves people's lives in places that need it most. The Agency has supported a number of PPP projects, particularly in infrastructure.

Public Sector Management A fundamental role of the World Bank Group is working with the governments of client countries to enhance the effectiveness of country systems and institutions to address difficult institutional problems. The Bank Group has a number of instruments and initiatives that seek to address critical governance issues, from investment and development policy financing, to analytical and advisory services, research, and knowledge products. The Governance Global Practice is responsible for the World Bank's governance and public sector strategy. The practice focuses on building efficient, open, and accountable institutions and governance systems through knowledge generation, documentation of global best practices, and tangible, hands-on, implementation support to Bank Group clients.

R

Reforms For the first time in several decades, the World Bank Group is undergoing a major internal reform. No longer regioncentric, the new structure, effective July 1, 2014, is organized around 14 Global Practices (Agriculture; Education; Energy and Extractives; Environment and Natural Resources; Finance and Markets; Governance; Health, Nutrition, and Population; Macroeconomics and Fiscal Management; Poverty; Social, Urban, Rural, and Resilience; Social Protection and Labor; Trade and Competitiveness; Transport and ICT; and Water) and 5 Cross-Cutting Solution Areas (Climate Change; Fragility, Conflict, and Violence; Gender; Jobs; and Public-Private Partnerships).

The new institutional architecture will help remove some of the "silos" that prevented staff members from sharing their knowledge more widely across Bank Group activities and kept them from applying the lessons of experience more broadly across multiple regions and sectors. A more efficient and focused institution will therefore be better equipped to respond to client needs more quickly and effectively and to meet its two overarching strategic goals—to reduce the number of people living in extreme poverty and to boost shared prosperity.

The World Bank Group also continues to advance other reforms to promote inclusiveness, innovation, efficiency, effectiveness, and accountability. It is expanding cooperation with the United Nations, the International Monetary Fund, other multilateral development banks, donor agencies, and civil society organizations. If the Bank Group is to respond effectively to the international economic realities of the 21st century, the reform efforts—including recognizing the expanding role and responsibility of stakeholders and increasing the voice and participation of developing countries—must maintain momentum on all fronts.

Increasing Voice and Participation

The World Bank Group is reforming to support greater representation of developing and transition countries in the institution, with an additional Board seat for Sub-Saharan Africa and an increase in the voting power of developing countries to at least 50 percent over time.

Promoting Accountability and Good Governance

Governance and anticorruption are now key lements in Bank Group operations across sectors and countries.

Improving Risk Management

A major effort is under way to reform the Bank Group's lending model so that it responds better to borrowers' needs and a changing global environment. The new approach calls for more focus on results and risks and for streamlined processing of low-risk operations, while paying more attention to supervision and higher-risk investments.

Reviewing Internal Governance

The "Review of Internal Governance" report sets out proposals for strengthening World Bank Group governance and overall effectiveness, including voice and participation, and for improving its responsiveness and adaptability to members' needs.

Development Committee
http://tinyurl.com/WBG035

Disclosure of Information Policy Paper
http://tinyurl.com/WBG034

Governance and Public Sector Management
http://tinyurl.com/WBG036

Organizational Chart
http://tinyurl.com/WBG031

Review of Internal Governance
http://tinyurl.com/WBG037

The Bank's Policy on Information Disclosure
http://tinyurl.com/WBG033

World Bank Group Senior Managers
http://www.worldbank.org/en/about/leadership/managers

World Bank Reform
http://tinyurl.com/WBG032

Regional Chief Economists Regional Chief Economists are the principal economic advisers to the Regional Vice Presidents (with accountability for the quality and relevance of regional economic and strategic work, and analytical and advisory services).

The Regional Chief Economists' duties include but are not limited to:

- Leading and inspiring the World Bank Group's economic research agenda, including through interacting with academic and policy communities inside the institution, in client countries, and internationally; liaising with the economic units of other international and bilateral agencies; and acting as the Bank's spokesperson for economic analysis

- Ensuring that the analytic and advisory activities portfolio of their region is strategic and reflects the latest and cutting-edge economic research findings from inside and outside the Bank, Group working with sector and country departments

- Leading a program of regional studies and regularly updating the regional management team and the Bank Group's governors on economic developments in the region

- Participating in and contributing to the discussions in the monthly Chief Economist Council meetings

Regional Vice Presidencies The World Bank has six Regional Vice Presidencies: Africa, East Asia and Pacific, Europe and Central Asia, Latin America and the Caribbean, the Middle East and North Africa, and South Asia.

Reimbursable Advisory Services In response to specific requests, the World Bank provides a variety of reimbursable advisory services (RAS) to clients beyond the analytic and advisory services that it can fund through its administrative budget or relevant trust funds. Typically, RAS engagements are provided in addition to other Word Bank Group activities; however, for nonborrowing member clients, RAS may be the single instrument through which the Bank Group provides services.

As a global cooperative, the World Bank brings international expertise and technical depth to bear through RAS engagements. As a long-term development partner, the World Bank Group goes beyond the standard contractual agreements offered by the private sector.

⮑ http://tinyurl.com/WBG038

Remittances Around the world, the money that migrants send home—remittances—is more than twice as large as foreign aid. Remittances to developing countries were estimated at $404 billion in 2013, up 3.5 percent compared with 2012. Growth in remittance flows to developing countries is expected to accelerate to an annual average of 8.4 percent over the next three years, raising flows to $436 billion in 2014 and $516 billion in 2016.

Recognizing the close links between remittances and development, the World Bank Group (WBG) is deepening its engagement on this broad agenda, including through the following activities:

• *Mobilizing diaspora financial resources for development.* The Bank Group is supporting client efforts to develop financing instruments for leveraging migration and remittances for national development purposes.

• *Improving data collection.* The Bank Group is working with statistics-gathering agencies to strengthen the collection of data on migration and remittance flows. The WBG publishes a comprehensive dataset on annual remittances data (inflows and outflows), monthly remittances data on selected countries, and estimates of bilateral migration and medical "brain drain" for over 200 countries.

• *Strengthening the links between remittances and financial inclusion.* The Bank Group is supporting efforts to enhance the integrity of money transfer systems and realize the potential of regular remittance flows to improve access to wider financial services for migrants and remittance recipients.

• *Measuring the global average cost of remittances.* Through the Remittance Prices Worldwide database, the WBG provides a tool for monitoring progress toward the G-20's 5x5 objective (that is, reducing the cost of remittances by five percentage points). The WBG chairs the Global Remittances Working Group, which was formed in 2008 at the request of G-8 countries to coordinate global activities on remittances.

• *Facilitating a reduction in the cost of making remittances.* The Bank Group is working to create an enabling environment for the reduction of remittance prices by helping to improve the infrastructure for domestic and cross-border payments, remove legal barriers to the development of sound remittance markets, and foster market competition.

⮑ http://tinyurl.com/WBG039

Replenishment IDA is funded largely by contributions from the governments of its richer member countries. Additional funds come from IBRD's and IFC's income and from borrowers' repayments of earlier IDA credits.

Partners meet every three years to replenish IDA funds and review IDA's policies. The most recent replenishment of IDA's resources, the 17th (IDA17), was finalized in December 2013, resulting in a record replenishment size of special drawing rights (SDR) 34.6 billion ($52.1 billion) to finance projects over the three-year period from July 1, 2014, to June 30, 2017. To increase openness and help ensure that IDA's policies are responsive to country needs and circumstances, representatives of borrower countries from each IDA region have been invited to take part in the replenishment negotiations since IDA13.

In addition, since IDA13, background policy papers have been publicly released, as well as drafts of the replenishment reports before their finalization.

⮑ http://www.worldbank.org/ida/ida-replenishments.html

Research The World Bank's principal research unit is the Development Economics Vice Presidency (DEC). Unlike operations and network departments, which also undertake research, its mandate includes research that may be cross-country and across sectors and reach beyond specific regional units or sectors. DEC researchers provide cross-support to World Bank operations to help ensure that the Bank's policy advice is firmly grounded in current knowledge.

With nine programs, it produces the majority of the Bank's research and enjoys a high international profile. The work of DEC researchers appears in academic journals, the World Bank Policy Research Working Paper Series, books, blogs, and special publications such as the Policy Research Reports.

⮑ http://go.worldbank.org/Q5IAP9GCZ0

Results-Based Financing Results-based financing (RBF) is an approach that links financing to predetermined results, whereby success is measured by the quality and quantity of actual services that health facilities deliver to people and not as inputs such as medical equipment or supplies. Experience so far indicates that RBF approaches can help strengthen core health systems, making them more accountable and able to deliver greater value for money, by shifting the focus from inputs to results.

⮑ http://tinyurl.com/WBG040

Results Measurement A focus on results is fundamental to the World Bank Group's approach to delivering programs and policy advice with partners in low-income and middle-income countries alike. Through financial assistance and technical knowledge, the Bank Group aims to help people around the world build a better future for themselves, their families, and their country.

A Dynamic Framework for Capturing Results
Results frameworks have long existed in World Bank Group–supported development operations. They are continuously improved to better capture data on results and see what did and did not work and why. The World Bank Group continues to fine-tune its systems for gathering and processing development information:

- The Corporate Scorecard is designed to provide a snapshot of the Bank's overall performance in a given fiscal year in the context of development results. It uses an integrated results and performance framework, which is organized in a three-tier structure that groups indicators along the results chain. It presents a high-level view and is not intended to provide country- or activity-level information. (*See* separate entry on the Corporate Scorecard.)

- All Bank Country Assistance Strategies now include key measurable assessments, allowing governments, donors, and stakeholders to collaborate more effectively in identifying and achieving common goals for development.

- All Bank projects rely on monitoring and results frameworks to guide implementation, make mid-course corrections as needed, measure impact, and cull lessons learned.

- IDA uses its Results Measurement System to identify and track development results in countries where policies and operations are being supported and to evaluate its performance in the process. Its system is designed to strengthen the focus of its activities on development outcomes and keep donors aware of IDA's effectiveness. The system measures results on four levels: IDA countries' progress, IDA-supported development results, IDA's operational effectiveness, and IDA's organizational effectiveness.

Special Initiatives

Several important initiatives at the corporate and project level are under way to strengthen the Bank Group's ability to monitor and measure the quantitative and qualitative results of IDA and IBRD support:

- *Core sector indicators.* Since July 2009, the Bank has strengthened how it measures results by introducing the standardized core sector indicators in 26 sectors and themes, along with project beneficiaries and private capital mobilized: education; health; roads; water supply; micro and small and medium enterprises; access to urban services; information and communication technology; biodiversity; conflict prevention and postconflict reconstruction; social inclusion; participation and civic engagement; social protection; irrigation and drainage; agriculture extension and research; thermal power generation; hydropower; other renewable energy; transmission and distribution of electricity; sanitation; wastewater collection and transportation; wastewater treatment and disposal; forestry; land administration and management; pollution management and environmental health; energy efficiency in heat and power; and oil and gas.

  Core sector indicators for additional sectors and themes are under discussion, and the scope of the exercise is being expanded to include the recipient-executed trust funds as well. This newly aggregated information supplements the more detailed project, country, and sector results data previously available. To facilitate the capture of these key data, Bank systems have been updated to allow teams to add relevant core sector indicators to the project results frameworks. These

form the basis for the World Bank and the World Bank Group Scorecards.

- *IDA at work and World Bank at work.* Quantitative data—enhanced by the core sector indicators—is complemented by qualitative overviews at the country, sector, thematic, and project levels. These qualitative reviews illustrate how IDA and IBRD are supporting government development programs that make a difference, whether the effort is bolstering governance to end extreme poverty in Bangladesh, boosting agricultural competitiveness in Burkina Faso, equipping the judicial system to promote justice in Ethiopia, or bringing clean water to communities in Rwanda.

- *Implementation completion reports.* When a project is completed and closed at the end of the loan disbursement period (a process that can take anywhere from 1 to 10 years), the World Bank and the borrower government document the results achieved, the problems encountered, the lessons learned, and the knowledge gained from carrying out the project. A World Bank operations team compiles this information and data in an Implementation Completion and Results Report, using input from the implementing government agency, cofinanciers, and other partners and stakeholders. The report is independently evaluated by the Independent Evaluation Group and is submitted to the Bank's Board of Executive Directors for information purposes. The knowledge gained from this results measurement process is intended to benefit similar projects in the future.

- *DIME.* Development Impact Evaluation is a global program hosted in the World Bank's Development Research Group. Its purpose is to increase the use of impact evaluation in the design and implementation of public policy and to increase the institutional capacity and motivation for evidence-based policy.

To ensure lasting gains, the World Bank Group helps partner countries develop the capacity to build their own statistical, information, and learning systems and design and implement effective programs. Financing and training are provided—for example, through the donor-supported Statistics for Results Facility—to upgrade government monitoring and evaluation systems and skills. This support is not limited to agencies that implement Bank-supported projects but also includes offices responsible for national planning and budgets. These important new efforts are strengthening the World Bank's ability to monitor and measure the size and quality of benefits flowing from World Bank Group support and to sustain achievements by building the capacity of partner countries through self-assessments in managing for development results.

IFC and Results Measurement

In addition to the Corporate Scorecard mentioned previously, IFC has several other tools for measuring the results of its development work:

- **DOTS.** IFC's Development Outcome Tracking System measures the development results of the Corporation's investment and advisory services. Measuring, monitoring, and evaluating IFC's results and those of its clients help assess the effectiveness of the Corporation's operations and improve them. It also helps IFC report on its performance in ways that reinforce public trust and expand its "license to operate." IFC clients thrive, for example, when they go beyond achieving above-market returns for shareholders and have a measurable development impact in their communities. IFC measures results because it benefits clients' businesses and benefits IFC as well.

- **IFC Development Goals.** The IFC Development Goals (IDGs) are corporate-level development goals that IFC began testing in 2011. They were inspired by the Millennium Development Goals as a way to better integrate IFC's results measurement with strategy. The IDGs are high-level targets for the incremental reach the Corporation aims to achieve through its investments and advisory services. IFC intends to use the IDGs to drive implementation of strategy and influence operational decision making, alongside volume targets.

- **New evaluation strategy.** The new evaluation strategy complements the work of the Independent Evaluation Group (IEG), which reports directly to the Board of Directors and is charged with providing its own assessments and lessons of experience. IEG's evaluations incorporate findings from IFC's own monitoring and evaluations. IFC's evaluation staff works closely with IEG to discuss work programs, share knowledge, and align efforts whenever possible.

- **Nonfinancial assurance.** IFC commissioned Ernst & Young to provide IFC's management with external assurance and commentary on certain nonfinancial aspects of its 2014 Annual Report, specifically the information on development effectiveness and economic, social, and environmental sustainability. IFC prepared the Annual Report and is solely responsible for its content.

MIGA and Results Measurement

MIGA, like the World Bank and IFC, is subject to periodic reviews by the Independent Evaluation Group, and its results are incorporated into the Corporate Scorecard.

MIGA's Development Effectiveness Indicator System (DEIS) measures and tracks the development impact of projects that the agency insures. Through this system, MIGA measures a common set of indicators across all projects: investment supported, direct employment, training expenditures, locally procured goods, and community investments. It also measures sector-specific indicators. In addition, the DEIS puts into place a process to measure projects' actual development outcomes three years from the time of contract signing. Starting in fiscal year 2014, MIGA began reporting these data for the cohort of active guarantees that it signed in fiscal 2011.

Corporate Scorecard
⮂ http://tinyurl.com/WBG042

Development Impact Evaluation
⮂ http://tinyurl.com/WBG043

DOTS
⮂ http://tinyurl.com/WBG044

Focus on Results
⮂ http://tinyurl.com/WBG041

IFC Development Goals
⮂ http://tinyurl.com/WBG045

Independent Evaluation Group
⮂ http://ieg.worldbankgroup.org

MIGA Development Results
⮂ http://www.miga.org/development-results

Nonfinancial Assurance
⮂ http://tinyurl.com/WBG046

Risk Management
World Bank and Risk Management
IBRD offers innovative risk management products and a choice of lending terms combining competitively priced, flexible financing with effective risk management tools and world-class technical expertise.

Today's IBRD loans are designed so clients can select currencies and fixed or floating interest rates (as well as customized repayment schedules) to mitigate financial risks at project inception and throughout the life of the loan. Similarly, public entities can customize loan terms for non-revenue generating projects or apply stand-alone hedging transactions to their portfolios. These options can reduce future vulnerabilities to foreign exchange risk and interest rate volatility. Treasury specialists can also assist clients to develop a public debt management strategy as a framework for using financial products and hedging strategies to manage debt and reduce risks.

Private sector financing for development projects can be difficult to attract, but World Bank guarantees can mitigate a range of risks to facilitate private investment and commercial borrowing by governments and public sector entities.

Natural disasters and adverse weather conditions can substantially affect public finances, especially in countries that have limited access to funding or market tools designed to manage these risks. The World Bank is working with middle and low income countries to develop customized, proactive risk-financing strategies, from immediate budget support and insurance-linked securities to sovereign budget and agriculture insurance programs. As recent examples:

• IBRD executed the largest weather and oil price derivative the market has ever seen to ensure the hydroelectric power company of Uruguay against drought and high oil prices.

• IBRD created a new IBRD Capital-at-Risk Notes Program allowing the Bank, as well as client countries, to hedge a large variety of risks, including catastrophe risk. The first transaction under this new program, a catastrophe bond completed in June 2014, enabled the 16 members of the Caribbean Catastrophe Risk Insurance Facility to obtain coverage for earthquake and tropical cyclones risk.

IFC and Risk Management

The objective of IFC's Global Risk Management advisory program is to strengthen financial institutions' risk management capacity and frameworks, loan portfolio monitoring, and nonperforming loan (NPL) management and workout capacity, while supporting the development of emerging distressed asset markets.

Although initially launched in response to the 2008 global financial crisis to address risk management and NPL challenges in emerging markets, the program now works with client financial institutions to help them implement better risk management systems and processes to increase their resilience to future crises. Through longer-term engagements and in-depth institutional building efforts, the program focuses on governance, market risk, liquidity risk, credit risk, operational risk, asset liability management, and capital adequacy.

At the sector level, IFC disseminates best practices and raises awareness of risk management issues. Since early 2009, IFC has held 150 risk management workshops and conferences for the financial section in 36 countries across all its regions, including Eastern Europe and Central Asia, Sub-Saharan Africa, South Asia, East Asia and Pacific, Latin America and the Caribbean, and the Middle East and North Africa.

As part of its knowledge management agenda, the program develops risk management tools to identify issues and support capacity-building work with client financial institutions. The program also supports the development of emerging distressed asset markets, especially in Europe and Central Asia, which is part of a wider sector-level initiative closely coordinated with the World Bank.

For more information on risk management, read the *World Development Report 2014: Risk and Opportunity Managing Risk for Development.*
➲ http://tinyurl.com/WBG073

Rural Development (*See* Agriculture; Social, Urban, Rural, and Resilience.)

S

Safeguards The World Bank's environmental and social safeguard policies are a cornerstone of its support to sustainable poverty reduction. The objective of these policies is to prevent and mitigate undue harm to people and their environment in the development process. These policies provide guidelines for Bank and borrower staffs in the identification, preparation, and implementation of programs and projects.

The effectiveness and development impact of projects and programs supported by the Bank has substantially increased as a result of attention to these policies. Safeguard policies have often provided a platform for the participation of stakeholders in project design and have been an important instrument for building ownership among local populations.

Bank projects and activities are governed by operational policies, which are designed to ensure that the projects are economically, financially, socially, and environmentally sound. The Bank's Operational Manual spells them out and provides guidance on how to comply with them ("Bank Procedures" and "Good Practices").

The Inspection Panel helps ensure compliance with Bank policies. The panel is an independent body to which individuals and communities can turn if they believe that their rights or interests have been or could be directly harmed by a Bank-financed project. The panel includes senior compliance experts who report directly to the Board of Executive Directors.

Environmental Safeguards

Environmental assessment is one of the 10 environmental, social, and legal safeguard policies of the World Bank. Environmental assessment helps identify, avoid, and mitigate the potential negative environmental impacts associated with Bank lending operations. The purpose of environmental assessment is to improve decision making, and to ensure that the project options under consideration are sound and sustainable and that potentially affected people have been properly consulted.

The Environmental Assessment Policy is considered the umbrella policy for the Bank's environmental safeguard policies, which include natural habitats, forests, pest management, physical cultural resources, and safety of dams. The details of this policy are described in the World Bank's Operational Manual.

Social Safeguards

Social safeguard policies on involuntary resettlement and indigenous peoples aim to promote inclusion of the most vulnerable groups, to protect indigenous peoples and those who may be involuntarily displaced, and to mitigate the effects of resettlement on those who have been involuntarily displaced. These two policies can be used as entry points for addressing the social issues involved in investment lending operations and to mitigate and compensate adverse impacts on indigenous peoples and persons displaced by development projects. The details of both policies are described in the World Bank's Operational Manual.

Safeguards Review

Evolution of policies. The current safeguard policies have served the Bank, its client countries, and the development community well over the past two decades. In the spirit of continuous improvement in the face of changing contexts and circumstances, the Bank is evolving these crucial policies to better address new development demands and challenges and to better meet the varied needs of borrowers that range from middle-income countries with well-developed institutions and capacities to low-income countries with weaker governance and institutions, and to fragile and conflict-affected situations where more tailored and coordinated interventions are required. The safeguards review and update is part of a larger modernization effort within the Bank that includes separate but complementary reviews of investment lending, to which the safeguard policies are applied, as well as operational procurement policies.

In 2012, the World Bank launched a multiphased process to review and update its environmental and social safeguard policies. Currently, the framework is being drafted, a process that will continue until early 2015.

The multistage review, supported by several periods of global consultations with stakeholders, is being undertaken in response to the need to better address environmental and social issues that countries face today, to deliver better environmental and social outcomes in the projects and programs the Bank supports, to ensure treatment and

coverage of environmental and social impacts and risks, to strengthen the ability to monitor and supervise actual impacts on people and the environment, to better meet the varied needs of borrowers, and to help strengthen country frameworks and institutions to deliver sustainable results on the ground.

IFC, MIGA, and Safeguards

As institutions engaged in private sector development, IFC and MIGA have adopted safeguards and standards applicable to the private sector. IFC's Sustainability Framework includes its Policy on Environmental and Social Sustainability, Performance Standards, and Access to Information Policy. MIGA also has a set of Performance Standards and a Policy on Environmental and Social Sustainability tailored to its specialized type of private sector investment. Both institutions adhere to the World Bank Group's Environmental, Health, and Safety Guidelines.

IFC's Environmental, Health, and Safety Guidelines

⟳ http://www.ifc.org/ehsguidelines

IFC's Performance Standards

⟳ http://tinyurl.com/WBG050

IFC's Sustainability Framework

⟳ http://tinyurl.com/WBG051

Inspection Panel

⟳ http://ewebapps.worldbank.org/apps/ip/Pages/Home.aspx

MIGA's Performance Standards

⟳ http://www.miga.org/projects/index.cfm?stid=1828

MIGA's Policy on Environmental and Social Sustainability

⟳ http://tinyurl.com/WBG052

World Bank Environmental and Social Safeguards

⟳ http://go.worldbank.org/WTA1ODE7T0

World Bank Operational Manual
⤳ http://tinyurl.com/WBG069

Safety Nets Recent food, fuel, and financial crises have amplified the importance of strong social safety nets to reduce poverty and vulnerability. Safety nets help poor people by boosting their incomes, increasing school attendance, improving nutrition, encouraging the use of health services, and providing job opportunities.

The World Bank Group supports sustainable and affordable safety net programs that protect families from shocks, help ensure that children grow up healthy and well-fed and stay in school, empower women and girls, and create jobs. Building sustainable and affordable safety nets in each developing country is a key component of the Bank Group's Social Protection and Labor Strategy 2012–2022, which is helping countries move from fragmented programs to affordable social protection systems that enable individuals to manage risk and improve resilience by investing in human capital and improving people's ability to access jobs.

The Bank Group works with countries to develop country-tailored tools and approaches; invest in knowledge, data, and analysis; and provide "on-time" policy advice and continuous technical assistance and capacity building. The Bank Group supports a diverse set of safety net interventions, ranging from cash transfers to labor-intensive public works to school feeding programs. In low-income countries, the Rapid Social Response program is particularly instrumental in addressing capacity constraints, developing effective delivery systems and communicating results.

The average annual World Bank Group commitment for social safety nets during fiscal 2007 to 2013 was $1.72 billion, a threefold increase from $567 million per year during fiscal 2002 to 2007. From fiscal 2007 to 2013, $12 billion in 273 lending operations across 93 countries were approved. About 21 percent of this financing was allocated for the world's poorest countries through IDA. Knowledge services comprise a critical component of supporting the safety nets agenda, especially in low-capacity contexts where implementation capacity is weak.

Recent trends in safety nets practice include:

- *Increase focus on low-income IDA countries.* Among the 93 countries represented in the portfolio, 42 had no or limited exposure to Bank Group safety nets engagement prior to fiscal 2007. Africa was the region with the highest number of countries newly introduced to the portfolio.

- *Increase in lending for systems-based approaches.* In fiscal 2013 alone, 26 projects with a social protections system-building component were approved. Prior to fiscal 2013, only a handful of systems-building projects existed.

⤳ http://www.worldbank.org/en/topic/safetynets

SAR (*See* South Asia.)

Scholarships World Bank scholarships and fellowship programs contribute to the Bank's mission of forging new dynamic approaches to capacity development and knowledge sharing in the developing world. They are also an important component of the Bank Group's efforts to promote economic development and shared prosperity through investing in education and developing human resources globally.

- *Joint Japan–World Bank Graduate Scholarship Program.* The Joint Japan–World Bank Graduate Scholarship Program is for graduate studies in subjects related to economic development. Each year, the program awards scholarships to individuals from World Bank member countries to undertake graduate studies at universities throughout member countries of the Bank. Scholars are required to return to their home countries on completion of their study programs and apply their enhanced knowledge and skills to contribute to the development process in their respective regions and communities.

- ***Japan Indonesia Presidential Scholarship Program.*** Funded by a grant from the government of Japan, the Japan Indonesia Presidential Scholarship Program supports PhD studies in an academic field of study covered by 10 Indonesian Centers of Excellence participating in the program. Each of the newly established Centers of Excellence is located at a leading higher education institution in the country with a demonstrated track record in the pursuit of excellence. The goal of the program is to promote excellence in research in these centers to support the Ministry of National Education in its mission to improve the quality of higher education and research in the country.

⟳ www.worldbank.org/wbi/scholarships

Small and Medium Enterprises Small and medium enterprises (SMEs) are an essential focus of IFC's work. As engines of job creation and growth in emerging markets, they are central to the larger equation of development. Supporting them is one of the most significant ways in which IFC promotes economic growth where it is most needed.

IFC provides investment and advisory services to help these businesses through their entire life cycle— from inception to growth and maturity. It assists in introducing more business-friendly regulatory, tax, and trade policies; building management skills; and supporting access to finance and markets. This integrated approach brings innovative solutions to some of the SME world's most difficult problems, fitting within IFC's larger efforts to promote sustainable and inclusive private sector development in the poorest countries. Since 2009, IFC has worked closely with the G-20 in scaling up successful models of SME finance, part of a larger agenda of improving access to financial services for the poor.

Small States More than a quarter of World Bank members are countries with a population under 1.5 million. These countries vary greatly in their level of development and in the size of their economies. They are also spread out geographically, with most of them clustered in the Caribbean, the Pacific, and Africa. Despite their diversity, these countries share a common set of development challenges: vulnerability to economic shocks and income volatility, limited capacity, difficulty accessing external capital, limited competitiveness, and susceptibility to natural disasters and climate change.

The World Bank tailors its assistance to the unique challenges of small states, drawing on an array of financial products and knowledge and learning services. Tailored country and regional programs help small states assess social and structural sources of vulnerability, address underlying policy and institutional weaknesses, and respond to and manage shocks. In addition, the World Bank works closely with small states to generate and share in-depth analysis on specific local challenges.

⟳ http://www.worldbank.org/en/country/smallstates/overview

Social Development (*See also* Social, Urban, Rural, and Resilience.) The World Bank supports social development by listening to poor people and promoting their voices in the development process; understanding and addressing their needs, priorities, and aspirations; and building formal and informal institutions. The Bank takes a bottom-up approach to development that brings voices of the underprivileged into the otherwise top-down development process. To promote social development, the Bank makes substantial evidence-based policy and program contributions through:

- Undertaking better and timelier social and political risk analysis, including poverty and social impact analyses

- Mainstreaming fragility and conflict sensitivity and responsiveness into analysis and operations

- Building a greater understanding of the resilience of communities and institutions to a range of natural and manmade shocks, whether they are economic crises, climate change, natural disasters, or violent conflict

- Promoting gender-differentiated social and economic empowerment programming for youth

- Strengthening links between citizens and their government representatives and promoting more accountable government structures

- Empowering communities in rural and urban settings by transferring the control over development decisions and resources for poverty reduction to the communities through a community-driven development approach

- Enhancing positive impacts, mitigating negative impacts, and managing social and political risks, including compliance with the Bank's social safeguard policies on indigenous peoples and involuntary resettlement

- Mainstreaming gender concerns and ensuring that operations are gender informed

⮎ http://tinyurl.com/WBG053

Social Media The World Bank Group shares live updates and interacts with audiences through events and various social media platforms including Facebook, Twitter, Tumblr, Instagram, LinkedIn, Google Plus, RSS, YouTube, Flickr, blogs, and mobile apps.

Social Protection and Labor (*See also* Global Practices.) One of 14 new World Bank Group Global Practices, Social Protection and Labor delivers operational approaches and evidence-based solutions to help individuals and families manage risk, cope with chronic or transitional poverty, and access better livelihoods.

World Bank Group and Social Protection and Labor
In a world filled with risk and potential, social protection and labor systems help people and families find jobs, improve productivity, cope with shocks, and invest in the health and education of their children as well as in protection for the aging population. Social protection programs, which comprise both social assistance (such as cash transfers, school feeding, targeted food assistance, and subsidies) and social insurance (such as old-age, survivorship, disability pensions, and unemployment insurance), are a powerful tool for reducing poverty and economic vulnerability. They can have a direct, positive impact on poor families by building human capital through better health, more schooling, and greater skills.

Jobs, too, are critical for reducing poverty and promoting prosperity. All countries, regardless of income, face challenges in creating and sustaining adequate job opportunities for their citizens. According to the World Development Report 2013: Jobs, advancing the global jobs agenda will require the right investment in people—the right skills for securing good jobs, the right protections against risks arising from volatile economies, and the right mechanisms for making smooth and safe transitions from one job to another. Reversing youth unemployment and underemployment trends is also crucial to boosting shared prosperity.

World Bank and Social Protection and Labor
The World Bank supports social protection and labor programs in developing countries as a central part of its mission to reduce poverty through sustainable and inclusive growth. The Bank has almost doubled its social protection and labor lending in the past few years to help countries respond to the food, fuel, and financial crises—from an

STAYING CONNECTED TO THE WORLD BANK GROUP

WORLD BANK

FACEBOOK

Explore, debate, and share the latest news.
➲ **https://facebook.com/worldbank**

TWITTER

Get real-time updates and interact with through Twitter feeds.
➲ **https://twitter.com/WorldBank**

TUMBLER

Discover data visualization from around the globe on development topics.
➲ **http://worldbank.tumblr.com**

INSTAGRAM

Follow for photo updates on the fight against poverty.
➲ **http://instagram.com/worldbank**

LINKEDIN

Stay updated and comment on the latest research, news, and career opportunities.
➲ **http://www.linkedin.com/company /the-world-bank**

GOOGLE PLUS

Discuss news and share multimedia in our circle and yours.
➲ **https://plus.google.com/+WorldBank**

RSS

Sign up for important global development issues with World Bank RSS feeds.
➲ **http://www.worldbank.org/rss**

YOUTUBE

Explore for the latest videos from around the world.
➲ **http://www.youtube.com/WorldBank**

FLICKR

Access our photostream, featuring Creative Commons licenses for sharing photos.
➲ **http://www.flickr.com/WorldBank**

MOBILE APPS

Download free mobile apps featuring access to economic data and the latest research.
➲ **http://apps.worldbank.org**

PODCASTS

Stay updated and comment on the latest research, news, and career opportunities.
➲ **https://soundcloud.com/worldbank**

(continued next page)

IFC

FACEBOOK

Explore, debate, and share the latest news.
➲ https://www.facebook.com/IFCwbg

TWITTER

Get real-time updates and interact with through Twitter feeds.
➲ https://twitter.com/IFC_org

YOUTUBE

Explore for the latest videos from around the world.
➲ http://www.youtube.com/user /IFCvideocasts

LINKEDIN

Stay updated and comment on the latest research, news, and career opportunities.
➲ http://www.linkedin.com/company /ifc---international-finance-corporation

MIGA

TWITTER

Get real-time updates and interact with through Twitter feeds.
➲ https://twitter.com/migaworldbank

YOUTUBE

Explore for the latest videos from around the world.
➲ http://www.youtube.com/user /MIGAWorldBank

LINKEDIN

Stay updated and comment on the latest research, news, and career opportunities.
➲ http://www.linkedin.com/company /mulitlateral-investment-guarantee -agency-miga

RSS

Sign up for important global development issues with World Bank RSS feeds.
➲ http://www.miga.org/news/rssfeeds.cfm

BLOGS

Read blogs on MIGA's current events.
➲ http://blogs.worldbank.org/miga

The Emergency Project to Assist Jordan Partially Mitigate Impact of Syrian Conflict provides supplies of vaccines and medicines for the growing population and ensures that Jordanians have affordable access to basic commodities such as bread and cooking gas. © World Bank / John Donelly (photographer). Permission required for reuse.

annual average of $1.6 billion in 1998–2008, to an annual average of $2.4 billion for 2012–13. Many social protection and labor programs are fragmented and lack harmonization, hampering their effectiveness.

The main objective of the World Bank's 10-year social protection and labor strategy is to help countries move from fragmented approaches to harmonized systems. It focuses on making these systems more inclusive of the vulnerable and more attuned to building people's capacities and improving the productivity of their work. The strategy lays out ways to deepen the Bank's involvement, capacity, knowledge, and impact in social protection and labor.

Rapid Social Response Program. The Rapid Social Response program provides catalytic resources

in relatively small amounts to help low-income countries build social protection and labor systems, so that they are prepared for future crises.

Open Data for Social Protection and Labor. In 2012, the Bank launched the Atlas of Social Protection with Indicators on Resilience and Equity (ASPIRE) as the first global compilation of data from household surveys documenting social protection. It provides a worldwide snapshot of social protection coverage, targeting, and impact on well-being by identifying countries' social protection programs, grouping them into categories, harmonizing core indicators, and detailing people's well-being. ASPIRE is currently being expanded to include indicators on social protection and labor program design and performance based on administrative records on social insurance, social assistance, and labor market programs. The Bank also offers cross-country data for mandatory pension systems around the world.

Youth Employment Inventory. In collaboration with the German Agency for International Cooperation, the Inter-American Development Bank, the Youth Employment Network, and the International Labour Organization, the Bank has also developed a Youth Employment Inventory that provides comparative information on more than 500 youth employment programs in some 90 countries.

IFC, MIGA, and Social Protection and Labor
Projects undertaken by IFC and MIGA create jobs in the private sector; both institutions promote social protections and labor best practices in their client companies, as spelled out in their performance standards.

Social, Urban, Rural, and Resilience (*See also* Global Practices.) One of 14 new World Bank Group Global Practices, Social, Urban, Rural, and Resilience helps developing countries build cities, villages, and communities that are inclusive, resilient, and sustainable.

World Bank Group and Social, Urban, Rural, and Resilience

Key statistics highlight development priorities for this Global Practice, which have strong links to ending extreme poverty, promoting shared prosperity, and ensuring sustainability:

- Seventy percent of the world's poor live in rural areas. Past rural development efforts have not been enough to significantly reduce the vulnerability and marginalization of the rural poor.

- Although 80 percent of gross national income is generated in urban areas, social exclusion and inequality are growing; 1 billion people live in slums today, and poverty is urbanizing. Another 1billion people are expected to move to cities by 2030.

- One and a half billion people live in countries affected by repeated cycles of violence.

- The number of people affected by natural disasters tripled to 2 billion in the past decade. Since 1980, low-income countries have accounted for only 9 percent of the disaster events but 48 percent of fatalities.

- The growth path of urban and rural areas has local and global implications for sustainability and climate change.

- Increasing the resilience of cities, villages, and communities is critical because the burden of disasters, conflict, crime, and violence falls disproportionately on the poor and vulnerable.

- Marginalized and vulnerable segments of society need to have a say in their development path.

To address these challenges, the Social, Urban, Rural, and Resilience Global Practice will work across the World Bank Group and with partners in social inclusion and sustainability; mainstreaming resilience in all dimensions of development; territorial and rural development; and urban planning, services, and institutions.

World Bank and Social, Urban, Rural, and Resilience

The World Bank's strategy for social development is to "put people first," aiming to replace top-down development processes with a bottom-up approach that brings voices of the poor and underprivileged into analysis and operations by mainstreaming fragility and conflict-sensitivity and responsiveness; building a greater understanding of the resilience of communities and institutions to a range of natural and manmade shocks; promoting gender-differentiated social and economic empowerment programming for youth; strengthening links between citizens and their government representatives; and promoting more accountable government structures.

The Bank's urban strategy aims to ensure that rapid urbanization is managed well for resilient, inclusive, and sustainable growth that is grounded in an urbanization policy framework that distills lessons from the ongoing Urbanization Reviews program. The Bank's urban agenda places greater emphasis on addressing risks from climate change and improving services for the urban poor.

Over the past 10 years, the World Bank has emerged as the global leader in disaster risk management by supporting client countries in assessments of exposure to hazards and addressing disaster risks. The Bank provides technical and financial support for risk assessments, risk reduction, preparedness, financial protection, and resilient recovery and reconstruction, working with the Global Facility for Disaster Reduction and Recovery.

In rural development, the World Bank focuses on land governance, public service delivery, rural financial markets, microfinance, community infrastructure, and enhancing the productive capacity of the poor.

The Global Partnership for Output-Based Aid, funded by international donors and administered by

The Third Public Works Project provides basic infrastructure and temporary employment in the Republic of Yemen. Primary health services have been extended to more than 537,000 people, 256,000 new students have been able to enroll in school, 209,000 people have improved access to water, 503,000 people have access to an all-season road, and 5,400 individuals have graduated from 10 newly built vocational training centers. © World Bank / Abdullah Al-Khawlani (photographer). Permission required for reuse.

the World Bank, funds, designs, tests, and documents output-based aid approaches to ensure that the very poor are connected to basic services, including water, electricity, and sanitation.

IFC, MIGA, and Social, Urban, Rural, and Resilience

IFC's and MIGA's work in the private sector complements the work of the World Bank in supporting sustainable social, urban, rural, and resilient development.

Community-Driven Development

⟳ http://www.worldbank.org/en/topic/communitydriven development

Disaster Risk Managment

⟳ http://www.worldbank.org/en/topic/disasterriskmanagement

Indigenous Peoples

⟳ http://www.worldbank.org/en/topic/indigenouspeoples

Social Development

⟳ http://www.worldbank.org/en/topic/socialdevelopment

Urban Development

⟳ http://www.worldbank.org/en/topic/urbandevelopment

Social Sustainability (*See also* Environmental and Social Sustainability.) Social sustainability means improving responsiveness to local communities; ensuring that responses are tailored to specific country contexts; and promoting social inclusion, cohesion, and accountability. Social sustainability takes the larger worldview into consideration in relation to communities, culture, and globalization. At the project level, this entails undertaking adequate social analysis and assessment, which in turn allows for adequate identification of social opportunities, as well as adequate mitigation of social impacts and risks, including through the proper application of the Bank's social safeguard policies.

The Social Sustainability and Safeguards Cluster of the Social Development Department (SDV) aims to improve the operational dimensions of social sustainability and help task teams enhance social opportunities and mitigate social risks, including but not limited to those covered by the Bank's social safeguard policies on involuntary resettlement and indigenous peoples. This effort promotes the social inclusion of the most vulnerable groups, cohesion, and accountability, which are key to empowering people and overcoming poverty.

The Bank focuses on four important areas of social sustainability:

• Supporting the development of corporate policies on social sustainability and safeguards

• Building staff skills in both broad social analysis and social safeguards through training and mentoring programs

• Providing strategic operational support to regions and Bank Group staff on the application of the principles of social sustainability and safeguards in specific sectors, countries, and institutional contexts

• Producing knowledge and practical guidelines to support social sustainability and safeguards, including social safeguard policy reviews, guidance notes, toolkits, and case studies

South Asia
World Bank Group in South Asia

South Asia has experienced a long period of robust economic growth, averaging 6 percent a year over the past 20 years. This strong growth has translated into declining poverty and impressive improvements in human development. The percentage of people living on less than $1.25 a day fell in South Asia from 61 percent to 36 percent between 1981 and 2008. The proportion of poor is lower now in South Asia than any time since 1981.

Still, the South Asia region is home to many of the developing world's poor. According to the World Bank's most recent estimates, about 571 million people in the region survive on less than $1.25 a day, and they make up more than 44 percent of the developing world's poor.

South Asia has a young population and one of the lowest female participation rates in the labor force. As a result of this "demographic dividend," more workers will be entering the labor force in the future, and the region will need to add between 1 and 1.2 million additional jobs every month for the next 20 years to accommodate them. Creating jobs for these new workers will contribute to growth, equity, and peace in the region. It also provides a road map for accelerating growth and fostering human development.

SOUTH ASIA REGION SNAPSHOT

1,649.2 million	Total population
1.3 percent	Population growth
$1,437	Gross national income per capita
31.0 percent	Population living below $1.25 per day
67 years	Life expectancy at birth
61.4 percent	Adult (15+) literacy rate

This region includes the following countries:*

Afghanistan
Bangladesh
Bhutan
India
Maldives
Nepal
Pakistan
Sri Lanka

*Regions are defined for analytical and operational purposes and may differ from common geographic usage. Variances also exist across the five World Bank Group institutions.

Member Countries by WBG Institution
⟳ www.worldbank.org/en/about/leadership/members#1

World Bank in South Asia

The World Bank is a significant development partner in South Asia. The Bank approved $10.5 billion for the region for 42 projects in fiscal 2014. Support included $2.1 billion in IBRD loans and $8.5 billion in IDA commitments. The leading sectors were Energy and Mining ($2.4 billion); Transportation ($2.3 billion); and Education ($1.4 billion).

The Bank's Country Partnership Strategy for India (2013–17) aims to help India achieve its long-term vision of faster, more inclusive growth. As the first country strategy to set specific goals for reducing poverty and increasing prosperity for the poorest people, it significantly shifts support toward low-income and special-category states, where many of India's poor and disadvantaged live.

Strategy

Work in the South Asia region supports the Bank Group's overarching goals of reducing poverty and boosting shared prosperity. The strategy is based on five pillars:

- *Increasing employment and accelerating growth.* The World Bank and the entire World Bank Group are engaging with countries in the region to strengthen policies that are conducive to inclusive growth and that support access to opportunities for jobs and job success.

- *Enhancing human development and social welfare.* Building human capital by ensuring that the people of South Asia have access to education, health care, and social safety nets is key to this pillar of the strategy. A large share of the portfolio is results focused, linking financial support directly to the achievement of core milestones that improve service delivery. Education projects target raising school enrollment rates and ensuring the quality and equity of the training and education system. Health projects seek to increase the use of skilled birth attendants and ensure that pregnant women, adolescent girls, and children under age five receive basic nutrition services. Given the alarming levels of infant and child malnutrition, the Bank emphasizes policy dialogue, diagnostic studies, and start-up financing support in this area.

- *Strengthening governance and accountability.* The Bank is working in South Asia to help make governments more accountable and transparent by building the capacity of legislative bodies and supreme audit institutions into their budget oversight roles. It is also helping to implement e-procurement systems and better delivery of public services and to craft right-to-information regulations.

- *Reducing weather, disaster, and food vulnerability.* South Asia suffered more than any other region during previous food and fuel crises. To help the region withstand future food crises, the Bank is working with governments to provide more irrigation and drainage services and to reforest land that had been logged. It also is working to increase the region's resilience to extreme weather events, natural disasters, and climate change.

- *Enhancing regional cooperation.* Regional cooperation and integration are key strategic priorities for South Asia, as limited intraregional trade; poor air, road, and rail connectivity; and scant trade in energy impede growth in the region.

IFC in South Asia

Continued strong growth in South Asia offers the best prospect for poverty reduction, but it depends on expanding social infrastructure and improving environmental sustainability so that the benefits of growth are widely shared and the growth is sustainable.

South Asia receives the lowest amount of foreign direct investment as a proportion of gross national product of any region in the world. Growth is generated largely by domestic investment, fueled by rising savings rates. Recently, India's strong growth and relatively well-developed capital markets have attracted record inflows of portfolio capital and private equity.

To grow opportunities for the underserved, IFC has concentrated on low-income, rural, and fragile regions in South Asia, while building infrastructure and assisting public-private partnerships; facilitating renewable energy generation; promoting cleaner production, energy, and water efficiency; supporting agriculture; creating growth opportunities for small businesses; reforming the investment climate;

encouraging low-income housing; and making affordable health care accessible.

IFC is focusing its business development efforts on finding investment opportunities in frontier countries in the region and in frontier regions within India. Prospects for new investments in Bangladesh, Nepal, and Sri Lanka are improving rapidly.

Through strategic investments and advisory efforts in the region, IFC aims to promote inclusive growth, particularly in the low-income states of India and postconflict and frontier parts of the region; help address the impacts of climate change; and encourage global and regional integration, including facilitating investments from South Asia into Africa.

IFC's commitments in the region totaled nearly $1.9 billion, including more than $300 million mobilized from other investors. IFC is working to expand access to services and sustainable infrastructure and to boost regional integration, with a special focus on frontier regions.

In fiscal 2014, IFC's clients in South Asia cared for 15.5 million patients and provided 130.6 million phone connections. In the financial sector, IFC supported about 6.7 million loans to micro, small, and medium enterprises.

MIGA in South Asia

MIGA provides political risk insurance (guarantees) for projects in a broad range of sectors in developing member countries, covering all regions of the world. Recent guarantees issued by MIGA for companies investing in South Asia support agribusiness and telecommunications in Afghanistan; power in Bangladesh; and power, banking, and manufacturing in Pakistan.

Data Resources on South Asia
⮑ http://data.worldbank.org/region/SAR

Research on South Asia
⮑ http://www.worldbank.org/en/region/sar/research

South-South Investment South-South investment—that is, the movement of capital from one developing or middle-income country to another—is an increasingly important way to deepen financial markets, generate growth, and put new sources of funds to use. It is also a strategic priority for IFC. Over the past eight years, such investment has accounted for up to 20 percent of IFC's projects and commitment volumes—increasingly in the poorest countries—in Africa and in the Middle East. According to the Independent Evaluation Group, it has yielded strong development outcomes and helped raise environmental and social standards.

Speaker's Bureau The Speaker's Bureau serves as the official liaison between the World Bank Group and its visitors, including students and teachers, youth organizations, business leaders, governmental representatives, and other professionals. It also responds to invitations to conferences and participates in guest lectures.
⮑ http://www.worldbank.org/en/about/speakers-bureau

Spring Meetings Each spring, thousands of government officials, journalists, representatives of civil society organizations, and invited participants from academia and the private sector gather in Washington, D.C., for the Spring Meetings of the IMF and the World Bank Group. At the heart of the gathering are meetings of the IMF's International Monetary and Financial Committee and the joint World Bank–IMF Development Committee, which discuss progress on the work of the IMF and the World Bank Group. Also featured are seminars, regional briefings, press conferences, and many other events focused on the global economy, international development, and the world's financial markets.

Staff Association The World Bank Group Staff Association (SA), founded in 1972, is an organization of staff members dedicated to furthering two broad objectives:

- To foster a sense of common purpose among staff in promoting the aims and objectives of the World Bank Group

- To promote and safeguard the rights, interests, and welfare of staff

The SA is also a strong and unified body whose aim is to reach an understanding between the staff and the Bank Group management, ensure that staff members are treated as full and equal partners in an environment of openness and transparency, and improve the staff's capacity to perform their jobs.

Sustainable Development The World Bank Group recognizes that growth must be both inclusive and environmentally sound to reduce poverty and build shared prosperity for today's population and to continue to meet the needs of future generations. It must be efficient with resources and carefully planned to deliver immediate and long-term benefits for people, planet, and prosperity.

Over the past two decades, economic growth has lifted more than 660 million people out of poverty and has raised the income levels of millions more, but too often it has come at the expense of the environment and poor communities.

Through a variety of market, policy, and institutional failures, the earth's natural capital has been used in ways that are economically inefficient and wasteful, without sufficient reckoning of the true costs of resource depletion. The burning of fossil fuels supported rapid growth for decades but set up dangerous consequences, with climate change today threatening to roll back decades of development progress. At the same time, growth patterns have left hundreds of millions of people behind: 1.2 billion still lack access to electricity, 870 million are malnourished, and 780 million are still without access to clean, safe drinking water.

Sustainable development recognizes that growth must be both inclusive and environmentally sound to reduce poverty and build shared prosperity for today's population and to continue to meet the needs of future generations. The three pillars of sustainable development—economic growth, environmental stewardship, and social inclusion—carry across all sectors of development, from cities facing rapid urbanization to agriculture, infrastructure, energy development and use, water availability, and transportation. Cities are embracing low-carbon growth and public transportation. Farmers are adopting the practices of climate-smart agriculture. Countries are recognizing the value of their natural resources. And industries are realizing how much they can save through energy and supply chain efficiency.

 ⮕ http://www.worldbank.org/en/topic/sustainabledevelopment

Syndications (*See also* Products and Services.) IFC offers commercial banks and other financial institutions the opportunity to lend to IFC-financed projects. These loans are a key part of IFC's efforts to mobilize additional private sector financing in developing countries, thereby broadening the Corporation's developmental impact. Through this mechanism, financial institutions share fully in the commercial credit risk of projects, while IFC remains the lender of record.

IFC's Syndicated Loan Program is the oldest and largest among multilateral development banks. In fiscal 2014, it accounted for 61 percent of the funds mobilized by IFC.

In fiscal 2014, IFC syndicated about $3.1 billion in B-loans, parallel loans, and Managed Co-Lending Portfolio Program loans, provided by more than 80 financial institutions. These included commercial banks, institutional investors, development finance institutions, and an emerging-markets central bank. A record $1.1 billion was provided by co-financiers in emerging markets. The syndicated loan portfolio stood at $15.2 billion.

Borrowers in the infrastructure sector received 44 percent of the total volume. More than a quarter of the financing IFC provided through syndications—$816 million in all—went to borrowers in IDA countries.

⟳ http://tinyurl.com/WBG061

Systematic Country Diagnostic As part of the restructuring of the institution, the World Bank Group endorsed, in July 2014, the proposal of a new Country Partnership Framework (CPF) to define World Bank Group country engagement. Under the new approach, Bank Group country engagements will continue to draw upon the national development strategies of the country. They will also draw upon a Systematic Country Diagnostic (SCD), which will be prepared by Bank Group staff in close consultation with national authorities and other stakeholders.

The SCD is intended to become a reference point for client consultations on priorities for Bank Group country engagement. It is intended to help the country government, the Bank Group, and other development partners establish a dialogue to focus their efforts around goals and activities that have high impact and are aligned with the global goals of ending extreme poverty and boosting shared prosperity in a sustainable manner.

The Systematic Country Diagnostic is:

- *Conducted by Bank Group staff in close consultation with national authorities* and other stakeholders. It identifies key challenges and opportunities for a country for accelerating progress toward the goals at the country level. It will not be limited a priori to areas or sectors where the Bank Group is currently active or expects government demand.

- *Conducted upstream of the CPF* to inform strategic discussions with clients about priority areas for Bank Group interventions in support of the twin goals. The SCD for every country will be aligned with CPF preparation and, where possible, with the preparation of key national development planning documents.

- *Based on the best possible analysis, drawing on available evidence.* It also identifies critical data and knowledge gaps that merit attention.

- *Informed by citizens' input and feedback.* Bank Group staff will seek to involve country partners (private sector, governments, researchers, or institutions) in SCD preparation.

- *Prepared by Bank Group country teams, including technical experts*, led by a Task Team Leader with proven integrative skills and drawing upon expertise across the appropriate networks or Global Practices and Cross-Cutting Solution Areas. (For Bank Group country teams preparing joint SCDs, IFC regional/country teams will lead IFC engagement, provide oversight with the Bank team and private sector perspectives, and draw on other expertise from IFC staff).

- *Subject to a corporate review* process similar to high visibility, flagship regional economic and sector work (ESW) with Bank-wide concept stage and decision stage review meetings chaired by the Regional Vice President (or delegate). Global Practices and Cross-Cutting Solution Areas are expected to participate actively in these review meetings.

- *Expected to be made publicly available* following Regional Vice President approval, following the Access to Information Policy on disclosure of ESW.

Any Country Management Unit taking a Country Strategy to a concept review after June 30, 2014, will be required to produce a CPF that is preceded by a SCD. Any strategy going to the Board after the second quarter of fiscal 2015 must be a CPF.

T

Technical Assistance (*See also* Advisory Services; Products and Services.)

World Bank and Technical Assistance

The World Bank provides professional technical advice that supports legal, policy, management, governance, and other reforms needed for a country's development goals. The Bank's wide-ranging knowledge and skills are used to help countries build accountable, efficient public sector institutions to sustain development in ways that will benefit their citizens over the long term. The Bank offers advice and supports governments in the preparation of documents, such as draft legislation, institutional development plans, country-level strategies, and implementation action plans. It can also assist governments in shaping or putting new policies and programs in place.

IFC and Technical Assistance

IFC's technical assistance—called advisory services—supports private sector development. Most of these activities are funded in partnership with donor countries; many involve close collaboration with the World Bank. These services include advising national and local governments on how to improve their investment climate and strengthen

basic infrastructure and helping companies improve corporate governance, strengthen risk management, and become more financially, environmentally, and socially sustainable. IFC's four broad types of advisory services are access to finance, business climate, sustainable business, and public-private partnerships.

MIGA and Technical Assistance

MIGA equips investment promotion intermediaries with leading-edge tools and techniques to strengthen their capacity to attract and retain foreign direct investment (FDI). MIGA's hands-on technical assistance emphasizes the transfer of best practices in FDI promotion, while MIGA's online information services leverage these capacity-building efforts by linking investors directly to relevant information on investment opportunities and business operating conditions. Services include, among others, program planning, market research, investor targeting, investor servicing and aftercare, and website development.

Tokyo International Conference on African Development Tokyo International Conference on African Development (TICAD) is a summit meeting on African development organized jointly by the government of Japan, the UN, the World Bank Group, the United Nations Development Programme, and the African Union Commission. TICAD has since evolved into a major global framework to facilitate the implementation of initiatives for promoting African development under the dual principle of African "ownership" and international "partnership." A central feature of this framework is the cooperation between Asia and Africa.

The objectives of TICAD are twofold:

- To promote high-level policy dialogue between African leaders and their partners

- To mobilize support for African-owned development initiatives

⟳ http://www.ticad.net

Trade
World Bank Group and Trade
Trade is an important tool for eradicating extreme poverty and boosting shared prosperity. The World Bank Group works to help countries take advantage of the benefits of international trade, specifically by improving developing country access to developed country markets and supporting a rules-based, predictable trading system. The aim is to make the world trading system more supportive of development and to help countries benefit from increased globalization by:

- Supporting the conclusion of pro-development trade agreements (multilateral, regional, and bilateral)

- Emphasizing trade and competitiveness at the core of national development strategies

- Promoting trade-related reforms through effective Aid for Trade programs

World Bank and Trade
The World Bank is the largest multilateral provider of Aid for Trade, providing $7.4 billion per year since fiscal 2003. Excluding infrastructure, which only indirectly affects trade, new World Bank trade-related lending reached $2.7 billion in fiscal 2013, which exceeded the amount of new lending in fiscal 2012 ($1.9 billion) and is nearly a fivefold increase from the fiscal 2003 level of $566 million. Given the importance of trade as a cross-cutting theme, the share of Aid for Trade in total newly approved Bank lending has steadily grown from 3 percent in fiscal 2003 to 8.6 percent in fiscal 2013.

The second Multi-Donor Trust Fund for Trade and Development is the largest source of donor funds to support analytical trade work across the World Bank. From 2012 to 2015, it will support work programs developed annually by the regions, networks, and other operational units of the WBG that work on trade.

IFC and Trade
IFC's Global Trade Finance Program (GTFP) extends and complements the capacity of banks to deliver trade financing by providing risk mitigation in new or challenging markets where trade lines may be constrained.

The GTFP offers confirming banks partial or full guarantees covering payment risk on banks in the emerging markets for trade-related transactions. These guarantees are transaction-specific and may be evidenced by a variety of underlying instruments such as letters of credit, trade-related promissory notes, accepted drafts, bills of exchange, guarantees, bid and performance bonds, and advance payment guarantees. The guarantees are available for all private sector trade transactions that meet IFC's eligibility criteria.

Through the GTFP bank network, local financial institutions can establish working partnerships with a vast number of major international banks in the program, thus broadening their access to finance and reducing their cash collateral requirements. This arrangement enables the continued flow of trade credit into the market at a time when imports may be critical and the country's exports can generate much-needed foreign exchange. In fiscal 2014, trade finance accounted for more than $7 billion of the commitments IFC made from its own account. The Global Trade Liquidity Program has supported $32 billion in trade in developing countries since it was launched in 2009.

Trade and Competitiveness (*See also* Global Practices.) One of 14 new World Bank Group Global Practices, Trade and Competitiveness brings together more than 500 leading technical experts in the field of trade, investment, innovation, and private sector development, with extensive policy expertise, sector-specific knowledge, and practical experience in implementation.

Spurring the creation of sustainable jobs is fundamental to the World Bank Group's goals of eliminating extreme poverty and boosting shared prosperity. The joint Trade and Competitiveness

Global Practice (T&C) provides a comprehensive array of solutions to support the efforts of client governments to boost trade and investment, to improve productivity and competitiveness at the national and industry levels, and to create a better environment in general for business operations. T&C works with governments to design policies that promote private sector growth, while helping them identify and remove impediments to the smooth functioning of markets.

More than 1.5 billion people—especially women and young people—are jobless or underemployed. Within 15 years, 600 million new jobs must be created to keep up with the surging global population. The private sector must create 90 percent of those new jobs. A vibrant private sector is the most important engine of economic growth and is thus a key driver of poverty reduction. Both least-developed and middle-income countries face an array of challenges in their efforts to establish an enabling environment to support the emergence of an innovative, inclusive, and globally competitive private sector: trade and investment policy barriers, as well as lack of innovation, keep firms and industries from accessing market opportunities that arise from newly emerging trade patterns; domestic regulatory frameworks may hinder investment and competition and raise barriers to productive, job-creating investments; and market failures may restrict the prospects for firm entry and growth. Infusions of money from donor countries and international institutions will not, by themselves, solve

The Georgia Regional Development project aims to help develop a tourism-based economy in the Kakheti region while also promoting the area's cultural heritage. The project has upgraded the water supply system, sewage networks, lighting systems, and several city parks in the region. © World Bank. Permission required for reuse.

the problem. Strengthening a country's position in trade and competitiveness is critical to helping it achieve economic growth.

The Trade and Competitiveness Global Practice offers an integrated package of solutions—including policy advice, technical assistance, financing, and capacity building—the Practice brings global knowledge to the design and implementation of projects tailored to the specific needs of client countries, whether fast-growing emerging economies, middle-income countries, or fragile or conflict-affected situations. With global specialists constituting half of its staff members and the other half serving in the regions, T&C has a wide footprint across the globe. Using different instruments, T&C delivers tailored, integrated solutions from diagnostics through implementation.

Transport and ICT (*See also* Global Practices.) One of 14 new World Bank Group Global Practices, Transport and ICT provides clients with infrastructure and policies to improve connectivity and competitiveness and to link people to markets and social services to stimulate economic growth, increase climate resilience, and reduce carbon footprint.

World Bank Group and Transport and ICT

Virtual and physical connectivity is a critical factor of competitiveness and economic growth. However, a third of the world's population lacks access to an all-weather road, and two-thirds of people in developing countries are more than an hour away from a large city. Of the world's population, 60 percent lack Internet access, and even where broadband access is available, many of the poorest cannot afford it. More and better investment in transport and information and communication technology (ICT) is needed to end extreme poverty and boost shared prosperity.

The Transport and ICT Global Practice provides clients with infrastructure lending and policy advice to improve connectivity and competitiveness and to link people to markets and social services, thereby stimulating economic growth, increasing climate resilience, and reducing the carbon footprint. The World Bank Group achieves its goals by financing infrastructure such as transport assets and corridors; providing policy advice on topics like public-private partnerships and road asset management; and supporting global public goods, such as the Global Road Safety Facility.

World Bank and Transport and ICT

In transport, the World Bank focuses on four main areas: urban mobility, road safety and safe transport, low-emissions transport, and trade logistics and facilitation. Its financing supports railway system expansions, rural and interurban roads, air transport, asset management, ports, and waterborne transport. Another major theme is the support of development corridors and regional integration by leveraging funding from public-private partnerships.

In ICT, the Bank focuses on extending affordable access to broadband and promoting e-government, open data, and smart cities. Its loans and credits support improvements in education, disaster risk reduction, digital access, climate-smart development, agricultural productivity, civil society engagement, health care, and business innovation.

IFC and Transport and ICT

IFC's investments in ports, airports, roads, railways, and other transport infrastructure support private transportation projects and public-private partnerships (PPPs) that bring benefits to communities, governments, and local businesses.

IFC provides financing and advisory services to private businesses in the telecoms, media, and technology sectors. Its clients range from tech start-up firms to global mobile operators. For smaller firms, IFC offers venture financing, encouraging private sector investment in markets traditionally

The Road Climate Resilience Project for Timor-Leste is working to deliver climate resilient road infrastructure to communities between Dili-Ainaro and to ensure roads are better protected against natural disasters. Reduced road closures will allow improved access to local and regional markets and towns. © World Bank / Joao Dos Santos (photographer). Permission required for reuse.

considered too risky. For larger firms, IFC offers debt, syndication, and loan guarantees. IFC coordinates closely with the World Bank's policy team that works with governments on telecom and ICT regulation and policy.

MIGA and Transport and ICT
Through its guarantees, MIGA is supporting a number of transport and ICT investments: a highway in Vietnam, marine transport and a tram line project in Turkey, a passenger-car ferry in Tunisia, a metro line in Panama, a bridge in Côte d'Ivoire, and telecommunications in Afghanistan, Cameroon, the Democratic Republic of Congo, Guinea-Bissau, and Iraq.

Treasury With more than 60 years of experience in financing the IBRD and investing its reserves and pension fund, the World Bank Treasury has developed substantial expertise in asset and liability management. During this time, it has achieved a global reputation as a prudent and innovative borrower, investor, and risk manager. Treasury also develops innovative lending products to meet World Bank clients' requests for customized financing—loans, derivatives, market hedges, and other instruments—for their development programs.

Asset Management and Advisory

Treasury now manages $70–75 billion in global liquidity portfolios and balanced funds for the World Bank Group, the staff pension fund, central banks, and other multilateral organizations. The asset management business is supported by state-of-the-art portfolio and risk management analytics and systems and also offers its clients extensive training opportunities and advice. Treasury's historical investment record in obtaining index-plus returns on very low risk has earned it an enviable reputation in this area.

Bond and Investment Products

From the international capital markets, Treasury currently borrows around $25–35 billion annually in about 20 currencies. It has offered World Bank bonds and notes in over 50 different currencies and opened up new markets for international investors through its issuance in emerging market currencies. Treasury is an extensive user of interest rate and currency swaps for hedging purposes, with about $30 billion in annual volume and a swap book totaling around $250 billion.

Financing and Risk Management

Treasury also develops innovative products to meet World Bank clients' requests for customized financing and risk management—loans, contingent financing, guarantees, hedging products, and catastrophe risk financing—for development programs. Treasury's financial practitioners work directly with clients to structure and deliver custom financial solutions to meet development program and debt management objectives.

Debt Management and Financial Advisory

A dedicated team of debt management practitioners and market specialists provides a range of capacity-building services to public sector entities in a partnership to promote best practice in debt management and asset and liability management. Services are complemented with original research, interactive workshops, and networking opportunities, plus an extensive portfolio of resources for practitioners.

➲ http:// treasury.worldbank.org

Trust Funds
World Bank and Trust Funds

Trust funds are financial arrangements between the World Bank and a donor or a group of donors under which the donor entrusts the Bank with funds for a specific development-related activity. Trust funds enable the Bank, along with bilateral and multilateral donors, to expand their response to specific needs, as in the case of fragile states or natural disasters or in support of global public goods.

Bank-administered trust funds support poverty reduction activities across a wide range of sectors and regions, thereby supporting clients in achieving development results at the global, regional, and country levels. Much of the recent growth in these funds reflects the international community's desire for the Bank to help manage broad global initiatives through multilateral partnerships, such as the Global Fund to Fight AIDS, Tuberculosis, and Malaria; the Global Environment Facility; the HIPC Initiative; and carbon funds. Trust funds also support the World Bank's own development operations and work programs.

➲ http://www.worldbank.org/cfp

IFC and Trust Funds

Much of IFC's advisory work is conducted by facilities managed by IFC but funded through partnerships with donor governments and other multilateral institutions. IFC's advisory services focus on access to finance, climate change, sustainable business, and public-private partnerships.

MIGA and Trust Funds

MIGA makes available special guarantee facilities and trust funds to encourage investment in areas of special need, working with partners to leverage the amount of coverage the Agency can provide. Currently, MIGA offers support through three trust funds: the Conflict-Affected and Fragile Economies Facility, the Environmental and Social Challenges Fund for Africa, and the West Bank and Gaza Investment Guarantee Trust Fund. MIGA also managed the Afghanistan Investment Guarantee Facility. The facility, now closed, provided cover for a total of five projects and for an overall guarantee amount of $11.7 million. MIGA also managed the European Union Investment Guarantee Trust Fund for Bosnia and Herzegovina. This $12 million fund has been fully utilized.

U·V

United Nations and Its Relationship to the World Bank Group Cooperation between the World Bank Group and the United Nations has been in place since the founding of the two organizations (in 1944 and 1945, respectively) and focuses on economic and social areas of mutual concern, such as reducing poverty, promoting sustainable development, and investing in people. In addition to a shared agenda, the Bank Group and the United Nations have almost the same membership: only a handful of UN member countries are not members of IBRD.

The World Bank's formal relationship with the United Nations is defined by a 1947 agreement that recognizes the Bank (now the Bank Group) as an independent specialized agency of the United Nations and as an observer in many UN bodies, including the General Assembly. In recent years, the Economic and Social Council has conducted a special high-level meeting with the World Bank Group, International Monetary Fund (IMF), World Trade Organization (WTO), and United Nations Conference on Trade and Development (UNCTAD) immediately after the Spring Meetings of the Bank Group and the IMF. The Bank Group President is also a member of the UN System Chief Executives Board for Coordination, which meets twice annually.

In addition, the Bank Group plays a key role in supporting United Nations–led processes, such as the International Conference on Financing for Development, the World Summit on Sustainable Development and the Post-2015 Development Agenda. It also provides knowledge about country-level challenges and helps formulate international policy recommendations.

In terms of operations, the Bank Group works with other UN funds and programs to coordinate policies, aid, and project implementation. It also helps prepare for and participates in most of the United Nations global conferences and plays an important role in follow-up, especially in relation to the implementation of goals at the country level.

↪ http://www.un.org

Universal Financial Inclusion The World Bank Group is committed to supporting countries in their efforts to bolster access to finance. It currently conducts financial inclusion projects with public and private partners in more than 70 countries. To promote financial inclusion responsibly, the World Bank Group urges policy makers to improve the standards for information disclosure and support innovative, well-designed financial products that

173

address market failures, meet consumer needs, and overcome some behavioral hurdles. Policy makers can also improve financial access by embracing new technologies, which include not only mobile banking but also other innovations, such as borrower identification based on fingerprinting and iris scans.

Recognizing that 2.5 billion adults worldwide are "unbanked" and that close to 200 million micro to medium enterprises in developing economies lack access to affordable financial services and credit, the World Bank Group put forward a vision for achieving universal financial access by 2020. As of late 2013, more than 50 countries had made commitments to financial inclusion targets. Setting and then achieving country-led national targets will open the way toward broadening financial inclusion. Adopting ambitious financial inclusion commitments can unleash private-sector innovation and investment, helping advance the goals of eliminating poverty and building shared prosperity.

Global Financial Development Report 2014: Financial Inclusion

⊃ https://openknowledge.worldbank.org/handle/10986/16238

The Global Financial Inclusion (Global Findex) Database

⊃ http://tinyurl.com/WBG087

Universal Health Coverage Under universal health coverage (UHC), all people can access the health care they need without suffering financial hardship by doing so. UHC—a continuation of the Millennium Development Goals—aims to achieve better health and development outcomes, to help prevent people from falling into poverty due to illness, and to give people the opportunity to lead healthier, more productive lives.

In recent years, the global UHC movement has gained momentum, with the World Health Assembly and the United Nations General Assembly calling on countries to increase efforts to accelerate the shift toward universal access to affordable and quality health care services. While the goal is universal, countries have much flexibility in determining how they reach that goal.

In December 2013, World Bank Group President Jim Yong Kim announced that the World Bank and the World Health Organization (WHO) would release a joint framework for monitoring progress toward universal health coverage with two targets:

- *For financial protection*, by 2020, the Bank and WHO propose to reduce by half the number of people who are impoverished due to out-of-pocket health care expenses. By 2030, no one should fall into poverty because of out-of-pocket health care expenses. Achieving this target will require moving from 100 million people impoverished every year at present to 50 million by 2020 and then to zero by 2030.

- *For service delivery*, the Bank and WHO propose to double the proportion of poor people in developing countries who have access to basic health services, such as vaccination for children or having a skilled attendant available at childbirth, from 40 percent today to 80 percent by 2030. In addition, by 2030, 80 percent of the poor will have access to other essential health services such as treatment for high blood pressure, diabetes, mental health, and injuries.

⊃ www.worldbank.org/en/topic/universalhealthcoverage

Upper-Middle-Income Countries (*See also* Classification of Countries.) The World Bank Group classifies upper-middle-income economies as those with a per capita gross national income of $4,036 to $12,475.

⊃ http://data.worldbank.org/about/country-and-lending -groups

Vice Presidential Units (*See also* Organizational Structure.) The Vice Presidential Unit (VPU) is the main organizational unit of the World Bank. VPUs operate under the leadership and direction of the President and organizational units responsible for regions, Global Practices and general management. Such units are commonly referred to as Vice Presidencies. With a few exceptions that report directly to the President, each of these units reports to a Managing Director or to the Bank Group's Chief Financial Officer (CFO).

Voting Power Member countries govern the Bank Group through the Boards of Governors and the Boards of Directors. The voting power of each Executive Director is determined by the value of the capital subscriptions held by the countries that he or she represents. For each of the four shareholding institutions—IBRD, IDA, IFC, and MIGA—the Executive Director for the United States has the greatest voting power, followed by the Executive Director for Japan.

⟳ http://tinyurl.com/WBG063

W

Water (*See also* Global Practices.) One of 14 new World Bank Group Global Practices, Water aims to help governments ensure basic access to water and sanitation services for even the poorest people.

World Bank Group and Water

The world will not be able to meet the great development challenges of the 21st century—human development, livable cities, climate change, food security, or energy security—without improving how countries manage their water resources and ensuring that people have access to reliable water and sanitation services. But mismanagement of this basic element of life has led to millions of deaths and billions of dollars in lost opportunities for economic growth every year, severely constraining countries' development potential.

Through its Global Practice on Water, the World Bank Group seeks to ensure that its water projects explicitly factor poverty reduction into project development:

- Early on, the world met the Millennium Development Goal (MDG) target of halving the proportion of people without access to safe water. Between 1990 and 2010, more than 2 billion people gained access to safe water. However, Africa will likely not attain its water MDG.

- Although the world will likely not meet the sanitation MDG by the 2015 deadline, progress is being made: 1.9 billion people gained access to sanitation between 1990 and 2010, and 500 million gained access just in the past several years.

- However, there is still a long way to go, with 2.5 billion people still lacking access to sanitation.

In response to these challenges, the Bank Group is placing particular emphasis on key themes: water resources management, water supply, sanitation, irrigation and drainage, and hydropower.

In fiscal 2013, the World Bank Group committed $3 billion for the water sector. In the past three years (fiscal 2011–13), the World Bank's commitment for water projects totaled $17 billion, comprising 56 percent for water supply and sanitation, 16 percent for hydropower, 15 percent for irrigation and drainage, and 13 percent for flood protection. In fiscal 2013, IFC lent $214 million for water infrastructure projects. MIGA provided guarantees totaling $704 million for water supply, water treatment, and hydropower investments in Ghana, Jordan, and Angola, respectively.

The Ayeyarwady Integrated River Basin Management Project for Myanmar wishes to increase the river's productivity with investments in a hydro-meteorological observation system and services to support agricultural productivity, water-related disaster risk management, and navigation enhancements to promote transport. © World Bank. Permission required for reuse.

However, with massive water challenges, financing from the public sector and development aid are not enough. The Bank seeks to leverage financing from other sources, including the domestic private sector and public-private partnerships.

World Bank and Water

The World Bank is the largest external source of financing for water projects. A strategic review of the World Bank's involvement in the water sector, "Sustaining Water for All in a Changing Climate" (2010), reaffirmed the relevance of core business themes: infrastructure for access, integrated water resources management, and capacity building for results-based decision making. In this context, the World Bank is defining a new vision for water that places increased emphasis on five strategic goals:

- Preparing client countries for a future of higher food and energy prices, more volatility, and more extreme weather

- Helping countries get water "right" in other sectors, such as energy, agriculture, and the environment

- Adopting an integrated "nexus" approach to water, initially in six geographic areas: India, Kenya, megacities in Latin America, the Mekong Delta, Nigeria, and the Western Balkans

- Advancing global knowledge on water and building stronger institutional frameworks for water management across sectors, as well as national and regional boundaries

- Committing to longer-term engagements, focusing on water basins

IFC and Water

Water, wastewater, solid waste, and district heating are fundamentally linked to the quality of life and efforts to alleviate poverty in developing countries. IFC supports both public and private projects that increase access and efficiency for water and waste services at an affordable and sustainable cost to consumers.

One of the ways IFC is responding to these challenges is by enabling partnerships between governments and private operators to bring the needed capital, expertise, and technology to improve water access and services. Working alongside government, civil society, and other stakeholders, the private sector can provide complementary knowledge, experience, insights, and convening power to address critical issues of water resource management.

IFC's track record in structuring public-private partnerships (PPPs) in water is strong. Long-term evaluations of its projects prove that concessions can have a positive impact on both access and quality of services for the population. Properly structured PPPs can play an important part in responding to the global water issues of today.

MIGA and Water

MIGA guarantees are well suited to mitigating the particular risks associated with investing in water and sanitation projects in developing countries. These guarantees, covering both new investments and project expansions, help ensure that investors are able to operate in a stable and predictable environment. In addition, MIGA's support can help mobilize investment in critically needed infrastructure, including hydropower. MIGA's support to projects helps unlock market access to commercial finance, allowing projects to achieve a positive development impact for the country.

Water Resources Practically every development challenge of the 21st century—food and energy security, rapid urbanization, environmental protection, adaptation to climate change—requires urgent attention to the management of water resources. The World Bank Group places water resources management at the center of its efforts to help countries adapt to and mitigate the effects of climate change.

The World Bank is one of the key external financiers in water resources management and one of the leading providers of knowledge and technical assistance on water. Overall, water lending accounts for 15 percent of the Bank's portfolio. World Bank funding has responded to the need to address both water development and management issues by promoting integrated water resources planning and by tackling institutional reforms along with infrastructure upgrades in various sectors. These sectors include contributions to flood management, hydropower, agricultural water management, pollution control, transboundary water management, and climate change adaptation and mitigation activities. The World Bank will continue to play a key role by working across sectors and countries and with institutions and diverse stakeholders to help countries build resilience to climate change through water resources management.

⮑ http://tinyurl.com/WBG064

Water Supply and Sanitation Water is vital to maintaining health, to growing food, to managing the environment, and to creating jobs. Yet over

783 million people in the world are still without access to improved water sources, 2.5 billion people live without access to improved sanitation, and 1.1 billion people practice open defecation. Despite significant gains, sanitation remains one of the most off-track Millennium Development Goals globally.

The World Bank Group is committed to helping client countries build competent, efficient, businesslike, customer-oriented water and sanitation services. These services must ensure affordable and sustainable services to all, particularly the poor.

The Bank is also engaged in two ongoing partnerships on water:

- The Water and Sanitation Program (WSP) is a 33-year-old partnership hosted by the Bank to help governments scale up improved water supply, sanitation services, and hygiene programs for poor people. It provides technical assistance and capacity building and leverages knowledge and partnerships through 125 technical staff members in 24 countries.

- The Water Partnership Program is a multidonor program aimed at strengthening the Bank's efforts to reduce poverty through improved water resources management and water service delivery.

  http://water.worldbank.org/water-supply-and-sanitation

Wolfensohn, James D. (*See* Presidents of the World Bank Group.)

Wolfowitz, Paul D. (*See* Presidents of the World Bank Group.)

Woods, George (*See* Presidents of the World Bank Group.)

World Bank (*See also* International Bank for Reconstruction and Development and International Development Association.) The World Bank is a vital source of financial and technical assistance to developing countries around the world. Through its loans, risk management, and other financial services; its policy advice; and its technical assistance, the World Bank supports a broad range of programs aimed at eliminating extreme poverty and boosting the shared prosperity of the bottom 40 percent of the population in every developing country. It divides its work between IBRD, which works with middle-income and creditworthy poorer countries, and IDA, which focuses exclusively on the world's poorest countries. The terms World Bank and Bank refer only to IBRD and IDA.

  http://www.worldbank.org

World Bank DataFinder The World Bank DataFinder app highlights the progress that has been made at the Bank since the Open Data Initiative was launched in April 2010. For the first time, the Bank's data are available to users on any of the three major mobile platforms and in four languages.

  http://data.worldbank.org/apps

World Bank Economic Review (*See also* Journals.) Published by Oxford University Press on behalf of the World Bank, the *World Bank Economic Review* (WBER) is one of the most widely read scholarly economics journals in the world. It is the only journal of its kind that specializes in quantitative development policy analysis. Subject to strict refereeing, articles examine policy choices and therefore emphasize policy relevance rather than theory or methodology. Readers include economists and other social scientists in government, business, international agencies, universities, and research institutions. WBER seeks to provide the most current and best research in the field of economic development.

  http://elibrary.worldbank.org/loi/wber

World Bank eLibrary The World Bank eLibrary is a subscription-based website for institutions that is designed to meet the unique needs of researchers and librarians. Launched in 2003, the eLibrary offers full-text access to the complete backlist of all books, working papers, and journal articles published by the World Bank since the 1990s. Users of eLibrary are assured full and immediate access to all academic research and scholarship published by the World Bank, the majority made available through Creative Commons Attribution (CC BY) license.

The eLibrary offers a variety of tools and added functionality, saving users valuable time. Special tools and conveniences include individual accounts for personalization, ePUB files and chapter-level access for the most recent titles, citation exporting, MARC records for libraries, and indexing with major library discovery services. The World Bank eLibrary is used by the world's top academic institutions, international and governmental agencies, think tanks, multinational corporations, and nongovernmental organizations.

↪ **www.elibrary.worldbank.org**

World Bank Group (*See also* IBRD; IDA; IFC; MIGA; ICSID; World Bank.) The World Bank Group consists of five institutions: the International Bank for Reconstruction and Development (IBRD), the International Development Association (IDA), the International Finance Corporation (IFC), the International Centre for Settlement of Investment Disputes (ICSID), and the Multilateral Investment Guarantee Agency (MIGA). IBRD and IDA together are known as the World Bank. The term World Bank Group refers collectively to all five of the institutions. Although each institution has a distinct purpose, history, and set of founding documents, they have a common commitment to reducing poverty, increasing shared prosperity, and promoting sustainable development.

Jim Yong Kim is the 12th and current President of the World Bank Group. He is chairman of the Bank's Board of Executive Directors and President of the five interrelated organizations:

- **IBRD.** The International Bank for Reconstruction and Development aims to reduce poverty in middle-income countries and creditworthy poorer countries by promoting sustainable development through loans, guarantees, risk management products, and analytical and advisory services. Established in 1944 as the original institution of the World Bank Group, IBRD is structured like a cooperative that is owned and operated for the benefit of its 188 member countries. IBRD raises most of its funds on the world's financial markets and has become one of the most established borrowers since issuing its first bond in 1947. The income that IBRD has generated over the years has allowed it to fund development activities and to ensure its financial strength, which enables it to borrow at low cost and offer clients good borrowing terms.

- **ICSID.** The International Centre for Settlement of Investment Disputes provides international facilities for conciliation and arbitration of investment disputes.

- **IDA.** The International Development Association is the part of the World Bank that helps the world's poorest countries. Established in 1960, IDA aims to reduce poverty by providing loans (called "credits"), grants, and guarantees for programs that boost economic growth, reduce inequalities, and improve people's living conditions. IBRD and IDA share the same staff and headquarters and evaluate projects with the same rigorous standards.

- **IFC.** The International Finance Corporation is the largest global development institution focused exclusively on the private sector. It helps developing countries achieve sustainable growth by financing investment, mobilizing capital in international financial markets, and providing advisory services to businesses and governments.

- **MIGA.** The Multilateral Investment Guarantee Agency was created in 1988 to promote foreign direct investment into developing countries to support economic growth, reduce poverty, and improve people's lives. MIGA fulfills this mandate by offering political risk insurance (guarantees) to investors and lenders.

World Bank Group Strategy At the 2013 Annual Meetings of the World Bank Group and the International Monetary Fund, the World Bank Group adopted a strategy titled *Building A Solutions World Bank Group* focused on aligning all of the institution's work with the twin goals of eliminating extreme poverty and boosting shared prosperity in a sustainable manner. The two goals are now at the heart of the World Bank Group's work. The first calls for reducing, by 2030, the share of the world's population living on less than $1.25 per day to no more than 3 percent. To accelerate progress, the Bank Group has also set an interim goal of cutting extreme poverty to 9 percent of the world's population by 2020.

The second goal of boosting shared prosperity will require promoting income growth of the bottom 40 percent of each developing country's population.

Implementation of the strategy supporting these goals involves sweeping institutional changes designed to significantly raise the World Bank Group's financial capacity as well as its operational efficiency. Under the new structures, the institutions of the World Bank Group—the International Bank for Reconstruction and Development (IBRD), the International Development Association (IDA), the International Finance Corporation (IFC), and the Multilateral Investment Guarantee Agency (MIGA)—will strengthen their collaboration to deliver effective solutions that bring global knowledge to bear on local challenges. Leveraging the strengths and resources of all four institutions will produce a stronger, more nimble, and financially sustainable Bank Group that is better able to deliver proven development solutions to its clients.

Delivering Results for Clients

The World Bank Group strategy comprises three pillars:

- The Bank Group will deliver results for its clients through country programs and regional and global engagements by offering knowledge and solutions to the toughest development challenges.

- Closer collaboration across the Bank Group will multiply the strengths of each institution by using their combined resources and expertise to serve clients as the "Solutions World Bank Group."

- Leveraging the partnerships, resources, and expertise of the private sector and other development actors will help the Bank Group maximize the impact of development in alignment with the twin goals.

A prominent change derived from the strategy is the development of Global Practices and Cross-Cutting Solution Areas, which are designed to reflect the institution's comparative advantages and better complement the existing strengths of its regional units and country offices. The Global Practices will improve the sharing across all regions of technical expertise and knowledge in 14 specialized areas of development: agriculture; education; energy and extractives; environment and natural resources; finance and markets; governance; health, nutrition, and population; macroeconomics and fiscal management; poverty; social, urban, rural, and resilience; social protection and labor; trade and competitiveness; transportation and information and communications technology; and water.

The Cross-Cutting Solution Areas will address development challenges that require integration across five areas of specialization: climate change; fragility, conflict, and violence; gender; jobs; and public-private partnerships.

The World Bank—composed of IBRD and IDA—has also adopted a new country engagement model that is designed to tailor policies and programs to the needs and priorities of individual countries. The model is centered on new Country Partnership Frameworks, which will be underpinned by evidence-based analysis and will help Bank Group programs selectively address areas that have the most impact in supporting countries' efforts to achieve the twin goals. This approach will include coordination with IFC and MIGA and will provide the basis for selective and focused engagements across the World Bank Group. Regular meetings of regional management from the World Bank, IFC, and MIGA will determine the appropriate level of engagement for each institution and identify where joint implementation mechanisms are needed.

The new approach will remain country focused, grounded in national priorities, owned by the country, and developed in coordination with other partners. Emphasis will shift from an approvals culture to a results delivery culture centered on implementation, real-time citizen feedback, and midcourse evaluation and correction.

Improving Financial Capacity and Sustainability
To ensure the availability of adequate resources that are aligned with the twin goals and its strategy, the World Bank Group is undertaking significant financial reforms that will increase its capacity to provide financial services to clients while strengthening its financial resilience. Through efforts to become more efficient and shore up its revenue base, the Bank Group will improve its financial sustainability and build a strong foundation for years to come.

Over the next decade, the World Bank Group will increase its financing capacity from an annual average of $45–50 billion to more than $70 billion. The additional financing is made possible by the record IDA17 replenishment, which will ensure IDA's lending capacity over fiscal 2015–17. On the revenue side, IBRD will strengthen its margins for maneuvering by increasing its single-borrower limit by $2.5 billion for Brazil, China, India, Indonesia, and Mexico, with a 50-basis-point surcharge on the incremental amount; lowering IBRD's equity-to-loan ratio percentage to reflect improvements in its portfolio credit quality; expanding the menu of loan maturities, including extending the maximum maturity; and restoring commitment fees on undisbursed balances.

A World Bank Group–wide expenditure review, which has identified cost-saving measures of at least $400 million on the annual cost base to be achieved over fiscal 2015–17, will result in increased lending capacity and budget flexibility and will optimize the cost structure of the Bank Group. The cost savings are being designed to ensure that the Bank Group's operational capacities and its ability to deliver services to clients will not be compromised. In addition, a new budget and strategic planning process—simpler and more flexible—is helping to align resources more directly with the World Bank Group strategy and twin goals. It focuses on promoting selectivity, linking budgets to results, and carrying out medium-term planning.

Increased collaboration among the four institutions of the World Bank Group will simplify procedures and reduce overlapping administrative functions while magnifying the development impact of its work with clients. One early example of collaboration is an innovative exposure swap between IBRD and MIGA of up to $100 million of principal that will enable each institution to do more business in Brazil and Panama.

An Agenda for Change

Other efforts to improve operations will continue beyond fiscal 2014. For example, in November 2013, the Board considered an outline of a new framework for procurement in World Bank investment project finance and endorsed a vision statement and principles to guide its implementation. The next phase will articulate details of the new policy and implementation. Work also continues on the review of the World Bank's safeguard policies, begun in 2012, to update the policy framework that helps avoid or mitigate harm to people and the environment. A second round of global consultations with stakeholders on the proposed new framework is planned for the second half of 2014.

Changes now under way across the World Bank Group are the most extensive and important in decades. They are intended to align all of the institutions' work with the twin goals within the context of its strategy. The result will be a Bank Group that is financially strong; a recognized leader in knowledge and talent; fast and responsive; internally integrated, globally connected, and locally engaged; and focused on achieving its goals of ending extreme poverty and boosting shared prosperity.

⊃ http://tinyurl.com/WBG072

World Bank Institute (*See also* Leadership, Learning, and Innovation Vice Presidency.) The World Bank Institute—now the Leadership, Learning, and Innovation Vice Presidency—is a global connector of knowledge, learning, and innovation for poverty reduction.

⊃ http://wbi.worldbank.org/wbi

World Bank Research Observer (*See also* Journals.) Written to be accessible to nonspecialist readers, the *World Bank Research Observer* is intended for anyone with a professional interest in development. Contributors examine key issues in development economics, survey the literature and the latest World Bank research, and debate issues of development policy. It is published by Oxford University Press on behalf of the World Bank.

⊃ http://elibrary.worldbank.org/toc/wbro/22/1

World Development Indicators World Development Indicators is a database of the primary World Bank collection of development indicators. Compiled from officially recognized international sources, it presents the most current and accurate global development data available and includes national, regional, and global estimates.

⊃ http://tinyurl.com/WBG088

World Development Report The *World Development Report* provides a wide international readership with an extraordinary window on development economics. Each year, the report focuses on a specific aspect of development. The World Bank's *World Development Report*, published annually since 1978, is an invaluable guide to the economic, social, and environmental state of the world today. Each report provides in-depth analysis and policy recommendations on a specific and important aspect of development—from agriculture, the role of the state, transition economies, and labor to infrastructure, health, the environment, and poverty. Through the quality and timeliness of the information it provides, the report has become a highly influential publication that is used by many multilateral and bilateral international organizations, national governments, scholars, civil society networks and groups, and other global thought leaders to support their decision-making processes. This corporate flagship undergoes extensive internal and external review and is one of the key outputs of the World Bank's Development Economics Vice Presidency.

⊃ www.openknowledge.worldbank.org/handle/10986/2124

World Health Organization The World Health Organization (WHO) is the directing and coordinating authority for health within the United Nations system. WHO is responsible for providing leadership on global health matters, shaping the health research agenda, setting norms and standards, articulating evidence-based policy options, providing technical support to countries, and monitoring and assessing health trends.

⟳ http://www.who.int

World Integrated Trade Solution The World Integrated Trade Solution (WITS) software provides access to data on international merchandise trade, tariff, and nontariff measures. Users can browse the country profile and related pages to view trade (exports and imports with countries and by product groups), tariff, and relevant development data. WITS also features built-in analytical tools that help assess the impact of tariff cuts.

⟳ http://wits.worldbank.org

World Trade Organization The World Trade Organization (WTO) is the only global international organization that deals with the rules of trade between nations. At its heart are the WTO agreements, negotiated and signed by the bulk of the world's trading nations and ratified in their parliaments. The goal is to help producers of goods and services, exporters, and importers conduct their business and ensure that trade flows as smoothly, predictably, and freely as possible.

⟳ http://www.wto.org

Y·Z

Young Professionals Program For more than 50 years, the World Bank's Young Professionals Program has been the preeminent program preparing global development leaders. The program is designed for highly qualified and motivated people who are skilled in areas relevant to the World Bank's operations, such as economics, finance, education, public health, social sciences, engineering, urban planning, and natural resource management. In order to be competitive for this highly selective program, candidates need to demonstrate a commitment to development, proven academic success, professional achievement, and leadership capability.

⮑ http://www.worldbank.org/jobs

Youth to Youth Community Youth to Youth Community (YTY) is a network of young World Bank Group employees aiming to channel fresh ideas and perspectives into Bank Group operations and to engage, inspire, and empower youth in development. The group was formed as a response to growing recognition of the critical role that youth play in development, both as a target group and as a partner. Y2Y was launched in February 2004 with a mission to bring fresh ideas from young Bank staff to the forefront and to increase and improve the investments affecting young people.

The Community serves as a mechanism to:

- Channel the ideas of internal young staff into the Bank

- Channel the ideas of external young people into the Bank

- Build partnerships between these two groups

The Community also provides a professional and social network for young professionals interested in development, as well as a place to enhance learning opportunities.

⮑ http://tinyurl.com/WBG067

Zoellick, Robert B. (*See* Presidents of the World Bank Group.)

APPENDICES

APPENDIX A

ABBREVIATIONS

ABCDE	Annual Bank Conference on Development Economics
AFR	Sub-Saharan Africa
AI	Access to Information (World Bank Policy)
AIDS	acquired immune deficiency syndrome
AIP	Access to Information Policy (IFC)
AMC	Asset Management Company
ASPIRE	Atlas of Social Protection with Indicators on Resilience and Equity
AUC	African Union Commision
BOT	build-operate-transfer
BRICs	Brazil, the Russian Federation, India, and China
CAO	Compliance Advisor Ombudsman
CAS	Country Assistance Strategy
CC BY	Creative Commons Attribution (license)
CCSA	Cross-Cutting Solution Area
CCSD	Center on Conflict, Security, and Development
CCT	conditional cash transfer
CDF	Comprehensive Development Framework
CEM	Country Economic Memorandum
CFP	Concessional Finance and Global Partnerships
CGAP	Consultative Group to Assist the Poor
CGIAR	Consultative Group on International Agricultural Research
CMU	Country Management Unit
CPF	Country Partnership Framework
CPIA	Country Policy and Institutional Assessment
CPS	Country Partnership Strategy
CRS	Conflict Resolution System
CSO	civil society organization
DCMI	Dublin Core Metadata Initiaive
DEC	Development Economics (Vice Presidency)

DEIS	Development Effectiveness Indicator System
DFi	Development Finance (Vice Presidency)
DFI	development finance institution
DIME	Development Impact Evaluation
DM	Development Marketplace
DOTS	Development Outcome Tracking System
DPL	Development Policy Lending
DRM	disaster risk management
DRP	Dispute Resolution and Prevention
EAP	East Asia and Pacific
EBC	Office of Ethics and Business Conduct
ECA	Europe and Central Asia
ECR	External and Corporate Relations (Vice Presidency)
ECRPK	Publishing and Knowledge Division of the External and Corporate Relations Vice Presidency
EFA	Education for All
EITI	Extractive Industries Transparency Initiative
ESW	economic sector work
EXTOP	Office of the Publisher
FCS	fragile and conflict-affected situations
FDI	foreign direct investment
FIRST	Financial Sector Reform and Strengthening Initiative
FM	Financial Management (Sector)
FMSB	Financial Management Sector Board
GAFSP	Global Agriculture and Food Security Program
GAVI	Global Alliance for Vaccines and Immunization
GBV	gender-based violence
GDLN	Global Development Learning Network
GEF	Global Environment Facility
GFATM	Global Fund to Fight AIDS, Tuberculosis and Malaria
GFDR	Global Financial Development Report
GFRP	Global Food Crisis Response Program
GIF	Global Infrastructure Facility
GNI	gross national income
GPE	Global Partnership for Education
GPOBA	Global Partnership on Output-Based Aid
GSD	General Services Department
GTFP	Global Trade Finance Program
GWP	Global Water Partnership
HHA	Harmonization for Health in Africa
HIPC	Heavily Indebted Poor Countries (Initiative)
HIV	human immunodeficiency virus
HNP	Health, Nutrition, and Population (Global Practice)

HR	Human Resource (Vice Presidencies)
HRF	Haiti Reconstruction Fund
IAD	Internal Audit (Vice Presidency)
IBRD	International Bank for Reconstruction and Development
ICSID	International Centre for Settlement of Investment Disputes
ICT	Information and Communication Technologies
IDA	International Development Association
IDG	IFC Development Goal
IEG	Independent Evaluation Group
IFC	International Finance Corporation
ILO	International Labour Organization
IMF	International Monetary Fund
INT	Integrity (Vice Presidency)
IPF	investment project financing
ITS	Information Technology Solutions
ITS	Intelligent Transport Systems
J4P	Justice for the Poor
KNOMAD	Global Knowledge Partnership on Migration and Development
LAC	Latin America and the Caribbean
LICUS	low-income countries under stress
LLI	Leadership, Learning, and Innovation Vice Presidency
MDB	multilateral development bank
MDG	Millennium Development Goal
MENA	Middle East and North Africa
MIGA	Multilateral Investment Guarantee Agency
NGO	nongovernmental organization
NPL	nonperforming loan
OAI-PMH	Open Archives Initiatives Protocol for Metadata Harvesting
OCP	Onchocerciasis Control Program
OECD	Organisation for Economic Co-operation and Development
OKR	Open Knowledge Repository
OPCS	Operations Policy and Country Services
PforR	Program for Results
PIH	Partners in Health
PPP	public-private partnership
PRSP	Poverty Reduction Strategy Paper
RAS	reimbursable advisory services
RBF	results-based financing
READ	Rural Education and Development (Project)
REAP	Renewable Energy and Rural Electricity Access Project
SABER	Systems Approach for Better Education Results
SAR	South Asia
SCD	Systematic Country Diagnostics

SDR	special drawing rights
SDV	Social Development Department
SEB	Skandinaviska Enskilda Banken
SE4ALL	Sustainable Energy for All Initiative
SLCP	short-lived climate pollutants
SMEs	small and medium enterprises
StAR	Stolen Asset Recovery Initiative
TA	technical assistance
T&C	Trade and Competitiveness Global Practice
TICAD	Tokyo International Conference on African Development
UHC	universal health coverage
UN	United Nations
UNDG	United Nations Development Group
UNDP	United Nations Development Programme
UNEP	United Nations Environment Programme
VPU	Vice Presidential Unit
WBER	*World Bank Economics Review*
WBG	World Bank Group
WDI	World Development Indicators
WDS	World Development Sources
WHO	World Health Organization
WITS	World Integrated Trade Solution
WSP	Water and Sanitation Program
WTO	World Trade Organization

CONTACTING THE WORLD BANK GROUP

To obtain general information about any of the World Bank Group institutions, use the contact information below.

THE WORLD BANK HEADQUARTERS

1818 H Street NW
Washington, DC 20433
Phone: (202) 473-1000
Fax: (202) 477-6391

GENERAL INQUIRIES
➲ http://go.worldbank.org/1MZIWY6AB0

MULTILATERAL INVESTMENT GUARANTEE AGENCY

Use the World Bank Headquarters address.
Phone: (202) 473-1000
Fax: (202) 477-6391

GENERAL INQUIRIES
migainquiry@worldbank.org

INTERNATIONAL FINANCE CORPORATION

2121 Pennsylvania Avenue NW
Washington, DC 20433

GENERAL INQUIRIES
Phone: (202) 473-3800
Fax: (202) 974-4384

INTERNATIONAL CENTRE FOR SETTLEMENT OF INVESTMENT DISPUTES

Use the World Bank Headquarters address.

GENERAL INQUIRIES
Phone: (202) 458-1534
Fax: (202) 522-2615
ICSIDsecretariat@worldbank.org

THE WORLD BANK GROUP
FROM PAST TO PRESENT

The following pages present a historical timeline of the major events and activities of the World Bank Group from 1944 to the present. It graphically shows how the World Bank expanded from a single institution to an associated group of coordinated development institutions, as well as how the Bank's mission evolved from facilitator of post-war reconstruction and development to its present day mandate of worldwide poverty alleviation.

Timeline entries have been categorized as follows:

- Policy/Operational
- Internal
- Loans/Credit
- Committees/Meetings

Other resources include the following:

Interactive timeline of the World Bank Group. This online timeline highlights major WBG events and activities since 1944.

⮑ http://www.worldbank.org/wb/about/timeline

World Bank Group Historical Chronology. A comprehensive timeline of key events in WBG history, by decade, with salient world events highlighted at the beginning of each year. Many of the items in the chronology are "firsts," such as the first lending for each member country, the first meetings of consultative groups, or the first lending in a particular sector. The chronology also indicates the date when each member country joined each WBG institution.

⮑ http://go.worldbank.org/GGMLF575S0

World Bank Group History: Exploring the Archives. This video examines the major events and strategic shifts in the Bank Group's history in four short parts: Introduction; Building the Bank, 1944–1968; Confronting Poverty, 1968–1995; and Supporting Social Development, 1995–present.

⮑ http://go.worldbank.org/GGMLF575S0

1944

- Twenty eight governments sign Articles of Agreement in Washington. The primary purpose of the new institution was to rebuild Europe.

- United Nations Monetary and Financial Conference draws up Bank Articles of Agreement at Bretton Woods—44 countries represented.

1945

IBRD—International Bank for Reconstruction and Development
Member countries: 40

1946

- First loan applications (from Czechoslovakia, Denmark, France, Luxembourg, Poland and Chile).

Eugene Meyer, President
- World Bank formally begins operations June 25.

1947

- First bond offering— $250 million in New York City.
- First loan—$250 million to France.

John J. McCloy, President
- Established first Resident Mission—Paris, France

1948

- First development loan— $13.5 million to Chile.

1949

Eugene R. Black, President

1940s

World Population in 1950: 2.5 billion	**1950**	● First loan to a national development bank— $2 million to Ethiopia.
	1951	● Finland and Yugoslavia repay first Bank loans in full.
	1952	● Japan and Federal Republic of Germany become members.
● First three loans to Japan totaling $40.2 million, are approved.	**1953**	
	1955	● Economic Development Institute (now World Bank Institute), serving as Bank's staff college, is established.
IFC—International Finance Corporation Member countries: 45	**1956**	● **International Finance Corporation (IFC)** is established as an affiliate of the Bank, with authorized capital of $100 million, to provide finance to private companies.
● IFC makes first investment— $2 million in siemens in Brazil to expand manufacturing.	**1957**	

1950s

1960

● **International Development Association (IDA)** is established as an affiliate of the Bank, with an initial subscription of $912.7 million, to provide financing to the poor, newly independent counties not creditworthy enough to borrow from the Bank.

World Population in 1960: 3 billion

IDA—International Development Association Member countries: 55

1961

● IDA extends first development credit—$9 million to Honduras for highway development.

1962

● First education loan—a $5 million IDA credit to Tunisia for school construction.

1963

● Bank launches the junior professional recruitment and training program (now Young Professionals program).

George D. Woods, President

● Eighteen newly independent African countries join the Bank.

1966

● **International Centre for Settlement of Investment Disputes (ICSID)** is established as a WBG agency to encourage a larger flow of private international investment by offering facilities for the resolution of disputes.

ICSID —International Center for Settlement of Investment Disputes Member countries: 23

1967

● France, Germany, Japan, the United Kingdom, and the United States form the Group of 5 to convene meetings of finance ministers and governors of central banks. The group became G-8 over time.

● Developing countries form the Group of 77 as a convention and negotiation arm.

1968

Robert S. McNamara, President

1960s

World Population in 1970:
3.8 billion

1970

Number of member countries by institution
IBRD: 115 • IDA: 105 • IFC: 84 • ICSID: 57

- First loan for populationplanning—
$2 million for Jamaica.

1971

- First loan for pollution control—$15 million for Brazil.

1972

- Bank redeploys projects and programs staff into regional departments to enable the institution to function more effectively.

- World Bank Group Staff Association comes into existence.

- First arbitration case filed at ICSID.

1974

- Interim Committee (of the IMF) and the Development Committee are established to advise the Board of Governors.

- Position of Director General of Operation Evaluation is established to ensure independent evaluation of projects and programs.

- President McNamara delivers Annual Meeting speech in which, for the first time, poverty is placed at top of Bank's agenda. The President wanted to combat the widespread suffering of the poor he had seen in many countries.

1975

- IBRD and IDA commit nearly $1 billion in one fiscal year for rural development projects.

- Shirley Boskey is appointed as the first female Director (International Relations Department).

1978

- First *World Development Report* team published report with the theme of accelerating growth and alleviating poverty.

- New Bank policy to assess the environment impact of Bank-assisted projects.

1979

- Bank's new commitments exceed $10 billion for the first time.

- Bank begins lending for health projects.

1970s

Number of member countries by institution
IBRD: 130 • IDA: 119 • IFC: 100 • ICSID: 77

● Structural adjustment lending initiated to provide balance of payment support to governments to restructure national economies and overcome heavy debt burdens.

1980

World Population in 1980:
4.5 billion

● First structural adjustment loan is approved—$200 million for Turkey.

● People's Republic of China assumes representation for China and quickly becomes one of the largest borrowers.

1981

A.W. Clausen, President

● Position of Ombudsman is established.

● Anne Krueger is appointed as first female Vice President (Economics and Research).

1982

● Bank establishes "small grants" program to fund activities to promote cooperation among nongovernmental organizations (NGOs), governments, academics, and media.

1983

1984

● IFC establishes $20 billion Special Fund to stimulate private sector development.

Barber B. Conable, President

1986

● NGO Working Group is established to build consensus among NGOs worldwide regarding the World Bank as well as to provide a forum for dialogue about development issues.

Multilateral Investment Guarantee Agency (MIGA), newest affiliate of the Bank Group, is established to provide investors with insurance against political risks of investing in developing countries.

1988

MIGA—Multilateral Investment Guarantee Agency
Member countries: 35

1980s

World Population in 1990: 5.3 billion

1990

Number of member countries by institution
IBRD: 145 • IDA: 140 • IFC: 125 • ICSID: 92
MIGA: 60

1991

● China replaces India as the largest IDA borrower. It will later "graduate" from IDA in 1999/2000.

Lewis T. Preston, President

● The Global Environmental Facility is launched.

1992

● New diversity strategy recommends an increase in the proportion of women at higher grade levels, and is later extended (1998) to include gender, nationality, race, sexual orientation and disabilities.

● Work-Family Agenda recommends ways to achieve a more flexible, family-supportive working environment.

● Russian Federation and 12 republics of the former Soviet Union become members of IBRD and IDA.

1993

● An independent Inspection Panel is established to investigate external complaints from individual groups negatively affected by Bank-funded projects, responding to concerns from NGOs and civil society groups about adverse environmental and social consequences of Bank-assisted projects and worries that Bank staff and management were not following the agreed upon policies.

● Institutional Development Fund is established to support innovative capacity-building initiatives.

1994

● First Public Information Center opened.

● WBG celebrates 50th anniversary while being widely criticized by NGOs and member governments.

1995

● Ghana Country Assistance Review is released, the first in a series of IEG studies that evaluate the relevance and efficacy of the Bank's overall Country Assistance Strategy and the effectiveness of various Bank lending and nonlending instruments.

James D. Wolfensohn, President

● The Global Environmental Facility is launched.

1990s

1996

● Quality Assurance Group (QAG) is established to provide real-time information on quality of the Bank's work.

● President Wolfensohn gives a ground-breaking "cancer of corruption" speech at the World Bank/ IMF Annual Meetings to show corruption is a major burden for the poor in developing countries.

● Knowledge Management is launched to connect those who need to know with those who do know, to collect know-how, and to make knowledge accessible.

● IMF, World Bank, and donors launch the Heavily Indebted Poor Counties (HIPC) Initiative to alleviate debt in response to the acute debt crisis in the world's poorest countries. The framework is significantly enhanced in 1999.

1997

● Board approves the Strategic Compact—a fundamental organization renewal effort— to improve technical excellence and be closer and more responsive to clients. It follows the 1987 reorganization that formed country departments and broke staff's lifetime employment and is complemented by the 1999 Comprehensive Development Framework (CDF) that ensured holistic development and national ownership of programs.

● Governance Action Plan is introduced. After just 2 years, over 600 specific governance and "clean government" initiatives are started in almost 100 borrower countries.

● Bank approves loan of $3 billion to South Korea and other loans to economies affected by the financial crisis to restore investor confidence and minimize social costs of the crisis.

1998

● Knowledge Bank Initiative is launched.

1999

● Bank's vision for the new millennium is articulated: "Our dream is a world free of poverty."

1990s

Number of member countries by institution
IBRD: 181 • IDA: 160 • IFC: 174 • ICSID: 129 • MIGA: 146

2000

World Population in 2000: 6 billion

● World Bank and its partners create Global Development Gateway, a portal on development where users can find and contribute information and resources.

● The IMF and World Bank present a new approach to linking debt relief/concessional lending and poverty reduction to urge national governments and citizens to develop national Poverty Reduction Strategy Papers (PRSPs) in partnership with all donors.

● World Bank releases *Voices of the Poor: Can Anyone Hear Us?* a new study on the causes and effects of global poverty with personal accounts from more than 60,000 people living in 60 countries.

● Bank holds first "Development Marketplace" to reward innovation and development.

2002

● WBG participates in the first UN International Conference on Financing Development in Monterrey, Mexico.

2003

● First Doing Business report is published.

● Ten leading commercial banks adopt the Equator Principles, choosing to follow World Bank and IFC environmental and social guidelines for all their investment work in developing countries.

● The World Bank and other multilateral and bilateral donors meet at the High-Level Forum on Harmonization in Rome to streamline procedures that guide delivery of aid worldwide.

2004

● The Bank and the IMF adopt a more comprehensive and integrated approach to fighting money laundering and terrorism financing in member countries.

2005

● The Bank publishes its first annual report investigating fraud and corruption both internally and in Bank-financed projects.

Paul Wolfowitz, President

2006

● A new Bank Gender Action Plan, a four-year $24.5 million plan to enhance women's economic power in key economic sectors.

2007

Robert B. Zoellick, President

● IFC donates $150 million to IDA, the first such contribution by the private sector arm of the World Bank Group.

2008

● The Bank responds to the food price crisis through the Global Food Crisis Response Programs (GFRP), providing support to 49 countries and reaching 66 million people.

2000s

2010

Number of member countries by institution
IBRD: 188 • IDA: 184 • IFC: 179
ICSID: 172 • MIGA: 149

● The World Bank adopts a comprehensive Access to Information Policy and launches the Open Data Initiative to commit the WBG to transparency and accountability by making all information available to the public, including Bank operations and board proceedings. The Open Data Initiative provides free and open access to development statistics.

World Population in 2010: [to come]

● In response to the financial crisis, the worst global downturn in 50 years, which left 114 million more people in extreme poverty by 2010, the WBG committed $128 billion in two years; more than any other international financial institution.

● IFC's Banking on Women program expands access to finance for women entrepreneurs.

2011

● MIGA's convention expands its development effectiveness by mobilizing $1 billion in insurance capacity for the Middle East and North Africa.

2012

● South Sudan becomes a member following decades of conflict. The WBG advances a $75 million trust fund.

● IFC's investments in Africa near $4 billion, more than double the level of investment in 2007.

Jim Yong Kim, President

● Climate change challenges become part of all new country assistance and partnership strategies, making climate change a priority of Bank-financed projects.

2013

● The World Bank and United Nations join forces to help the World's most fragile regions. WBG President Jim Kim and UN Secretary-General Ban Ki-Moon travel through Africa, committing $1 billion to the most vulnerable countries.

● Fragile and conflict-affected countries receive $2.6 billion IDA financial assistance to support more than $1.5 billion people in 36 countries and territories affected by violent conflict, about 52 percent of the world's poor.

2014

Number of member countries by institution
IBRD: 188 • IDA: 184 • IFC: 180
ICSID: 173 • MIGA: 150

● WBG restructuring implemented July 1, 2014, with the creation of 14 Global Practices and 5 Cross-Cutting Solution Areas.

2015

World population (projected): 7.2 billion

2010s

INDEX

Boxes and figures are indicated by "b" and "f" following page numbers; photographs are indicated by italicized page numbers.

Environmental Benefit nt

The World Bank Group is to reducing its environmental footprint. In support of this commitm blishing and Knowledge Division leverages electronic publishing optio -on-demand technology, which is located in regional hubs worldwide. se initiatives enable print runs to be lowered and shipping distances de ulting in reduced paper consumption, chemical use, greenhouse gas nd waste.

The Publishing ge Division follows the recommended standards for paper use set by the G en ss Initiative. Whenever possible, books are printed on 50 percent to 100 percent postconsumer recycled paper, and at least 50 percent of the fiber in our book paper is either unbleached or bleached using Totally Chlorine Free (TCF), Processed Chlorine Free (PCF), or Enhanced Elemental Chlorine Free (EECF) processes.

More information about the Bank's environmental philosophy can be found at http://crinfo.worldbank.org/wbcrinfo/node/4.